The American Utopian Adventure

AUTOBIOGRAPHY OF A SHAKER

FREDERICK W. EVANS.

MOUNT LEBANON.

Columbia Co. New York. U.S.A.

AUTOBIOGRAPHY OF A SHAKER,

AND

Revelation of the Apocalypse.

WITH AN APPENDIX.

FREDERICK W. EVANS

New and Enlarged Edition, with Portrait.

"THE SPIRIT SEARCHETH ALL THINGS, YEA, THE DEEP
THINGS OF GOD."

PORCUPINE PRESS, INC.
Philadelphia 1972

Library of Congress Cataloging in Publication Data

[Evans, Frederick William] 1808-1893.
  Autobiography of a Shaker.

  (The American Utopian adventure)
  Reprint of the 1888 ed.
  1. Evans, Frederick William, 1808-1893.
2. Shakers. 3. Bible. N. T. Revelation--Prophecies
I. Title. II. Title: Revelation of the Apocalypse.
BX9793.E8A3   1972   289.8'092'4 [B]   79-187481
ISBN 0-87991-002-X

First edition 1869. Enlarged edition 1888 (Glasgow: United Publishing Co., 1888)

Reprinted 1972 by PORCUPINE PRESS, INC., 1317 Filbert St., Philadelphia
Pa. 19107, from a copy in the collections of the Duke University Library

Manufactured in the United States of America

PREFACE.

———

As may be gathered from the work, this "little book" owes its origin to a demand, on the part of the public, for definite and reliable information respecting the present status—doctrines and principles—of *Shakerism*, together with the design and ultimate object of the system, whether it be applicable to the *race*, or only to an "*elect*" *few* in this world, and to the *whole race* in the world to come.

The author having been a *Materialist*, easily sympathises with *that phase* of human thought, which is far more prevalent and wide-spread than is generally imagined.

Heretofore, Shakerism, of all religious systems, has, by this class of mind, been esteemed the extreme of ignorance and fanaticism — as *the one* entirely outside the pale of philosophical and logical investigation—the *rejected stone*.

During the first fifty years of its history, the fact itself, that men and women did live in an intimate

47676

social relation, above the plane of sexual, generative lusts and affections (illegal or legal) was strenuously denied as an absurdity — a human impossibility. More recently this fact has been tacitly or sullenly admitted; still, not many practical inferences affecting the constitutions of civil and religious organisations have been deduced therefrom. *Now*, the fact is not only freely conceded, but the law involved therein is demanded and sought with avidity.

We cordially invite both Rationalists and Religionists to "eat"—"read and inwardly digest"—this "*little book*." It is "written within and *without*," or "on the back side" of this world,—connecting with eternity.

INTRODUCTION.

An introduction to parties so widely divergent as
are the Shakers and the Public, appears proper and
appropriate.

Have we not come before the great Church of
America in an acceptable time? Is not the advent
to earth again of the Christ Spirit to all Christendom
the absorbingly-expectant event?

This day, do not the modern prophets—the most
learned interpreters of Scripture—(who have sought
out, calculated, and set down, to a year, a month, a
day, when, how, and where, the "Redeemer should
come to Zion") stand before a disappointed world,
utterly confounded! with their erudite knowledge
and wisdom brought to naught? — MILLER, NOEL,
CUMMING, SHIMEALL, the last links of a long chain,
reaching back to the very age of Jesus himself. The
latter—SHIMEALL—speaking " of the doctrine of the
Second Coming of the LORD JESUS CHRIST in resurrection power," as held by all Christians—Catholic,

Greek, and Protestant, says,—"Nevertheless, from an early period of her history, the Christian Church has been at issue with herself on the great question regarding the nature and purposes of that event, and of the period when it shall take place."

Of the *time*, the Shakers differ but little from either of those named, and exactly coincide with CUMMING, that the great prophetic period of *time* ended (and will be "no more") in 1792. But, "in the nature and purposes of that event," to be carried out, they differ immeasurably.

Did not JESUS and the Apostles also agree in the *time* set by the same class of men—Prophets and the learned Jewish Rabbis—interpreters and calculators —who had created so general an expectation of the coming of the Messiah, that windows and doors were left open to admit him? but which were afterwards closed and shut in his face when he did appear in a "nature, and for purposes not found in their books, nor dreamt of in their philosophy or religion."

In the Church and world *then*, as in the Church and world *now*, marriage, private property, and war, were permanent institutions, no less of the subdued and prostrate Jews than of the conquering and tri- umphant Romans.

Of *war*, the "New York Tribune," in a recent editorial, writes,—"War, unhappily, is not likely to pass away from the usages of people calling themselves civilised, and bearing the name of *Christian*. Nay! it seems to be as prevalent as ever. The art of war is studied, and the machinery of war is perfected to an extent never dreamt of until this generation. The engines of destruction are numerous and fearful beyond precedent."

That generative lusts, the root out of which war grows, and selfish private property, *for which* it is waged, are equally intrenched in the creeds of the Churches, and the constitutions of nations, there can be no shadow of doubt. While the affirmation of JESUS remains a standing truth, that, were his "kingdom" like other kingdoms "*of this world*," then, as in *them*, his subjects and "servants would" also practise war, and "fight" and marry, and not live in love, as now they do, having "all things common" in gospel community.

Has not JESUS—his doctrines, precepts, and principles, which (on a small scale) were incarnated in the Pentecostal Church—been rejected by the Babel-builders of all the civil and ecclesiastical structures upon the face of the earth, excepting only that of the Millennial Church, now in process of erection by

the Shakers, who have adopted "the man JESUS" as
the very Head of the corner in the foundations of
the "Second Temple," which they are industriously
laying "in troublous times" (as was by the Spirit
foreseen), to the salvation of man from sin, sickness,
and poverty, to the glory of God, and the well-being
and honour of humanity?

For the Shaker Order is the source and medium
of spiritual religious light to the world ; the seed-bed
of radical truths ; the fountain of progressive ideas.
For "in CHRIST are hid all the treasures of wisdom
and knowledge," with which to bless and redeem the
race from every form of evil, and from every cause of
human misery and suffering, unto GOD.

June, 1869.

CONTENTS.

APPENDIX TO FIRST EDITION.

APPENDIX TO NEW EDITION.

SHAKER LITERATURE.

Extracts from Books written by Elder Evans.

"Shaker Communism."

Rudimental Principles of the Patriarchal Era.

EXTRACTS FROM "ANN LEE: A BIOGRAPHY."

BY ELDER F. W. EVANS.

SHAKER LECTURES.

SHAKERISM IN LONDON.

THE SHAKER SYSTEM.

SHAKERS AS FARMERS.

THE SHAKERS AND SPIRITUALISM.

LIFE WITH THE SHAKERS.

SHAKER MISSION TO SCOTLAND AND ENGLAND.

MOUNT LEBANON.

SHAKERS AND SHAKERISM.

NOTE TO NEW EDITION.

HESTER M. Poole in the closing lines of this Book says.—"The Shakers *practise* as well as preach a temperance and a religion well worthy of respectful attention." The publishers of this Book being of this opinion, consider this a good reason for its re-issue in this country so recently visited by its author.

Many readers and thinkers in Scotland and England have had their minds drawn to "The Shakers" by recent letters—notably in the *Scotsman*—by Dr. Walter C. Smith; and in a London paper, *The Weekly Times and Echo*—by a sympathetic writer.

This book will interest the few earnest people who still think it is possible to obey the Law of Christ—the command to "*Love thy neighbour as thyself.*"

A recent writer when quoting these words of Christ,—"For if any man come to me and hate not his father and mother, and wife and children, and brethren and sisters, yea, *and his own life also*, he *cannot be my disciple*," says, "they have never been acted upon yet." This writer and some others may read with interest this "Autobiography of a Shaker," who obeys these laws of Christ.

The following quotations are given to shew the current of present thought in this country, and seem very appropriate when presenting this picture of Shaker Life and Work,—

"Traditional beliefs will be modified without irritation and passion when it is made clear that the new creed conserves the spiritual and moral forces of the old, and when it is made equally clear that the surrender removes real difficulties of belief, and is made in obedience to the claims of Truth, and not to those of a passing and peremptory tyranny. Till then new views will have to encounter a blinding fundamental antipathy."— *From British Weekly, 8th June, 1888, being "the moral" of article—"The Apology of the Narrow Minded."*

"Those who, from fear of a public opinion impregnated with impurity, shrink from grappling with the disease inherent in the generative and reproductive principle of the universe, after they have become convinced that the only hope of the worlds redemption lies in its purification, will reap the reward of their timidity when they pass into another life, and find the problem of their own purification presented to them under conditions much more trying than those which surrounded it here. But those who are willing, inspired by love for humanity, to place themselves in God's hands as ready sacrifices for the advancement of this great work, will find a consolation in the supreme peace and joy which will flood them, that will more than compensate for the rage that will be concentrated upon them by the infernals, and which will find expression through their agents in this world, generally among those most noted for what is called their "piety" and "good works." As in the days of Christ, so will it be again; the most bitter enemies of him who tries to bring new life and love into the world from the source of light and love, will be the churches, and the Pharisees by whom they are haunted."—*From page 251-2 of Laurence Oliphant's new Book, "Scientific Religion."*

"NOT EVEN NOW ARE YE ABLE TO BEAR IT, FOR YE ARE
CARNAL."

We regret to note a number of small errata—grammatical and typographical—in the earlier sheets of this work. On page 56, a Civil Government, etc., should be (having a balance of power, being composed equally of *intellectual celibate* men and women; perhaps the Senate being the *female* branch of the government, as the *House* will be the *male* branch, and the Presidents a man and a woman, the Executive.) On page 60, read "For this cause was the Gospel preached to them *that were dead,* that they might be judged."

The "Photogravure" is from a negative taken by R. T. Dodd, of Glasgow, in July, 1887.

Glasgow, July, 1888.

AUTOBIOGRAPHY OF A SHAKER.

PART I.

THE NATURAL MAN.

IN consequence of the Shakers having held a convention in Boston on November 11th and 12th, 1868, to which I was a delegate, I received (from Friend J. T. FIELDS) a note, in which occurs the following paragraph:

"How would it do for you to write an article for our *Atlantic Monthly Magazine*, which should be an autobiographical account of your experience as a seeker after truth, and should give the 'reason of the hope that is in you,' that people may understand precisely the meaning of a sect which has lately been brought into notoriety by the writings of Dixon and Vincent?"

I can see great importance in a *principle*, very little in an individual. Not of myself should I write *of* myself; but in the hope that others may be advantaged thereby, I acquiesce in the foregoing suggestion.

I have always lived much in the future, yet my present life has been a practical success; while my work has ever been before me, my reward has always been with me. I am satisfied with the continued realizations of the prophetical spirit within—of the abstract principles that have been my inner life.

2

My father's family were of the middle class in
England. They were long-lived, my grandmother
reaching the advanced age of one hundred and four,
and my grandfather approaching one hundred. My
father, George Evans, was the youngest of twelve
children, and died comparatively young ; he was sent
into the English army, was under Sir Ralph Aber-
crombie in the Egyptian expedition, coöperating with
the fleet under Nelson, and held a commission in the
service.

My mother was of a class a little above, so that the
marriage caused a perpetual breach between the two
families. Her name was Sarah White. I was born
in Leominster, Worcestershire, England, on the 9th of
June, 1808. The first *fact* that I can *remember* may
be of some interest to the student in anthropology.
When I came of age, and on my return to England,
in 1830, I was relating to an aunt on my father's side,
whom I had never before seen, that I had always had
stored up in my memory one thing which I could not
account for ; I could remember nothing before or
after it to give it a meaning, and none of my mother's
relatives knew anything about it. *I saw the inside of
a coach, and was handed out of it from a woman's
arms into those of some other person.* My aunt was
utterly astonished, and stated that my mother was
coming down from London to Birmingham, when I
was not more than *six months old*, that something
happened to the horses which frightened the party
badly, and that I was handed out (just as I had seen
and remembered) by my mother into the arms of
another person.

When I was four years of age my mother died, and I was thrown among her relatives, who sent me to school at Stourbridge, where there were some two hundred scholars; and the position the master assigned me was that of the poorest scholar in the school, which effected my release from the schoolroom, to my great satisfaction and peace of mind ; for, if there was one thing more than another that I hated, it was school-books and an English schoolmaster, with his flogging proclivities. I was then about eight years old.

Henceforth my lot was cast with my uncles and aunts at Chadwick Hall, near Licky Hill, the scene of one of Cromwell's battles, where a systematic arrangement of all things obtained, from the different breeds of dogs,—the watchdog in his kennel, the water spaniel, the terrier of rat-catching propensities, the greyhound, the pointer, and the bulldog,—to the diversity of horses for the farm, the road, the saddle, and hunting ; there were five hundred sheep, with a regular hereditary shepherd to change them from pasture to pasture in summer, and to attend to all their wants, and fold them in the turnip-fields all the winter. Every field on the farm was subject to a rotation of crops as regular as the seasons, which are generally bad enough for the English farmer.

The farm was very hilly and woody, and dotted with five fish-ponds formed from a stream that ran through it. There was plenty of fish and game, and the woods were vocal with the great variety of singing birds, from the jackdaw to the nightingale.

As my friends had given up all attempts and hopes to educate, and thereby fit me for good society, I was allowed to follow my own instincts and affinities ; and these led me to associate almost exclusively with the servants, of whom eight or ten were kept on the place, there being two distinct classes of human beings, and two separate establishments, at Chadwick Hall, as on a Southern plantation in the olden times of *seven years ago*. Here I was allowed to educate myself to my heart's content, reading and studying the vegetables and fruits (and of these there were variety and abundance, including the apple and pear to the apricot and gooseberry), in all of which I was deeply *interested*. The land and its crops, the animals and the servants who attended them, together with those who officiated indoors, were all my school-masters and mistresses, and the servants were not less my particular friends, for I was a Democrat.

When almost twelve years of age, my father and brother, whom I did not know, appeared at Chadwick Hall, not to me among the servants, but to my uncle and aunts in the parlour, and to my grandmother, who had *not* given me up for lost, as had the others (so far as a school education was concerned), but had taught me to say my prayers before going to bed, and when I rose in the morning ; had caused me to learn the Collect on Sunday ; and required the servants to take me to the national Episcopal Church to learn the text, and patiently endure an occasional gentle knock on the head from the sexton's long wand. For all of this I had a proper respect ; but an organ (which I heard for the first time) in another church alarmed me, and caused me to cry out in a fright, to the amazement of a large congregation.

My father, brother, and uncles and aunts, as I subsequently learned, had a sharp contention about taking me off to America, of which I only knew so much as I used to hear the common people sing in a doggerel originating at a time recruits for the Revolutionary war were being raised :

" The sun will burn your nose off,
And the frost will freeze your toes off ;
But we must away,
To fight our friends and our relations
In North America."

The different parties became warm in their feelings, and quarrelled, each party laying claim to me ; and, as neither would give way, Englishmen-like, they agreed to settle the matter on this wise : I, Frederick, was to be called into the parlour, no word upon the subject to be spoken to me previously, and uncle was to put a question to me, which he did, as follows : " Frederick, will you go to America with these men (who are your father and brother), or will you stay with us?" "I will go to America with my father and brother," was my instant reply, and that settled it. I was soon "fixed off," and on my way to Liverpool. This was in the year 1820, and I attained my twelfth year at sea.

I was hardy and healthy, and liked to work ; I barely knew my letters, and detested paper books. I had not been poisoned with saleratus, or American knick-knacks or candies; nor with American superfine flour bread ; nor with the great variety and dreadful mixtures with which the systems of children and young persons in this nation are duly prepared for Plantation Bitters, and the long, endless train of bitters resulting from dyspeptic diet and stimulating drinks,—the natural result of excess of land, and of material wealth being in advance of the moral and mental development of the inhabitants of a country ; thus creating a hotbed of physical vice, which is well calculated to check the increase of population.

The next ten years were spent in America, in such intimate relations with my brother, G. H. Evans, that some reference to him seems indispensable. He was two years older than me, and had received a scholastic education ; so that, in literary knowledge, we were the two extremes of learning and ignorance. But we were brothers in a higher meaning of the term. We were Radicals in civil government, and in religion, we were Materialists. He is now deceased ; but he made his mark upon the page of history, which has recorded the current of thought as it flowed down from the *founders* of the American government to the election of Grant as President of these United *Reconstructing* States, upon principles more nearly realising the abstract truisms affirmed in the Declaration of Independence than were ever before reduced to practice.

George started the Land-Reform movement in this country, on the basis of the principle laid down by Jefferson, that " the land belongs to man *in usufruct* only." And *that idea* was, doubtless, entertained by all the signers of the Declaration of Independence. George was contemporary with Horace Greeley in his younger days ; and, at the time of starting the *New York Tribune*, they were fast friends.

Another important point of agreement between the founders of the government and G. H. E., was that they were all, so far as I know (excepting Thomas Carroll, of Carrollton, who was a Catholic), infidels to the existing so-called Christianity of the world. Jefferson, Thomas Paine, Franklin, and Washington (who has been somewhat white-washed by the sectarian priesthood), were Materialists, Deists, Unitarians, etc. These made provision that no priest of *any denomination* should hold any place of trust, or office, under this government.

This school of mind had progressed up to the Community theories of Fourier and Owen, and the attempts to realise them in various places in Europe and America were most rife about the year 1830.

The right *to be* and the right *to land*, each included the other; we held that they were identical; and hence we waged a fierce and relentless war against all forms of property accumulation that owed their origin to land monopoly, speculation, or usury.

While still an apprentice at Ithaca, G. H. E. published *The Man*. Afterwards I combined my means with his, and we published, successively, *The Workingman's Advocate*, *The Daily Sentinel*, and finally, *Young America*, besides a great variety of other publications, including *The Bible of Reason*, etc., etc.; none of which, in a pecuniary point of view, were very successful; for G. H. E. was a poor financier, and we had a tremendous current of conservatism to stem. But that these publications had a controlling influence upon the American press may be inferred from the very frequent quotations in other papers from the editorials of *Young America*, and also from the fact that six hundred papers indorsed the following measures, which were printed at the head of *Young America* :—

"*First.*—The right of man to the soil : 'Vote yourself a farm.'

" *Second.*—Down with monopolies, especially the United States Bank.

" *Third.*—Freedom of the public lands.

" *Fourth.*—Homesteads made inalienable.

" *Fifth.*—Abolition of all laws for the collection of debts.

" *Sixth.*—A general bankrupt law.

" *Seventh.*—A lien of the labourer upon his own work for his wages.

" *Eighth.*—Abolition of imprisonment for debt.

" *Ninth.*—Equal rights for women with men in all respects.

" *Tenth.*—Abolition of chattel slavery and of wages slavery.

" *Eleventh.*—Land limitation to one hundred and sixty acres ; no person, after the passage of the law, to become possessed of more than that amount of land. But, when a land monopolist died, his heirs were to take each his legal number of acres, and be compelled to sell the overplus, using the proceeds as they pleased.

" *Twelfth.*—Mails in the United States to run on the Sabbath."

These, and similar views and principles, we held and propagated to the very best of our ability; for our whole hearts and souls were in them.

This Spartan band was few in number, but there were deep thinkers among them ; and all were earnest, practical workers in behalf of the down-trodden masses of humanity. It was war between abstract right and conventional rights. We held the Constitution to be only a compromise between the first principles of the American government, as they were set forth in the Declaration of Independence, drawn up by Jefferson, and the then existing vested rights of property-holders and conservatives of all sorts, secular and religious ; and we contended that the mutual, well-understood intention and design of the founders of the government was, that, as soon as was possible, the Constitution should be amended, so as to conform more and more to the ideal pattern set forth in the declaration of rights inherent in humanity, it being a question *only* as to *how long* an acknowledged *wrong* should be permitted.

Our little party gradually and steadily increased, and acquired the title of " The Locofoco Party" in the following manner : On the evening of the 29th of October, 1825, a great meeting was to be held in Tammany Hall, by the Democratic party (which was then and there split into two, and in which the Radical Land Reformers triumphed, taking with them a large portion of the party). The Conservative leaders came up the back stairs into the hall, and secured the fore part of the meeting, and elected a chairman and committee. But these were finally entirely out-voted by the thousands of workingmen who crowded into and filled the hall, ejecting Isaac L. Varian, whom the monopolists had installed, and putting in

Joel Curtis as chairman. Then the Conservatives retired in disgust down the back stairs as they came in, and revengefully turned off the gas, leaving the densely-packed hall in total darkness. The cry was raised, " Let there be light," and " there was light "; for locofoco matches were ignited all over the room, and applied to candles, when a fine illumination ensued, creating great enthusiasm, which finally resulted in the election of Andrew Jackson and R. M. Johnson as President and Vice-President of the United States. For it was soon found that the Loco- foco party held the balance of power ; and they offered their entire vote to whichever of the parties would put at the head of their great party papers the twelve measures above enumerated, and the offer was accepted by the Democratic party.

Thus, during the last thirty-eight years, have been accomplished the following among our progressive purposes, viz. :

Second.—The United States Bank overthrown.

Third.—Freedom of public lands to actual settlers secured.

Fourth.—Homestead laws in nearly all of the States.

Sixth.—General bankrupt laws passed by the United States.

Seventh.—Lien of labourers upon work to a great extent secured.

Eighth.—Abolition of imprisonment for debt in most of the States.

Tenth.—Abolition of chattel slavery in the United States entire.

Ninth.—Equal rights for women is next in order.

I will now return to the scenes of my boyhood ; for it is a truth that "the boy is father to the man."

The example of the order and economy practised at Chadwick Hall was not lost upon me. Two uncles, John and James, managed the farm. One remained at home mostly ; the other attended the fairs and markets, which latter are held once a week at the principal towns. Here the farmers and dealers meet to sell and buy all the products of their farms ; the grain being bought and sold by samples. The fairs were much the same thing, but the sales were principally of live stock on a large scale. On these occasions, servants (male and female) congregated together, and hired themselves out for the ensuing year, each one producing his " character " on paper from his former employer.

To these markets and fairs my uncle John used frequently to take me ; and there I learned somewhat of the relative value of property, and how to buy and sell. At home I learned to take care of horses, cattle, and sheep. Everything moved as if by machinery. For instance, there were some twenty horses, and in the morning, at a regular hour, they were all turned out to water, as we now turn out cows. Whilst they were gone, their mangers were cleaned, and the racks emptied of any hay left in them over night ; this was put aside to be aired, and fresh hay was given ; at night, however, the aired hay was first fed out ; nothing was wasted or lost.

In the house it was the same. Once a month they washed ; once a week they baked bread made from unbolted wheat, black enough, but *sweet*, especially when, as often happens in that unfortunate climate, the wheat is grown ; then the bread is *sweetish*. But the people are not dyspeptic ; nor do they *in the country* commonly eat pills.

When my father and brother had fairly possession of me, they found they had " caught a Tartar." I had a good constitution, and, before they converted me into a " young gentleman," could stand a great deal of discipline.

We came over in the ship called the *Favorite*, laden with salt and iron. The captain said, that in twenty-two voyages, he had never experienced one so rough. Three times was the jibboom broken off close to the prow of the ship. At one time the ship sprang a leak, and it was " All hands to the pumps ! " There were several feet of water in her hold ; but the storm abated just in time to save the vessel, which was lost on her next voyage.

Landing at New York, we went up to Newburgh, where we hired three teams to remove our baggage to Binghamton, at which place two uncles were already located. This became *my home* in America, from whence I went and came until I found a Shaker home. And here, in the company of young folks belonging to the three families, I was again the black sheep. Several of the young men became editors, while I could barely *read* a little. But one of my aunts, one evening, when we were all together, prophesied of me, that " of the company present, Frederick would yet occupy the most desirable position in life ;" which has come to pass.

I now took a sudden turn in respect to books and learning. I saw that "knowledge was" not only "power," but that it was respect and consideration. I made up my mind that I would learn to read, and *love* to read. My first *dose* was the *Life of Nelson ;* then I set myself to reading the Bible through by course ; and I did it ; and here I made a discovery (or rather my friends did), that my memory was so retentive, that whatever I read was, as it were, pictured on my brain. I had only to look at the picture to see it in all its minutest particulars, without any effort. And (as Lincoln would say) this reminds me of what a woman I met on a Hudson boat said ; that in coming from California she was nearly drowned, but before consciousness was gone, all the sins of her life was present to her view ; not one, however small, was missing.

I next went to Ithaca, and put myself to school to an Episcopal minister, who proved a real friend. One of his first lessons was to teach me how to *think*. He had only a dozen scholars, and we were well attended to. I became with him a great favourite, and the times of intermission were largely devoted to my special instruction and benefit. At parting, he advised me "always so to live, that I could respect myself ;" and that has ever since been my life motto. Next I apprenticed myself at Sherburne Four Corners, N. Y., to learn the hatting business. There I had access to a library of valuable books, and I took to reading Rollin's *Ancient History*, Plutarch's *Lives of Great Men*, the *Tatler* and *Spectator*, and Zimmerman, Shakespeare, Young, Watts, Thomson Socrates,

and Plato.   I also took up theology, and asked myself, why was I a Christian, and not a Mahometan or
a follower of Confucius?—for I had read the Koran
and the Bibles of all peoples that I could obtain.   I
read Locke on the *Human Understanding, and the
Being of a God.*   This laid in me the foundation of
Materialism; for I came to the conclusion that matter
was eternal, had never been created.   Thomas Paine's
Crisis and *Rights of Man*, together with Volney and
Voltaire, were among my friends.

I became a settled and firm Materialist, a believer
in *matter*, as I then understood it, the object of my
external senses; for I then did not know that I had
any other senses.   This continued to be my condition
until I met with the Shakers, some five years afterwards.   I possessed this one great advantage, that
what I *did* believe was *true*, however much there
might be true that I did *not* believe.

Starting from such a basis, it was not strange that
I early became a convert to the Socialistic theories
which, about the year 1830, were so enthusiastically
advocated by their respective adherents, as the grand
panacea for all the wrongs perpetrated by Church
and State.   To all my other radical ideas I now
added Socialistic-Communism ; and I walked eight
hundred miles (starting from New York) to join a
Community at Massilon, Ohio.   On this journey I
was the recipient of many acts of kindness and
hospitality from so great a variety of persons, entire
strangers, that, to this day, I cannot think of the
Western people without emotions of gratitude and
pleasure.   At first, my feet swelled, and became very

sore ; but at length I could walk quite comfortably forty miles a day.

Reaching the Community, I found Dr. Underhill at the head of it, and a goodly number of congenial spirits, — infidels (like myself) and philosophers,— lovers of wisdom ; there also were *some Christians ;* and these were considered the cause of the breaking up of the Community, which occurred within about two months after my arrival.

A dozen or so of us,—young men,—looking into the causes which had destroyed so many Communities (some of us had been in five or six different ones, and were well acquainted with the whole movement), con- cluded to found another upon a proper basis, purely philosophical, and not to allow in it a single Christian.

But, in the meantime, I had to make a voyage to England ; and, in the spring of 1829, I started on a raft, from the village of Chatauqua, drifting down the Monongahela and Ohio to Cincinnati, and thence on a flat-boat down the Mississippi to New Orleans. This gave me an opportunity of seeing life as it ex- isted in the then slave States, and I formed my own private opinion of Jefferson's remark, when he said, he "trembled for his country, when he reflected that God was just," which was, that he saw the end from the beginning of slavery.

Sailing from New Orleans, and landing in New York, I soon after embarked for England ; and, after ten years' absence, I found, at Chadwick Hall, no more change in persons or things than would usually occur in a similar place in America in a single year.

I returned to New York in January, 1830, when

we perfected our plans for the new Community; and
I was deputed to travel for information, and to find
a suitable location in which to start. At this time
we had in New York a Hall of Science, and Robert
Dale Owen and Fanny Wright were among its great
lights.

Calling one day in the month of June (3rd), 1830,
at the office in Mount Lebanon, I was directed to
the North House as the proper place for inquirers.
I was kindly received by those who, at that time, I
supposed were the most ignorant and fanatical people
in existence. And knowing by experience how touchy
and sensitive *religious* persons were to any ideas not
in unison with their own, and how extremely reluc-
tant they were to have either their dogmas or practices tested by logic or common sense, I was very
wary and careful as to what I said, and in the questions I propounded. But I was agreeably surprised
and impressed by the air of candor and openness, the
quiet self-repose, with which I was met. I remained
here two or three days, but failed to find the touchy
place where anathemas supply the place of reasoning,
proof, and evidence ; I have now been here some
thirty-eight years, and have yet to find it. In fact,
after about a week's inquiry, I pronounced them a
society of infidels ; which indeed was paying them the
highest compliment of which I was capable.

My reason for so concluding was, that all that I, as
a philosopher, had repudiated and denounced, in the
past religious history of mankind, as false and abominable, and as having turned this earth into a real
hell, while they were cutting each other's throats

about imaginary heavens and hells, the Shakers also repudiated and denounced, only in stronger terms than I was master of; the power of a man or people for truth and good being measured by their capacity for indignation, and for the "wrath of God revealed from heaven against" falsehood and evil, in all their multifarious forms.

I found here one brother, Abel Knight, who had been a Quaker, then a Socialist, and whose house in Philadelphia had been the head-quarters of Communists and infidels; a man of standing, in all the known relations of life; he was a brother indeed, and a father too.

I have stated that I was a Materialist; and to some it may be interesting to know how I was converted. Well, it was not by the might of reasoning, nor by the power of argument, but by Spiritualism in the *right place,*—the Church of God; and put to the *right use,*—the conversion of a soul from an earthly to a spiritual condition.

The Shakers prayed for me, and I was met in my own path just as the Apostle Paul was met in *his* own path, by spiritual manifestations made to myself when quite alone, from time to time, during several weeks, until my reason was as entirely convinced, by the evidence received, of the existence of a spirit-world, as I am, by evidence that is presented to my outward senses, of the existence of our material earth. Not only so; but I came to a conception of the inner world as being the most substantial, and of the inner man as being the real man; the outward world being only the shadow of the invisible world

3

of causation. I also saw a meaning in the words of Paul : " We look not at the things which are seen, but at the things that are not seen ; for the things which are seen are temporal, but the things that are not seen are eternal."

Some persons may be curious to know what particular kind of spiritual manifestation it was that could convince so confirmed an infidel and Materialist. It was so spiritual that, while it fully met my case, I never have seen how I could put it into words, and do justice to the heavenly visitants or myself. In fact, I have always felt much as did a tribe of negroes whom Livingstone found in the interior of Africa, and whom he designates the " African Quakers," because they will not fight. When he began to act the *missionary* to them, by preaching his kind of religion, they replied to him in a whisper, " Hush ! hush ! " It was too sacred a subject for them to clothe in audible words. Even the *Jews* would never utter the sacred word " JEHOVAH "— *He-She*—except in a whisper.

In one of the first meetings that I attended, I saw a brother exercised in a slight way outwardly ; and it gave me the first *evidence* that began to produce in me faith in the *spiritual*. For I held that no person could believe, or disbelieve, at his or her own option ; *belief* being solely the result of evidence.

One night, soon after retiring, I heard a rustling sound, as of the wind of a flock of doves flying through the window (which was closed) towards my bed ; and, that I believed it to be supernatural, and that the faith in the supernatural, which the servants had planted in my soul, by their oft-told *ghost* stories, had not wholly died out under my Materialism, was evidenced by the fact that I was frightened, and hid my head beneath the bed-clothes. For this faith was never planted by the priest whose text I used to learn ; nor by the sexton who now and then gave me a rap on the head ; because neither the priest nor his people (who informed me every time I met with them, that they had, during the past week, been doing " those things which they ought *not* to have done," and that also they had " left undone those things which they ought to have done ;" and that they were " *miserable sinners* ") had succeeded in attracting my attention to, or in the least degree interesting me in, supernatural or spiritual existences of another world.

I soon recovered my self-possession, and found that a singular mental phenomenon was going on. I was positively *illuminated*. My reasoning powers were enhanced a hundred-fold. I could see a chain of problems, or propositions, as in a book, all spread out before me at once, starting from a fact that I *did* admit and believe ; and leading me, step by step, mathematically, to a given conclusion, which I had *not* hitherto believed. I then discovered that I had powers within me that I knew not of. I was multiplied and magnified, and intensely interested. I was *reasoning* as I never before reasoned. Doubting was at a discount ; for here were facts, something of which my senses were cognisant—my physical, mental, rational, and spiritual senses ; and I *knew* that intelligences not clothed in what I had called *matter* were present with me, reasoning with me more purely and logically than hitherto had any intelligences in the body ever done, or than any mere mortal man or woman has ever done since. This first visitation of angels to me continued till about one o'clock in the morning, having lasted several hours. I now had *new* material for *thought*.

The next night they came again. This time it was spirit acting upon matter. Something began at my feet, and operated as palpably as water, or fire, or electricity; but it was neither; to me it was a new force, or element, or power,—call it what you please. I reasoned upon it. There was no pain, but *fact*. It passed quite slowly upward throughout my whole body.

These visitations recurred nightly for three weeks, always different, always kind and pleasant; but were addressed directly to my rationality, showing me the facts of the existence of a spiritual world, of the immortality of the human soul, and of the possibility and reality of intercommunication between souls in and spirits out of the mortal body.

At about this time I had the following dream :—I saw a great fire, and a nude man, perfect in his physical organism, standing by it; he stepped into its very midst, the flames completely encircling his whole body. The next thing I observed was, that while he was perfect in *living beauty*, he was so organically changed that no "fig-leaf" covering was required.

Although a Materialist, I had never presumed to deny what others might know or had experienced to be true. But I would not believe, or rather *pro-fess* to believe, things of which I did not know, or of which I had received no evidence. This was the extent of my infidelity ; and I still hold fast to the same position, as to a rock upon which to build. " How can we reason but from what we know ? "

At the end of the three weeks, I was one day thinking of the wonderful condescension of my spirit friends, and how I had been met, to repletion, by evidence addressed to all my senses, powers, and faculties of body and mind : and I said to myself, " It is enough;" and from that moment the manifes-tations entirely ceased ; thus adding, as a seal, still another proof, that intelligent beings, who perfectly understood all of my mental processes, had me in charge.

Among the people (Believers) themselves, I had, for the *first time*, found religionists who were also rationalists, ready to " render a reason for the faith and hope that was in them ; " and who were willing to have that *reason* tested by the strictest rules of logical ratiocination. And they could appeal to me, as a Materialist, as did the Nazarene to unbelievers, " If ye believe not my words " (and the validity of my arguments), yet " believe for the very works' sake."

I had objected to other religious people and preachers, that, whereas they professed to believe in God, in the immortality of the soul, in an eternal heaven and hell, their lives and actions, as logical sequences, were inconsistent with such premises ; and I often said to them : " If I believed what you profess to believe, I would devote all my time to a preparation for eternity." Here, however, was a people, unknown by the world, doing that very thing. Their whole life was a religious one ; all their temporal, no less than their spiritual, affairs, being the exponent of their religion. Here was, first, faith in a Supreme Being, not as a dry, unsympathizing Trinity of three male 'persons, but a *Dual God*—a Father, the Fountain of wisdom and power, and a Mother, the Fountain of goodness and love to humanity. Here was faith in Divine communication — revelation — from the Parents primarily of all souls, not only to the man Jesus, as the " first-born " of humanity, in the *male* line, eighteen hundred years ago ; but also to the woman Ann, the first-born of humanity in the *female* line, in modern times. "Why not ? " I said. Theoretically, I was just as ready to believe the one as the other ; especially when, in the present, as in the former case, I found the principles identical, and the works similar.

Moses was a land reformer. The Jews held land as do the people of Vineland, by allotment, each one having his little family homestead. The early Christians, being all Jews, easily went one step further, and held their land "in common ;" and thus did the Shakers, viewing them as a body politic complete in themselves. For all the principles of Materialistic Socialism were in practical operation—their "works;" where is possessed and enjoyed "freedom of the public lands," and of all lands, and "land limitation," and "homesteads inalienable ;" where is fully carried out "abolition of slavery, both chattel and wages," including poverty and riches,—monopoly in all its forms, together with speculation, usury, and competition in business; where is abolished "imprisonment for debt," or for any other cause; for in each Community (or family) not only are there no "laws for the collection of debts," but debt itself is impossible; where "Woman's Rights" are fully recognised, by first giving her a Mother in Deity, to explain and protect them; where equal suffrage for men and women, and equal participation in the government of an Order founded by a woman, was an inevitable necessity.

These were the works for the sake of which I was compelled to believe that there really was a God, and that revelation, or communication, existed between that God and those whom I had supposed were the extremely ignorant and very fanatical Shakers.

As a Materialist, accustomed to be governed by *common sense*, the Shakers had to convince me by evidence, addressed to my own senses and reasoning faculties, that a God did exist; and that they received *from him* revelations upon which a rational man, in the most important business relations of life, might safely depend, before I could think of believing the Bible or any other record of what men and women (who possessed no more nor better faculties or senses than I did), in the dark ages of ignorance and superstition, in the early history of the human race, had seen, or heard, or felt, or smelt, or tasted, or said,—experienced.

If a God exists in our own time, then, certainly, men and women, as perfect as were those of olden times, also exist. Moreover, it is generally claimed

that great progress has been made by mankind as a
race ; therefore, and as a natural consequence, this
progress should in nothing be more palpable than in
his religion (his relation to God), and the relation of
man to his fellow-man. And why, therefore, should
there not be (if there ever was) a living intercommunication between God and man *to-day*, as well as
on long-ago by-gone days? was the question to be
answered ; and the Shakers did answer it in a sensible
and rational manner, by words and *facts* not (by me)
to be gainsaid.

I was not required to believe the imperfectly-
recorded experiences of spiritual men and women,
but to attain to an experience of my own. I had
received a revelation as truly as ever did Peter, or
Paul, or Jesus, or Ann ; and I therefore *believed*, not
from the words of others, but (like the people of
Samaria) because I had seen, and heard, and felt, for
myself.

This *rock*—revelation from a Christ Spirit in each
individual — is the true foundation of the Shaker
Church. "Night calleth unto night, and day unto
day." There is nothing that will so illumine the
pages of a true record of a *past* revelation as will a
present and superior revelation shining thereupon ; for
it separates the chaff from the wheat, the false from
the true, darkness from light.

After three months' absence, I returned to New
York, to face, for the first time, my astounded Materialistic friends, to whom a more incomprehensible
change could not have happened than my apparent
defection from their ranks.

As soon as my arrival in the city was known, there was a gathering at my brother's office. The room was well filled; many older than myself, to whom I had looked as my superiors in knowledge and experience, were present. At first there was a little disposition shown by a few to be querulous and bantering, while the greater part took it as a serious matter, to be righted by solid argument.

I called the attention of the company, and inquired whether any of them wished to give me any information concerning Materialism — its principles? All said No! you do not need it. I then inquired if any one present was acquainted with *Shakerism?* and again the answer was No! Then, gentlemen, I replied, it is for *you* to listen, and for *me* to speak. And I *did* speak; and gave them as simple an account of my experience thus far as I was able.

I also had a separate interview with Robert Dale Owen at the Hall of Science. At its close he remarked: "I will come up to New Lebanon, and stay two months; and if I find things as they now appear, I will become a Shaker." I still await his arrival.

In course of time all of them became Spiritualists. Who sowed the seed?

I joined myself to the Order, and became a Shaker. I have now had thirty-eight years' experience, and feel "satisfied with the goodness of God" and his people to me. I have gained a degree of victory over *self*, which causes my peace to "flow as a river," and which fills me with sympathy for *all* "seekers after truth" and righteousness, whoever and wherever they may be.

PART II.

THE SPIRITUAL MAN.

IN Part I. I have given an outline of my auto-biography in the external world ; and of my convincement—by means of the spiritual phenomena presented *to* and operating *in* me, as a worldly man, a materialist—that the Shaker Order was the highest mediator between God and man.

But here I am again embarrassed, by my own reali-zation of the unprepared state of many to appreciate the more interior religious exercises of soul involved in such a work of conversion. To it Jesus referred : " Neither cast ye your pearls before swine, lest they " —not comprehending their intrinsic value—" trample them under [the] foot" of their understanding ; "give not [lightly] that which is holy unto the dogs, [opposers] lest they turn again and rend you," for not giving them such kind of food as their appetites crave.

However, I am encouraged, in regard to others, by my own experience. I often used to think, in the early days of my faith, when I saw the brethren and sisters exercised in the beautiful gifts of the Spirit, which worldly Christians hold to be impossible in modern times, " How can I ever attain thereunto ? " and, " If I can reach such a baptism, no other human being need doubt the possibility of a like attainment."

After being rationally convinced, by the above-mentioned spiritualistic manifestations, that the claims of the Order were founded upon the existence of a Supreme Being and a revelation of knowledge and power (unto salvation from wilful sin, and from its very nature), coming down to mankind through intervening spheres and media, I was also blessed with a Christ Spirit baptism, by which I was interiorly convinced that I was a sinner before God ; and in that light I saw light and darkness, and perceived that many things, held in high estimation by even the most zealous of worldly Christians, were an abomination in the sight of that Christ Spirit.

I had now come to a day and work of judgment that I could comprehend ; and I esteemed it as a sacred privilege to bring to the light of earthly witnesses all the deeds I had done in the body and soul, whether they were good, or whether they were evil. Then I began to grow in grace and in the knowledge of the character of the first Christian, Jesus.

And I saw, according to the record,—the Bible,— that Jesus went with all the Jews in Judea, confessing their sins and transgressions against Moses, as the exponent of natural law for the earth-life. And John heard him, and was thereby convinced that Jesus had lived even nearer to the Law than he himself had done ; and said : "I have need [rather to confess unto thee, and] to be baptized of thee."

After that, Jesus was baptized by the descent of a Christ Spirit ; and then occurred (for the sake of the multitude) the external spiritualistic appearance of a dove and a voice. This spirit was the Second or spiritual Adam, the Lord from heaven, *the Christ.*

As Jesus had done to John, so did Ann to Jane Wardley,—confessed her sins, and repented of them to the entire forsaking thereof. "Who so confesseth and forsaketh them shall have mercy ;" while those who sin, and continue to cover their sins, as is the practice of the Christians of Babylon, do not prosper in the work of overcoming sin ; they live and die in their sins ; · and therefore where Jesus is, in the spirit world, they can find no entrance until they have confessed their sins (which "follow after them ") to God's acceptance. The simple Shakers prefer sending their sins " beforehand to judgment."

As each particle of gold possesses every one of the chemical properties of all the gold upon or in the earth, so does each human being possess all the elements and properties of humanity in the aggregate. The same process that would separate the dross from one ounce of gold would also serve to separate the dross from all the gold in existence.

And when it is satisfactorily proved that one man was the author of the system of Christianity, and that one woman was the finisher of that system, that is, that JESUS laid (or is) the " Corner Stone," and that ANN placed (or is) the Capstone of the Temple, and that each of them became a perfect " pattern," or specimen of genuine Christianity, unadulterated, free from any Babylon mixture, from all extraneous worldly elements adverse or pertaining thereto, it cannot but be clearly seen why those two should sit as refiners of silver and purifiers of gold to the remainder of mankind ; and why they, or their representatives, should watch carefully the crucible,— Shaker Society,—to see that each man and woman coming into it continue in the fire until, like the silver or the gold, the faces of the refiners become perfectly reflected in them,—until the same character is formed, —and the same mind and spirit shall be in them that was in JESUS and in ANN, as the " first born " brother and the " first born " sister of the new creation.

From the moment of the interior conviction already referred to, my life has been " hid with CHRIST," among this people, " in God;" and as an individual, I have been so absorbed into the community, that my personal history, " my policy," has become identified with the history and principles of the Order.

For at least five years before visiting the Shakers, I had been quietly and firmly settled as a Materialist. And, while I was heartily disgusted with all religious ideas and doctrines, yet I respected sincerity of faith and devotion (however erroneous it might be) in all human beings. But I had no more *respect* for the Bible than for any other book ; and I informed the brethren when I first came, that it was useless quoting from that particular book, to confirm any proposition which they might advance. Consequently, my faith in Shakerism does *not* rest upon the *Bible ;* nor do I now hold *it* as the Word of God, but as simply a compendium of Jewish literature,—Law, History, Poetry, Philosophy (according to the knowledge of the times when written), Ethics (often no better than that of cotemporary Avatars of other nations), Chronicles, and an account, more or less imperfect, of the spiritualism of the nation ; and, lastly, a record of the religious experiences of its devout men and women,— Seers, Prophets, and Prophetesses, from Adam to Jesus, and his immediate successors ; together with their promises, prophecies and visions.

And all of the publications that the Society had issued were utterly useless in the work of enlightening and converting me to the principles and faith of the Shakers, for the simple reason that the authors so entirely rested all their arguments upon the Bible, which, together with the fact that all those authors who had written *against* Shakerism also invariably rested their arguments upon *their* interpretation of Scripture, at once dispelled all desire in me to read *them*. When I was in New York, my brother, as a last resort, brought me some such books to answer their charges and accusations. But the reading to him a *prayer* on the cover of one of them, and a religious homily in the Preface of another, amply sufficed, in our estimation, to refute all they had written. For, to know that *Christians* hated and reviled the Shakers and their doctrines, was strong presumptive evidence to us that Shakerism, if not entirely true, was at the least well worth "looking into."

Mother Ann received an independent revelation from a Christ Spirit, as did Jesus. The largest number of her people having been very religious, zealous Quakers, Methodists, Baptists, etc., believed because her gifts and teaching so remarkably accorded with the Scriptures ; whilst I accepted the principles upon their own logical merits, and was sorry they were so Bibleish.

I therefore did not read either the Bible or a Shaker book until after I had been at Mt. Lebanon long enough to be fully established in Shakerism as the basis and ultimate of a new and independent revelation.

But by far the most extraordinary and wonderful part of my religious experience was and has ever been (to me) the coincidence with the Scriptures of my religious ideas and theology, as I had been forming it for the last thirty-eight years, when, after a time, I came to read them in the light and under the influence of a Christ baptism.

I read and use the Bible merely to illustrate my own ideas with other persons' language ; the same as a Frenchman would learn and use English through which to convey his French ideas. And, although it is now many years since I became reconciled to the Bible, and religious terms and phrases, I nevertheless continue, cordially and thoroughly, to hate *cant*,— using sacred words, and tone, and carriage, with no practical ideas connected therewith,—the *absence of common sense.*

Of all the books in the Bible, there was one with which I could not connect a single principle, or doctrine, that I believed, and *that* was the book of *Revelation* (to the exposition of which Part III. is devoted). I let *it* alone, until a comparatively short time ago, when I was impressed to read it through, which I did several times in succession ; at first, with about the same result that a Dictionary would give.

After a time, I began to see a little method in it ; and the light in which I stood continuing to shine upon its pages, gradually it has opened to my view somewhat as John saw it. But not until the present time, and while writing for the *Atlantic Monthly*, have I ever been able to go through the Vision, and see the *soul* of it—the key that rendered the shut-up open ; the mysterious, simple; the dark, light; the tangled and confused, regular and logical.

For I am now fully satisfied, that it is the clearest sunshine—the purest Vision—from the seventh or Resurrection heaven, that has ever come down to this generative, sin-stricken, and soul-darkened earth. So pure indeed, that, while John was sufficiently *innocent* to be the medium thereof, unadulterated, no other man has ever been able to even look upon it, or to bear its light, in consequence of the self-condemnation it would inflict.

And, happily for humanity, unlike all other of the books of Scripture, this one has escaped the twisting and " wrenching " to make it agree with the *ideal* of Christian truth as existing in the minds of translators; for the reason that they knew not what use to put it.

It was not until the times of the Gentiles were fulfilled, and the " Woman who had gone forth into Babylon "—the wilderness—had been delivered, and had brought forth the Daughter of Man,—Ann Christ, —that a people could form the character that would break the seal, and open the Apocalypse to earth's expectant inhabitants.

For the Vision of all the Apocalypse has become as a " book that is sealed, which one handed to him that was (spiritually) unlearned, saying, Read this! He answered, I cannot ; for I am unlearned." Then it was "handed to him that was (naturally) learned," (as those we have named—Scott, and others) "saying, Read this! and he answered, Neither can I read it; for it is sealed." I can indeed read the language, even in the original Greek; but the *ideas* connected with the words are so different from any heretofore associated with them in my mind, that "*I do not understand it; and do not believe that any other man knows any more of it than myself.*"—(Adam Clarke.)

It is "the Plan" of Human Redemption and Resurrection. I have now but just broken the seals, and opened the book. I shall hereafter proceed and study it *for myself*, by bearing faithfully the cross of Christ against all that is adverse to the Holy Spirit of the seventh heaven.

Moses of olden time hath in every city those who preach him, being read in the synagogues every Sabbath-day. And Jesus, for nearly two thousand years has had his heralds and ambassadors proclaiming his name, and preaching his *male* "gospel to every creature."

And now one " like the Son of Man " sits upon and points to some eighteen *white clouds* not much larger than a man's hand, rising above the horizon in different parts of America.

These clouds, which have *a future*, are the eighteen societies of Believers, as follows, viz. :—

Mount Lebanon, Columbia Co., N.Y., two and a half miles from Lebanon Springs, twenty-five miles southeast of Albany. Address F. W. Evans.

Watervliet, seven miles north-east of Albany.

Groveland, Livingston Co., N. Y.

4

Hancock, Berkshire Co., Mass.
Tyringham, same county and State.
Enfield, Hartford Co., Conn.
Harvard, Worcester Co., Mass.
Shirley, Middlesex Co., Mass.
Canterbury, Merrimack Co., N. H.
Enfield, Grafton Co., N. H.
Alfred, York Co., Maine.
New Gloucester, Cumberland Co., Maine.
Union Village, Warren Co., Ohio.
Watervliet, Montgomery Co., Ohio.
White Water, Hamilton Co., Ohio.
North Union, Cleveland, Cuyahoga Co., Ohio.
Pleasant Hill, Mercer Co., Ky.
South Union, Logan Co., Ky.

Be it mine to speak the praises of the *Mother*
Church ; and to introduce the readers of this publication to a " new thing in the earth,"—" a woman "
who has established a millennial community ; thus
en-*compass*-ing the primordial spiritual object of " a
man,"—JESUS.

" Turn again, O Virgin of Israel ! turn again to
these thy cities." As yet they shall use *this speech*
in the land of Judah, and in the cities thereof, when
I shall bring again their captivity. " And there shall
dwell in Judah itself, and in all the cities "—communities—" thereof, together, husbandmen and they
that go forth with flocks. For I have satiated the
weary soul, and I have replenished every sorrowful
soul :"—

" The Lord bless thee, O habitation of Justice, and
Mountain of Holiness !"

ANN LEE.

Ann Lee was born February 29, 1736, in Toad Lane (now Todd's Street), Manchester, England. Her father, John Lee, was a blacksmith, and poor; with him she resided until she left England for America. Her mother was esteemed a very pious woman. They had eight children, who were, as was then common for poor children, brought up to work, instead of being sent to school; by which means Ann acquired a habit of industry, but could neither write nor read. During her childhood and youth, she was employed in a cotton factory, and was afterwards a cutter of hatters' fur; and then a cook in an infirmary. She was in every calling noted for her neatness, faithfulness, prudence, and economy.

Her complexion was fair, she had blue eyes, and light chestnut hair. Her countenance was expressive, but grave, inspiring confidence and respect. Many called her beautiful.

She possessed a strong and healthy physical constitution, and remarkable powers of mind. At times, when under the operation of the Holy Spirit, her form and actions appeared divinely beautiful. The influence of her spirit was then beyond description, and she spoke as " one having authority."

In childhood she exhibited a bright, sagacious, and active genius. She was not, like other children, addicted to play, but was serious and thoughtful. She was early the subject of religious impressions, and was often favoured with heavenly visions.

As she grew in years, she felt an innate repugnance to the marriage state, and often expressed these feelings to her mother, desiring to be preserved therefrom ; notwithstanding which (through the importunities of her relatives), she was married to Abraham Stanley, a blacksmith. The convictions of her youth, however, often returned upon her with much force, and at length brought her into excessive tribulation of soul, in which she earnestly sought for deliverance from the bondage of sin, and gave herself no rest day or night, but spent whole nights in labouring and crying to God to open some way of salvation.

In the year 1758, the twenty-third of her age, she joined a society of people who, because of their indignation against sin in themselves, often shook, and (by the Spirit) were shaken, and hence by the rabble were designated *Shakers*. The society was under the lead of Jane and James Wardley, formerly of the Quaker order. The people of that society were blameless in their deportment, and were distinguished for the clearness of their testimony against sin, the strictness of their moral discipline, and the purity of their lives.

The light of this people led them to make an open confession of every sin they had committed, and to take up finally and for ever the cross against everything they knew to be evil. This endowed them with great power over sin ; and here Ann found that protection she had so long desired, and which corresponded with her faith at that time. She was baptized into the same spirit, and by degrees attained to the full knowledge and experience of all the spiritual truths of the society.

Her statement is: "I felt such a sense of my sins that I was willing to confess them before the whole world. I confessed my sins to my elders, one by one, and repented of them in the same manner. When my elders reproved me I felt determined not to be reproved twice for the same thing, but to labour to overcome the evil for myself. Sometimes I went to bed and slept; but in the morning, if I could not feel that sense of the work of God that I did before I slept, I would labour all night. This I did many nights, and in the daytime I put my hands to work and my heart to God, and the refreshing operations of the power of God would release me, so that I felt able to go to my work again.

"Many times, when I was about my work, I have felt my soul overwhelmed with sorrow. I used to work as long as I could keep it concealed, and then would go out of sight, lest any one should pity me with that pity which was not of God. In my travail and tribulation my sufferings were so great that my flesh consumed upon my bones, bloody sweat pressed through the pores of my skin, and I became as helpless as an infant. And when I was brought through and born into the spiritual kingdom, I was like an infant just born into the natural world. They see colours and objects, but they know not what they see. It was so with me; but before I was twenty-four hours old I saw, and knew what I saw."

Ann was wrought upon after this manner for the space of nine years. Yet she often had intervals of releasement, in which her bodily strength and vigour were sometimes miraculously renewed; and her soul was filled with heavenly visions and divine revelations. By these means the way of God and the nature of his work gradually opened upon her mind with increasing light and understanding.

She spent much time in earnest and incessant cries to God to show her the foundation of man's loss,—what it was, and wherein it consisted,—and how the way of salvation could be discovered and effectually opened to mankind in their present condition, and how the great work of redemption was to be accomplished.

The ultimate effect of the labour and suffering of soul that Ann passed through was to purify and fitly prepare her for becoming a temple in which the Christ Spirit, that had made the *first* appearing to Jesus, and constituted him Jesus Christ, could make a *second* appearing; and through whom the God of heaven could set up a church, or "kingdom which should never be destroyed."

While Ann, for bearing her testimony against "fleshly lusts, which war against the soul," was imprisoned in Manchester, England, she saw Jesus Christ in open vision, who revealed to her the most astonishing views and divine manifestations of truth, in which she had a perfect and clear sight of the "mystery of iniquity," the root and foundation of all human depravity.

From the time of this appearing of Christ to Ann in prison (1770), she was received by the people as a mother in spiritual things, and was thenceforth by them called Mother Ann.

The exercises in their religious meetings were singing and dancing, shaking, turning, and shouting, speaking with new tongues, and prophesying, with all those various gifts of the Holy Spirit known in the Primitive Church. These gifts progressively increased until the time of the full organisation and establishment of the Shaker Church in America, in the year 1792.

On the 19th of May, 1774, Mother Ann, with eight of her followers, embarked in the ship *Mariah* for New York, where they arrived on the 6th of August following. They proceeded to Albany, and thence to Watervliet, which was at that time a wilderness, and called Niskeuna, where they remained very secluded for about three years and a half.

Mother Ann, having finished her work on earth, departed this life, at Watervliet, on the 8th day of September, 1784, aged forty-eight years and six months.

Thus it is an interesting fact, that Ann Lee, the ostensible founder of the Shaker system of Religious Socialism, was an uneducated woman—that is, according to the popular idea of education. But was she, therefore, uneducated, unlearned? Neither Confucius, nor Zoroaster, nor Plato, nor Homer, nor even the Prophets of Israel, would pass an examination in a sophomore class at college. Of Jesus it was asked, "How knoweth this man letters, having never learned?" And it is certain that Ann, in her normal state, could neither write nor read. Yet Shakerism *only* is successful Communism; and (so far as I am aware) is the only religious system that teaches science by Divine revelation; and it also teaches that all true science leads directly thereto,

as in the case of Swedenborg,—one of the most
learnedly-scientific men of his time—by whom it
evolved *Spiritualism*. He was contemporary with
Ann, who said he was her John the Baptist. He,
not the Fox girls, was the angel of modern Spiritualism, which is the last and highest of the sciences,
inasmuch as it teaches the geography of the spirit
world, resting, as does all science, upon facts—
supernatural phenomena. It is the very science that
Materialists should learn. It (as well as astronomy,
chemistry, agriculture, etc.) has always been an
element of Shakerism. There may be Spiritualism
without religion, but there can be no religion without
Spiritualism, which is as a bayou flowing out from
the great River of Divine Revelation, in Shakerism,
to the sea—world.

It was by spiritual manifestations (as I have stated
in Part I.) that I, in 1830, was converted to Shakerism.
In 1837 to 1844, there was an influx from the spirit
world, "confirming the faith of many disciples" who
had lived among believers for years, and extending
throughout all the eighteen societies, making media
by the dozen, whose various exercises, not to be
suppressed even in their public meetings, rendered it
imperatively necessary to close them all to the world
during a period of seven years, in consequence of the
then unprepared state of the people, to which the
whole of the manifestations, and the meetings, too,
would have been as unadulterated "foolishness," or as
inexplicable mysteries.

The spirits then declared, again and again, that,
when they had done their work amongst the inhabi-

tants of Zion, they would do a work in the world, of such magnitude, that not a palace nor a hamlet upon earth should remain unvisited by them.

After their mission amongst us was finished, we supposed that the manifestations would immediately begin in the outside world; but we were much disappointed; for we had to wait four years before the work began, as it finally did, at Rochester, N.Y. But the rapidity of its course throughout the nations of the earth (as also the social standing and intellectual importance of the converts) has far exceeded the predictions.

In Revelation (xviii.) it is said, an angel came "down from heaven, having great power, and the earth was lightened with his glory." That is *Spiritualism,* and Swedenborg was the type of it, just as Jesus was the type of Christianity in his day, and as Ann Lee was the type of Christianity in its second advent upon the earth.

It is a fact, patent to all observers, that what the religious world designated by the vague and (in many respects) unmeaning epithet of opprobrium, *Infidelity,* had made itself respectable and respected in such men as Hume, Volney, Voltaire, Frederick the Great of Prussia, and the whole host of writers of the French Encyclopædia—got up for the express purpose of overthrowing Christianity; for the signature with which Voltaire was in the habit of closing his articles for the press was "Crush the wretch!" meaning Jesus Christ. These were the "horns" that grew out of the beast, and that "hated the whore"— the "whore of Babylon," the Catholic Church—and tormented her with their fiery missiles of truth, ending in the French Revolution, the abolition of the Sabbath, and of all Church establishments and services, and the deification of *Reason*, personified in a young female, who was paraded through the streets of Paris in a state of nudity; thus undesignedly foreshadowing the coming Woman.

The "second beast" (which was the "image" of the first) "had two horns like a lamb"—Luther and Calvin—but "he spoke as a dragon, exercising all the persecuting power of the first beast" (unto whom he gave his power), as see Henry VIII., its head, who destroyed *two of his six wives*, and died a monster of depravity, after putting to death, by burning and hanging, for their *heresies*, "seventy-two thousand of his subjects"—(Blackwood). "He soaked the earth with Protestant blood"—(Cobbett).

Those same "horns" (powers), growing out of the "image of the beast,"—Protestantism,—produced the American Revolution. Thomas Paine, Washington, Franklin, Jefferson, and their compeers of the same class,—Deists, Materialists, Universalists, Unitarians, Freethinkers, Infidels, — framed the Declaration of Rights, or first principles of a Civil Government, and formed a Constitution, which was but a compromise, for the time being, between right and expediency, but which contained within itself the power of amendment,—of growth towards those first principles. And, if it did not abolish slavery, it did abolish "the beast" of Church and State; for it separated the Church from the Civil Government. It was "the earth opening its mouth to swallow up the flood" of religious persecution ; thus helping the woman, Ann Lee, to found an Order, or Church, in America, which could not exist even in England, much less in any other nation ; for hitherto, under the reign of the "beast and the image of the beast," the Civil Government had been the sword of the Chureh, by which to punish infidels and heretics. Yet these antagonistic "horns" grew out of the "beast." Now, a thing is supported by what it grows out of, and of which it is a component part; therefore it is added, "they ate her flesh,"—were part and parcel of Babylon.

The angel of Spiritualism has "great power" to act upon material things, by rapping, and moving tables, chairs, bells, musical instruments, etc.; thus "confounding the wisdom of the wise" and scientific Materialists, and converting them to a belief in God, a spirit world, the progressive nature and immortality of the human soul, and its sequences,—in short, doing with such men as Robert Owen and Robert Dale Owen—types of a class—what all the Churches in England had, for half a century, laboured in vain to do. These men made ten converts from the churches, while the churches were trying to make one from the ranks of the infidels. They were "lightened with the glory" of the angel of Spiritualism, and were enlightened and quickened by it, too, into more life than the "dead bodies" of the churches possessed.

Nor was this all, or the worst of it. For the Christians, who said, "We will go and do the will of God"—do right to humanity—did not do right ; but they, as their opponents said, "pointed to the heavens, and thither directed the attention of their hearers, while they took possession of the earth from under their feet;" and then, for the first time, in England, were built poor-houses and taverns, for the needy and travellers, instead (as was the case under the Catholic rule) of religious institutions, where the poor should be fed and cared for, and the wandering traveller lodged [Cobbett]; while the infidels, who denied the existence of the Christians' Triune God, said, "We will not do his bidding," did do good to humanity, and sought to establish communities, as at New Lanark and New Harmony, and a hundred other places, to restore (unwittingly) the Christian institution of "all things common," some of them spending their whole lives and immense fortunes to do what it was the first duty of a Christian priesthood to accomplish—fulfill the prophecy, and make provision for every man to "sit under his own vine and fig-tree," upon his own land, thus realising one of the beatitudes of Jesus, by causing the meek to "inherit the earth."

I had often heard of the "*plan of salvation;*" but to me it seemed a poor plan, as it had been arranged. For its elementary doctrines were, a Trinity of *male* Gods creating man, who sins; the birth, by a woman, of one of the Trinity; his final death as an atonement for man's sins; then the re-animation of his body to life, and the transmutation of his physical into a spiritual body; and then, finally, the ultimate re-animation of all the bodies of the human race, to undergo a like transformation. Then a similar change in the earth itself, on an external day of judgment, etc., etc. After all this, each and every

person would pass into a perfect heaven of the most
consummate purity and holiness, or be plunged into
a burning hell of veritable fire and brimstone, there
to remain for ever and ever; the event to depend
upon what they had or had not done during the
short term of their earth-life.

These doctrines I was taught when a child, and I
supposed that I believed them. But the truth of
the matter is, to such an extent are man and woman
and child "the creatures of circumstances" (as Owen
would put it) that a large proportion of them are
not accountable for their condition, physical, moral,
or religious. Therefore it would be decidedly wrong
to send them to any worse hell than their own state
constitutes. And what sort of a heaven would it be
that could admit such persons within its precincts?

The theology of Christendom had degenerated into
the mere doctrines of devils—of unreasoning authority; for Babylon "is become the habitation of devils,
and the hold of every foul spirit, and a cage of every
unclean and hateful bird." The deification of Reason
was but the swing of the pendulum to the other extreme. The Church was at war with science—with
astronomy, and was not willing that the earth should
turn upon its own axis; with *geology*, limiting all its
records to six thousand years; with *chemistry*, in con-
travention of the maxim, that "from nothing comes
nothing, and that not anything can be annihilated,"
claiming that all things were made out of nothing;
with *physiology*, by teaching that destructive plagues
(as cholera, small-pox, etc.) came of Divine appointment, and were to be stayed only by church rites;

with *agriculture*, by praying for good crops, without first enforcing, as indispensable requisites, drainage, subsoiling, fertilising, the protection of birds, and diligent attention to the laws of God in Nature.

In fine, Babylon, in her war upon Nature, upon science, upon human reason, has been worsted; and now she is like a whale with a thrasher on its back and a sword-fish under its belly; for she has Shakerism, with its Divine revelations, assailing her from above, and Spiritualism, embodying all the sciences, working upon her from below.

Therefore, with much propriety, did the *next angel*, who followed the angel of Spiritualism, and witnessed its effects, announce to a thankful and rejoicing universe, "Babylon is fallen, is fallen." As a "great millstone cast into the sea, thus with violence shall that great city Babylon," the adulterous mixture of Church and State, right and wrong, peace and war, humility and pride, monastic celibacy, and sacramental marriage, Hebraism and Mahometanism, Christianity and Heathenism, all commingled together in Christendom, be destroyed, and dissolved by the "fervent heat" generated by Divine revelation and human reason co-operating; yea, she "shall be utterly burned with fire" and consumed by the flame of scientific and revealed truth, "for strong is the Lord God who judgeth her," and mighty are the Church of God, and the earthly Civil Government of America, which will *execute the judgment* (to be finally passed upon every nation, kingdom, and state upon earth) by the spread of republican principles and the everlasting *Gospel of Jesus Christ and Mother Ann.* Thus will celibacy in the Shaker Order operate as a substitute for poverty, famine, disease, and war, in governing the unreasoning, unlimited principle of human reproduction.

Then there will be formed and established a legitimate union of the true Christian Church with a true Civil Government, each in its order, like soul and body. And then "out of Zion shall go forth the Law, and the Word of the Lord from Jerusalem,"—the Church of Christ's Second Appearing ; and the nations shall "not learn war any more" ; but, instead thereof, the people shall learn (and practise) agriculture, horticulture, manufacturing, and just commerce—exchange of equal values.

I understand that Emerson, in a recent lecture in Boston, made some statements relative to communities, the causes of their failure, etc. Robert Owen published his view of the causes of failure at New Harmony, as follows :—" There was not disinterested industry ; there was not mutual confidence ; there was not practical experience ; there was not unison of action, because there was not unanimity of counsel. These were the points of difference and dissension, the rock upon which the social bark struck, and was wrecked."

I will state my view, and endeavour to elucidate and defend it. A permanently successful community must necessarily be the external body of a true Christian Church of Christ's Second Appearing.

An angel said to Esdras : " For in the place where the Highest beginneth to show his city, there can no man's building be able to stand." Perhaps all professing Christians will agree, that the time when the

Lord God began to show his power the most directly
in organising and building them into a "city," was
on the day of Pentecost, when He gathered together
the people of one nation,—the Jews,—and, from
among them, individuals of one and the same class,
namely, spiritualists (religionists), who in that place
formed a community. In it, the males and females
were separated ; thus laying the foundation of the
two monastic orders of the Gentile Christian Church.
These (male and female) were the "two witnesses,"
within that Church, for the original order of the
Jewish Primitive Christian Church ; and the line of
the "heretics" (male and female), ending in the
Quakers, produced the "two witnesses," *outside* of the
national church, for the principles of that Primitive
Church ; celibacy, community, revelation, spiritualism,
non-resistance, simplicity of dress and language, and
health. For none of these *heretical* "witnesses" held
to *all* of these Christian principles ; and therefore
their Organization, resting upon them "in part" only,
could not possibly "stand ;" but have been, or will be,
(finally) "done away."

But suppose I present a succinct consecutive view
of the "Plan of Salvation," as seen from a Shaker
stand-point. I the more readily do this, because I
know that most theologians will agree with Dr.
Adam Clarke and Dr. Cumming, that "the only key
with which to unlock the mysteries of godliness,—
of prophecy and vision, and of the 'Revelation'—is
the actual occurrence of the central event, the Second
Appearance of Christ." And I have great satisfaction in being able to state that this important and

transcendently-glorious event took place in the year
1770 (see p. 38) ; and the permanent " setting-up,"
or establishment of his kingdom (or Church) upon
earth, occurred at the time—1792—assigned by Dr.
Cumming as the end of the twelve hundred and sixty
years,—the " reign of the beast ;" the period of time
during which the "woman" who "fled into the
wilderness" remained there ; and the period during
which the "two witnesses" prophesied ; all ending'
in the year 1792, when the "sanctuary" or church
was to be "cleansed, and an end made of sin." In
that very year the Shaker Church was founded. At
that time Believers were gathered into community
order by Joseph Meacham and Lucy Wright (called
Father Joseph and Mother Lucy), as Mother Ann,
previous to her decease, had said would be the
case.

Joseph Meacham and Luey Wright were among
the first of those in America who received faith in
the religious principles of Shakerism. Upon them
the leadership and government of the people (Shakers) devolved. Under their administration, the principles in regard to property and order in general
were fully carried out, and a community of goods
was established.

They gradually gathered the people from their
scattered condition into families. Orders, rules, and
regulations, in temporal and spiritual things, were
framed. Elders and deacons of both sexes were
appointed, and set in their proper order ; and a
Covenant was written and entered into, for the
mutual understanding and protection of the members.

Joseph Meacham was a Baptist preacher in New Lebanon, and a prominent leader in the religious revival out of which the Society of Mount Lebanon originated. He was born in Enfield, Connecticut, February 22, 1742, of one of the best families. He was a philosopher, intuitional and revelational, and was "learned in all the learning of the Egyptians." That he was a man of great executive ability is proved by his success in organising and establishing the Shaker community system. He died August the 16th, 1796.

Lucy Wright, who stood with him in that work, was born in Pittsfield, Massachusetts. She was of one of the most wealthy and influential families in the town, and was a beautiful woman, and of extra-ordinary intellectual and moral endowments. She succeeded Father Joseph as the head of the Society, and was designated Mother Lucy. She died February 7th, 1821.

But what *is* the Shaker Church? and what relation does it bear to the present and the future, and to the history of religious ideas, as they have descended with the tide of time from the beginning, and especially as they stand recorded in the Anglo-Saxon Bible? Is it a normal or an abnormal institution? I claim that it is the fruit of the tree of *humanity*, ripened under the laws of progressive development, operating ever since the world began.

SERPENT.

The medium of temptation to the first human pair was their physical, sensuous nature,—"the serpent" seducing them by the mere desire of pleasure, in the exercise of their creative powers, to ignore and do despite to the *law of use*, which is, "Whether ye eat or drink, or whatsoever ye do," let it be, not for the pleasurable sensations attending, but for the "honour and glory of God,"—*use*, as in the originating of an immortal soul. For simple generation, in and of itself, as originally instituted, was as innocent as eating and drinking. God and Nature made man upright; but he has sought the lusts of generation (the flesh), the lusts of eating and drinking, and finally added the lusts of the mind,—the intellectual faculties; so that, in the days of Jesus, "the serpent," which began in Eden by crawling upon the earth on his belly, had become a winged serpent or dragon, causing mankind to wax worse and worse, and was the symbol of Paganism in the aggregate.

In the *Third Epoch*, this dragon became a fiery, flying dragon, or serpent : the fall into self-hood had involved the spiritual faculties in humanity, so that the people, thinking to do God and humanity service, could perpetrate murder by torture.

FOUR DISPENSATIONS.

The same idea of progress by successive stages, is often used by the various Prophets, under different symbols : Ezekiel saw four issues of water from beneath the threshold of the temple : first, to the ankles ; second, to the knees ; third, to the loins ; the fourth was an impassable river,—the time when the Spirit should be poured out upon all flesh ; the old having dreams ; the young, visions of spiritual things ; the knowledge of the Lord covering the earth, as the waters do the land under the sea.

These four Epochs are again represented to John, the beloved disciple, by *four beasts*—a lion, a calf, a beast with a face like a man, and a flying eagle. These symbols portray the progress of man, from the lowest to the highest condition of natural humanity ; while the four outflowings of water represent the influxes from the Christ sphere, or seventh heaven, passing down through the six inferior generative heavens, and portray the progress of man from the lowest to the highest condition of *spiritual* humanity.

THE LION EPOCH.

The *Lion Epoch*, from Adam to Abraham, is the wild, animal phase of human progress,—when man lived by hunting, clothed himself in skins, and practised war as an exciting amusement, like the American Indians. During this Dispensation, the earth was filled with violence ; might made right. In those times there were giants ; and the mammoths and mastodons were to them as the horse and ox and elephant are to us.

THE CALF EPOCH.

The *Calf Epoch*, from Abraham to Jesus, is the second stage of progress, wherein food and clothing obtain, as under Moses, Confucius, Zoroaster, Romulus, the Pharaohs, and their contemporaries. In this Epoch, the arts and sciences are cultivated ; mechanics, mathematics, architecture,—it is the temple era ; pyramids are built, and great walls, like those of China ; and massive works, that remain for ages,—bridges, arches, and roads.

In Israel, while in the wilderness, the Lord called Bezaleel, and "filled him with the Spirit of God, in wisdom, and in understanding, and in knowledge, and in all manner of workmanship, to devise cunning works, to work in gold and in silver, and in brass, and in cutting of stones, to set them, and in carving of timber, to work in all manner of workmanship;" to the erection and embellishment of buildings, and the making of tools, etc. ; all culminating (in the days of Solomon) in the glorious kingdom of Israel, and the world-renowned and splendid temple, which was dedicated to, and sanctified by, the God of Israel, as a house of prayer for all nations ; which temple is said to have been composed of all known earthly sub-stances, as indicating that the good and true in all people will be incorporated into the final temple of God,—the *Church of* JESUS CHRIST *and* MOTHER ANN.

The same laws were in operation in all contempo-rary nations, producing similar results : a Saviour, a Bible, statutory laws, a temple, as of Jupiter, and Diana, and Apollo, in which the deities of the several nations were often manifested as really as in Israel's temple. But the God of Israel, though a God of mar-riage, and war, and slavery, was God of these gods, and Lord of their lords ; because Israel was the model and typical nation—progressive,—having prophecies and promises (a reflection from the Christ sphere, which was the true Pattern shown on the Mount, of things to come), up to the manifestation of John the Baptist, the harbinger of their Messiah—Jesus ; and to the appearing to him of the Christ Spirit, who, as his God and Guardian Angel, suddenly came to his prepared temple—the man Jesus.

This system of spiritual theology is not confined to this little earth, but is equally applicable to the inhabitants of all the material worlds within the universe of Nature, whether fallen or unfallen ; the Christ, or Resurrection Order,—the *seventh heaven*,—being the only Mediator, or intervening sphere, between souls in all worlds and the *Esse* of Life, or Final First Cause, the Eternal Father and Mother—GOD.

THE FACE-OF-A-MAN EPOCH.

The " *Face-of-a-Man* " *Epoch*, from Jesus to Ann Lee, is the third stage of the onward movement of humanity. There is the "beast," or animal, as a basis, as heretofore ; but now we have, on the surface of society, Christianity in name. Whole nations of Pagans are, under Constantine and his successors, converted by the sword ; the people are baptised by *force;* their temples are turned into churches, and their priests into a Christian priesthood ; their statues of gods and goddesses are converted into the likenesses of the various apostles and saints ; and, for the images of the Virgin Mary, the statues of Venus afford an ample supply.—(Mosheim.)

Thus do we find, in Christendom, a mixture of Hebraism, Paganism, and Mahometanism, with just enough of Christianity to gild it over. As Dixon puts it : " The truth is, we English and Americans have hardly yet embraced Christianity as a scheme of life. We find our religion at church; and when we have sung our psalms, and breathed our prayers, we go back into the streets to be governed, for another week, by our Pagan laws, derived from the Roman Pandects, or from the code of Justinian." "Foremost," says the same writer, "among the seekers after light are the Shaker brethren at Mount Lebanon, in the State of New York."

In a Mahometan country, Dixon asserts, the Koran is a law-book; but not so the Bible in Christendom. For the equalization of land by Moses, and the perfecting of the process of reproduction, this Third Epoch has substituted the monastic orders, with common property and celibacy for the few; and, for the clergy and the many, Pagan monopoly.

Hence the late Archbishop Hughes, when on a visit to Mount Lebanon, after investigating the Shaker system in the most searching manner, remarked: "The principles of your order have always been held by the Catholic Church. Celibacy is enjoined upon the clergy; common property is a monastic rule, as is also non-resistance. But your order is higher than ours, in that, what we require of a small number of our most advanced members in the Church, you expect and exact of all, from the greatest to the least."

THE FLYING-EAGLE EPOCH.

The *Flying-Eagle Epoch* is a compound and complex Dispensation, embracing a perfected *spiritual* government, and a perfected *civil* government in the natural order; embodying all the elements of Divine revelation in Nature, relating to reproduction, nutrition, clothing, architecture, agriculture,—all science applied to human happiness on the earth-plane,— Republicanism; the *eagle* being the ensign of true godly Republicanism, as was the *dragon* of Paganism; while the eagle, with wings superadded, the *flying eagle*, is the Resurrection Church,—*Shakerism*, —rising above the earthly order of a mere civil government (however just and orderly) into the pure and holy sphere of abstract Christianity.

These four living creatures are the four Dispensations, the complete history of humanity in the *external order*, from the beginning of time to the end of the human race,—*natural humanity*,—moving towards the millennial state, wherein there will be a spiritual order, the soul; and a natural order, the body of mankind; a Civil Government (having a balance of power, being composed equally of men and women; perhaps the Senate being the *female* branch of the government, as the House will be the *male* branch; and the President, as at present, the executive) enforcing, as the most important of all its functions, a strict observance of the natural law of generation, *intercourse for offspring only;* and as a logical sequence, "wars and fightings" will "cease to the ends of the earth."

Then the higher law of *celibacy*, from a ground of progress, will continually go from Zion, the spiritual order, to regulate the populative principle; and the Word of the Lord, through the President, as the executive of the Republic, enforcing the moral law in its entirety; and there will be no more sickness, or

premature death by fœticide and infanticide, or the
"social evil," or riches, or poverty, or over-population ;
for one order "will sing the song of Moses, the servant of God," and the other will "sing the song of
the Lamb"—Jesus.

These two lines of progress existed in each individual of the race, from the beginning, and were
marked in the race itself by the two sons of Adam,—
Cain and Abel, and their descendants. Cain was
begotten under the law of *lust;* Abel under the true
natural law.

The Pagan nations came of Cain, and descended
in Pharaoh,—Egypt,—passing through Ishmael, the
brother of Isaac, to his posterity, and on to Tiberius
Cæsar,—Rome,—who slew his righteous brother,
Jesus, as Cain did Abel ; then, continuing through
Judas, the antithesis of Jesus, to his posterity, culmi-
nated in the Pope, Luther, Calvin, Mahomet,—the
whole Antichristian world,—*Babylon.*

THE FOUR ISSUES OF WATER.

The *first* outflowing of the waters was only to the
ankles, beginning with Abel ; thus showing that
Divine revelation to man from the Christ heavens
was only a small beginning and weak ; existing
rather as a spirit of prophecy ; operating practically
to cause the righteous to observe the laws of Nature
in nutrition, to sustain the individual ; and in propagation, to continue the race.

The *second* outflowing of the waters was to the
knees,—from Abraham to Jesus. Here the revelation
from the Resurrection Order began more distinctly

to show its true character and design, by types and shadows of future things ; putting restraints upon the appetite respecting what to eat, and when and how to propagate; attaching penalties to sin either by fornication, or by disorderly, unnatural, and untimely sexual intercourse of married persons ; and exacting the offering up of children to the Lord, to be brought up in the temple as Nazarites,—celibates ; and requiring the mark of circumcision upon all males, as a prophetic sign that the Christ Spirit would ultimately lead the *true* descendants of Abel and Isaac to cut themselves off from the order and work of generation, by becoming circumcised in thought and imagination.

For in the *third* dispensation, propagation was a work which belonged exclusively to the *true* descendants of Cain and Ishmael, and not to the "seed of the woman," who were to "bruise the serpent's head," —the lust of generation—by "slaying" the innocent "lamb" of nature, generation itself ; thus effectually cutting themselves off "from the foundation of the world." In this manner they become "lambs of God," who are continually "taking away the sins of the world ;" "Saviours upon Mount Zion," to destroy in themselves the work of Esau—natural generation.

The *third* outflowing of the waters was to the loins. Now the waters—Christ elements—had become deep enough to enable many men and women to swim free from the earthly, animal work of physical reproduction; thus dividing the spiritual posterity of Jesus into two parts, as was divided the natural posterity of Adam in the instances of Cain and Abel, Isaac and Ishmael, and Jacob and Esau ; distinguishing those who (by means of having the sexes separated in monasteries and nunneries) lived a celibate life, as did Jesus, the twelve Apostles, and all of the Pentecostal Jewish Christian Church, from those who had been heathens,—Gentiles,—the posterity of Cain, Ishmael, Esau, and Judas, who, under the combined influences of Hebraism and Christianity, continued the order of marriage.

The early Christians held that no Pagan could become a Christian, without first becoming a Jew, and keeping intact the Law of Moses.

In this Third Epoch,—the first appearing of Christ, —the waters reached only to the seat of the generative life,—"the loins." One of the most perfect of the Prophets of the past said (lamentingly), "My loins are filled with a loathsome disease,"—lust. Of him even Peter affirmed, "David is not ascended into the [Resurrection] heavens."

And another, speaking of the saints of the Ankles-and-Knees Dispensation, declared, "These all died in faith, not having received the promises made from time to time by the Christ Spirit that followed them," and once in a long time found a Prophet through whom to portray a true Christian, and project hopes of future glory.

Their souls were in paradise, the Jewish heaven, into which Jesus (and the thief) entered immediately after passing out of the body, and preached to them as he had done to their posterity in Jerusalem ; and thousands of these faithful souls believed, and went with Jesus, as his witnesses, on his mission to the antideluvians, whence he " descended into their hell."

There Jesus and his disciples preached to those who, when upon earth, had been giants in wickedness, whose every thought and imagination had been only for sensual indulgence in eating and drinking, and in marrying and giving in marriage ; and who mocked Noah, while he, being spiritually instructed, was constructing a large ship, in which to save a seed of all living creatures upon earth, to contain them and their food during a period of forty days. And "for this cause was the Gospel preached to them, that they might be judged" in the same way and manner, by the truth preached, as were those who were still in the body and upon the earth, in Jerusalem.

After this, Jesus appeared (in spirit) to one of his friends, and informed her that he had not yet ascended to his own proper Resurrection heaven.

THE IMPASSABLE RIVER.

Now there is to be no more walking upon the earth, and at the same time wading in the water. The time of the Gentile Christians is "fulfilled," in which, "if they married, they did no sin," but they should "have trouble in the flesh."

Now there is required a full sacrifice of the Adamic man and woman, an "end of the world," which, with the lusts and elements thereof, shall be "melted," by the operation of the "fervent heat" of truth, and "pass away." Old things are to be done away, and all things are to become new ; a perpetual Sabbath of worship ; a continual "feast of tabernacles ;" a never-ending camp meeting ; a last supper or sacrament, where the guests no more separate to go and eat at the table of isolation, after having eaten as brethren and sisters "in common" at the Lord's table; a baptism in "the river of life," cleansing the soul from the "uncleannesses" of a generative nature, and "from the corruptions that are in the world through lust."

For as, "in the days of Noah, they were eating and drinking, marrying and giving in marriage, until the flood came and killed them all, *so* shall it be at the coming of the Son of Man," the second direct appearing of the Christ Spirit upon the earth. For whereas the flood arrested and cut them off from all those practices, by physical death, the operation of truth, by this manifestation of the Christ Spirit, more effectually arrests mankind by the death of the generative life itself; thus bringing the world to an end in them. "Ye are they upon whom the ends of the world are come"—the end of marriage, of selfish property, oaths, war, sickness, unbelief in Spiritualism and Divine Revelation.

———

In Part III. I intend giving a more full exposition of the theories and principles of *Shakerism ;* and will endeavour to show that they agree with and pervade the whole book of the *Apocalypse,* just as the soul of a man possesses and permeates all the parts of his physical body.

PART III.

REVELATION OF THE APOCALYPSE.

DR. ADAM CLARKE says, he is "satisfied that no certain mode of interpreting this book has yet been found out. I have read elaborate works upon the subject, and each seemed right until another was examined. I will not add another monument to the littleness and folly of the human mind by endeavouring to strike out a new course. I repeat: *I do not understand the book;* and I am satisfied that not one who has written on the subject knows any more of it than myself. Disappointment laughs at hope's career." That was not only candid, but *true.*

"Go and tell this people, Hear ye, indeed, but understand not; and see ye, indeed, but perceive not. Make the heart of this people fat (with learning), and make their ears heavy (earthy), and shut their eyes (seal their spiritual senses), lest they see with their eyes, and hear with their ears, and understand with their heart, and convert, and be healed" —saved.

Jesus said to his *followers,*—"Unto *you* it is given to know the *mysteries* of the kingdom of God; but to *others* I speak in parables, that though seeing, they might not see; and though hearing, they might not understand."

That the central event of that Vision was the Second direct Appearing of Christ is freely admitted by all the divines and commentators in Christendom. Clarke, Scott, Cumming, Noel, and (lastly) Shimeall, agree in this one thing.

Now, inasmuch as the Shakers claim that Christ *has* made his second appearing, they must also claim possession of the "keys" by which to unlock these mysteries, so far as history has progressed.

Therefore, all previous attempts to interpret the Vision have been premature, and were made upon the first principles of Antichrist: a trinity; direct communication of each soul with deity possible; atonement; physical resurrection; one heaven, one hell; no probationary state beyond this life; and no present revelation.

Whereas, our first principles are, Duality of Deity, and that there are seven heavens; each one, except the *seventh*, having its corresponding hell; and each one ascending as a spiritual world to the one below, or exterior to it; and that they are joined together by revelation—vision; so that, "where there is no vision, the people," in all worlds, "perish," as in the Protestant world, because they are disconnected with Deity from above.

These spheres, or heavens, exist one within another, as the spirit within the soul, and as the soul within the physical body. Each heaven has its God, a representative of Deity, who receives the Word of God by revelation from the heaven above him. "If ye called them gods unto whom" (only) "the Word of God came," as the God of Israel, and the gods of

the heathen nations, who were ministered unto by
the God of Israel, He being "God of gods;" as
the Gentile Christian Church was ministered to by
the Jewish Christian Church, from the Leaders of the
one to the Leaders of the other. Probation continues
throughout the six generative heavens; hence, even
"the heavens," being all generative, "are not clean in
thy sight;" that is, the souls in them have not been
resurrected.

There has not been, nor will there ever be, any
physical resurrection.

The *seventh* heaven is the Resurrection heaven.
Each heaven has also its Holy Spirit. A baptism
of the Holy Spirit of either of the first six heavens,
always operated to perfect the process (in the line of
the Messiah) of reproduction in those who received
it; as in the creation of Abel, Seth, Noah, and
Enoch; of Abraham, Isaac, and Jacob; of Samuel,
John the Baptist, and Jesus—fathers; with a corresponding class of mothers. While a baptism by the
Holy Christ Spirit was always *death to the generative
life* in those upon whom it rested, and made them
eunuchs and celibates—*virgins*—to the honour and
glory of God and humanity.

St. John received a revelation from God; but it
came through Jesus Christ; and then through "the
angel" by whom he sent it; and John passed it on
down to earthly, human beings. (See Revelation
i. 1.) This Revelation is a historical chart of the
past, present, and future history of the race; divided
into seven histories, and these again subdivided into
other sevens; like wheels within wheels, each wheel

a fac-simile of every other wheel ; so that the history of one cycle is the history of every other cycle ; "there being no prophecy of any private interpretation," as it will apply again and again in other cycles. The reason being, that the same general principles are applicable to every cycle, human nature being and remaining always the same.

That is why, in all ages, there have been efforts (plausible ones, too,) made to interpret finally the book of "*Revelation.*"

When Catholic missionaries first went to India, they found so great a resemblance between the religious ideas and temple ceremonies of the natives and those of their own Church, that they concluded the Devil had taught them to the Hindoos, in order to prevent their conversion by thus forestalling the true Catholic faith.

There was to be a day, the light of which "should be as the light of seven days." (See Isaiah xxx. 26 to end.)

"In the days of the voice of the seventh trumpet, the mystery of God" (in the Revelation) was to "be finished."

John mistook the angel sent by Jesus Christ unto him for the Deity, whereas he was only a fellow prophet.

The Seven Churches of Asia contain all the principles of good and evil involved in the whole history.

Revelation, i. 5.—" Jesus Christ, who is the faithful witness, and first begotten of the dead."

This is our starting-point, that Jesus was a faithful and true witness of *what* Christianity *is*, and an

6

example in himself of just what a Christian *should be*.
Mankind were all dead in sin, and in nature ; and
he was the *first* of the dead to be begotten by the
Christ Spirit ; the " first - born of many brethren."
This is the key to the whole of the book of Vision—
the Apocalypse. And as no child is born the first
time (into this world) without sufferings, of itself,
and its mother, and friends, and its first sound is
a cry ; so is it in being born a second time (into the
Christ sphere, or heaven). Therefore it is asserted,
" all kindreds shall wail because of him ;" for " out
of his *mouth* went a sharp two-edged sword "—words
—the testimony of Jesus.

Jesus was a microcosm of the race. The whole
Apocalypse is in each individual. All its epochs,
seals, trumpets, vials, plagues, and thunders, are the
travail of soul of the natural man and woman towards
the Resurrection Order. " I am he that *liveth*, and
WAS *dead* (not physically), and have the keys of hell
and of death." In each human soul exist the germs
of a Christ life. " Except a grain of wheat fall into
the ground and die, it abideth alone :" the whole
matter lies just here.

The life in a human soul seeks first to propagate
itself by *natural generation*. That life element *can
be inverted by death ;* for, as the grain of wheat dies
to transmit its life to its successors, so did Jesus *die*,
to be awoke, or resurrected, in the likeness of the
Christ Spirit. He was a new creature in a meaning
that mere theologians never dreamed of.

" He that overcometh, and keepeth my works, to
him will I give power over the nations, and he shall

rule them with a rod of iron ; as the vessels of a potter shall they be broken to pieces." What have we here? Precisely the same power ascribed to his disciples that had been, and is still being, ascribed by generative Christians to Jesus Christ alone : " As he is, so are we in this world."

But, overcometh *what?* Why, the power of a generative life ! When once this central idea is conceived of, then the sayings of this book are fraught with intense interest and profound spiritual significance. " He that overcometh shall be clothed in white raiment "—righteousness. " I will make him a pillar in the temple." " He shall sit with me on my throne, even as I also overcame, and am set down with my Father on his throne." As is Jesus, so is his disciple —one character.

Chap. v.—Here is " a little book, written within and on the back side, sealed with seven seals," which no mere natural man or woman could either open to read the inside, or endure " to look upon it," so as to be able to read the *outside* writing. What was the matter? Jesus, having been slain, or cut off from the foundation-principle of the world,—generation,—had no difficulty in breaking the seals, and reading. And then the four living creatures (Dispensations), the four and twenty elders, with harps and vials full of the prayers of saints in all time, could unite in singing a new song,—not the song of Moses,—and with the help of many angels round about the throne (ten thousand times ten thousand in number), and every creature on the earth and under it, united in saying, " Worthy is the Lamb—Jesus—that *was slain* " (not

by the Romans, but) by the Spirit of Christ, "to
receive power, and riches, and wisdom, and honour,
and glory, and blessing ; " because he had redeemed
unto God (by slaying them—destroying the generative
life) souls out of every nation, and kindred, and
tongue, and people, making them " kings and priests
unto God ; " and they should "reign on the earth,"
and over the earthly life in themselves.

This little book was simply the history of seven
churches, from the Pentecostal to the Shaker Church.
Each one and all of them, in succession, having been
acknowledged, by those who were in them, as the
Christian Church, it is revealed just what were the
principles of the first and last of them ; and wherein
the others agreed or disagreed therewith ; thus
explaining why the fruit of Gentile Christianity has
been so sour and unsatisfactory to mankind generally.

The *First Church,*—the Apostolical Church,—was
based upon the seven principles of Revelation,
including Spiritualism, Community, Peace, Repudi-
ation of Oaths, Oral Confession, Health of Body,
and Celibacy.   Only Jews, whom Moses had dis-
ciplined, could become members of the Apostolical
Church.

Second Church.—The Gentile Church, founded by
Peter and Cornelius, retained Marriage and Private
Property, under restrictions.   All its members had
been heathens, or Gentiles.

Third Church.—The Nicene Church, founded by
Constantine, retained Marriage, Private Property, and
War.

Fourth Church.—The Roman Catholic Church, founded by Leo the Great, retained Marriage, Private Property, War and Oaths ; forbade marriage to the clergy and monastic orders ; and commanded to abstain from flesh-meat on certain days and occasions ; practised persecution to death of heretics ; established the Inquisition, &c.

Fifth Church.—The Protestant Church, founded by Luther and Calvin, denied Spiritualism, substituting the Bible for the Word of God and all spiritual manifestations, or miracles ; abjured Celibacy and Oral Confession ; holding on to Marriage, War, and Swearing, and claiming that physical disease is from the Lord, and must be borne with Christian resignation.

The Roman Catholic Church committed adultery with the State, laden with all the "sins of the world," and thus became the "great Whore of Babylon, the Mother of Harlots ;" the English Episcopal Church being her eldest Daughter, and the elder Sister of all the Protestant sects.

The Apostacy was finished and *Babylon*—Christendom—had become "the habitation of devils, the hold of every foul spirit, and a cage of every hateful and unclean bird."

And "horns"—infidel powers—Rationalists—grew out of her. They hated the mongrel churches, Catholic and Protestant, all of them, tormented them with fire and sword, as in the French Revolution ; still eating her flesh, and being a component part of her, out of which they had grown.

It was the Puritanic element, combined with

Rationalism, that effected the American Revolution, and established the

Sixth Church,—the Infidel Church of America, which excludes the clergy of Babylon—Christendom —from civil power ; declaring that all human beings are born equal, possessing an inherent right to land ; and that, in religion, there being no Inquisition, all may believe what they please. This prepared the way for the

Seventh Church,—the Shaker Church of Christ's Second Appearing, in which *Revelation*, Spiritualism, Celibacy, Oral Confession, Community, Non-Resistance, Peace, Gift of Healing, Miracles, Physical Health, and Separation from the World, are the foundations of the " new heavens "; in which Religion and Science are inseparable friends for evermore ; and where the simple *word of a Believer* is of the same force as the *oath of a worldly, Gentile Christian*, Catholic or Protestant.

Chap. vi.—At the opening of the sixth seal, there was a great earthquake—Protestant Reformation; and the sun—Revelation—" became black as sackcloth of hair "; the canon of Scripture was closed ; no more spiritual gifts, or Divine revelation ; nothing left but a book, and a married priesthood for its interpreters,—Luther, himself a monk, marrying a nun— perjuring themselves. And the moon—Civil Government—was turned to blood—war. They fought until exhausted ; and then, " in time of peace, prepared " to fight again—*Christian wars ;* and the heaven—the Christ Witness Church—" departed as a scroll."

Chap. vii.—*Work in the Spirit-world*.—Twelve

thousand of each of the twelve tribes of Israel were sealed and saved, and formed a Jewish Christian Church in the Spirit-world. And then "a great multitude, which no man could number, of *all nations*, and kindreds, and peoples, and tongues, stood before the throne, clothed in white"—righteousness—"with palms of victory in their hands." They cried, "*Salvation !*"

"What are these? and whence came they?" inquired one. "These came out of great tribulation, and have washed their robes, — characters, — and made them white in the life of the Lamb,"—Jesus. He and his disciples had preached the Resurrection faith to them. They had died in sins of all kinds : pride, anger, malice, lusts of the flesh and of the mind, and many abominable propensities. These had caused them great tribulation,—*hell*. Now, by faith in confession and repentance, they had received the power of God, by which they were enabled to take up and bear a full cross against their evil deeds, wicked thoughts, and vile imaginations, which had made them hateful and disgusting ; and caused them to hate and loathe themselves and each other ; and they arose out of, and *died* to, their generative nature,—the flesh,—the root out of which all their evils had grown. "The works (or fruits) of the flesh are these : adultery, fornication, uncleanness, lasciviousness, idolatry, witchcraft, hatred, variance, emulations, wrath, strife, seditions, heresies, envyings, murders, drunkenness, revellings, and such like."

But now, being redeemed, "they hunger no more" after their former earthly, sensual, and devilish indulgences; "neither thirst any more" for the pleasures of the fashionable follies and vices of the popular Christianity on earth. Their hearts' affections and thoughts are changed, and turned into another channel; "and their life is hid with Christ in God."

Chap. viii.—At the opening of the seventh seal, "there was silence in heaven about the space of half an hour." This was the Quaker Order, the last of the witnesses; out of which arose the *Shaker Church*, which is now inviting all the witnesses—Quakers, Moravians, Methodists, Tunkers, Waldenses, Rappites, etc.—to come up higher into the Resurrection Church, and henceforth bear the full testimony of Jesus, that *not* "being weak through the flesh," they may reign with Christ for ever and ever.

Chap. x.—When the sixth angel sounded, a mighty angel, "whose face was as the sun, and his feet as pillars of fire, came down from the seventh heaven, and set his right foot upon the sea—the world— and his left upon the earth"—spiritual truth—the Churches; and then seven thunders uttered their voices; these were the seven Cycles (each with an increase of testimony against the "man of sin") of travel, in the Shaker Church, towards the perfected work of redemption. The angel then lifted up his hand to heaven, and swore by the Creator, and all that He had brought into existence, "that there should be *time no longer*."

"I saw a new heaven and a new earth; for the first heaven and the first earth were passed away; and there was no more sea"—world—generation and its concomitants. *Time* was passed. The prophetic period of twelve hundred and sixty days (years) was ended, and "the times of the Gentile Christian Church fulfilled." *Eternal life* on earth had begun. As Jesus said: "To know Thee, the only true God, and Jesus Christ,—his testimony,—is eternal life." Death has lost his sting,—*sin;* and the grave its victory. "In the days of the voice of the seventh angel, when he shall begin to sound, the mystery of God shall be finished." It *is* finished.

Chap. xi.—The holy city, the Pentecostal Church, with its celibacy, community, &c., is trodden down twelve hundred and sixty years, by the Gentile Churches, which retain marriage and its corollaries.

After this organization—temple—was destroyed, the two witnesses—male and female saints—individuals and scattered communities of Christians,—who retained the original faith and doctrines of the Pentecostal Church,—were *God's* Church—Candlesticks. And, when any individual fell back into generation, or war, or private property, the beast had killed him; the tail of the dragon—lust—had drawn a star down from heaven to earth. And, when a community or society of them had "finished their testimony," ceased to bear the true testimony of the Primitive Church, and had given their power to the beast, the beast had overcome them; they became rich, popular, and fashionable, spiritually "dead bodies" in Babylon. They sanctified marriage and war; and the Puritans under Cromwell, and the Methodists under Marlborough, became the best fighting material England ever produced.

When a revival of God's Spirit of Life shall occur, "they will arise, and stand," as at first, for "the faith once delivered to" them when they were "saints." And then they can and will hear the testimony of Christ's Second Church—temple—from heaven, calling them to "Come up hither." This, when they ascend, will cause an earthquake among their friends. Then "the nations were angry; for God's wrath had come" (being "revealed from heaven against all unrighteousness"), and "the time of the dead, that they should be judged," in the Spirit-world, by the gift from the temple of God that is opened in heaven upon the earth—the Resurrection Shaker Church. "Know ye not that we shall judge angels"—*souls out of the body.*

Chap. xii.—"There appeared a great wonder in heaven; a Woman clothed with the sun, and the moon under her feet, and upon her head a crown of twelve stars." This Woman was the Christ Order— sun to the earthly man—struggling to redeem Jesus and the twelve apostles to God. It was a success on the part of God. A true Christian man—Jesus—was born of the Spirit, and twelve men with him "in part." But a great red dragon—Rome—earthly government with sword of persecution—smote the Shepherd, and the sheep were scattered—the Pentecostal organization was destroyed.

The first Christian—Jesus—was cut off from the earth, and caught up to God in the Spirit-world, where he preached his faith to those who could no more kill the body; and converted thousands and tens of thousands of them to Christianity, during the

twelve hundred and sixty years that the Woman—
Christ's Church—was in the wilderness-state of the
"two" scattered "witnesses."

And, although this scattering was not effected in
the Church of the Spirit-world, it was not prevented
without a contest. "There was war in heaven;
Michael (he that contendeth for Christian perfection
—"Be ye perfect, even as your Father in heaven is
perfect"—) and his angels fought against the dragon
—lusts of the mind, which had been developed out of
the lusts of the flesh—the old Eden snake. And the
dragon fought, and his angels, and prevailed not;
neither was their place found any more in heaven.
"And the great dragon was cast out" (of the Christian Church in heaven, or the Spirit-world); "that
old serpent, called the devil and Satan, which
deceiveth the whole world. He was cast out into the
earth, and his angels were cast out with him."

"In this mountain"—Church in the Spirit-world—
"shall the Lord of hosts make unto all people, a
spiritual feast of fat things. And" in *this other*
mountain—*Mount Lebanon*—the Shaker Order—"He
will destroy the face of the covering"—Gentile Christian generation—"cast over all people" in Christendom, "and the vail" of the flesh "that is spread over
all nations. . . . For in this mountain shall the
hand—power—of the Lord rest."

Then was heard "a loud voice *in heaven* (in the
Spirit-world), saying: Now is come salvation, and
strength, and the kingdom of our God, and the power
of his Christ: for the accuser of our brethren,"—
generation and generative lust,—"is cast down, which

accused them before God day and night" continually, both priests and people, under the Law. For if a Jew could not *know* even his lawful wife without being accused of sin (see Leviticus xii. and xv., 16 to 33), how much less could a professing Christian be defiled therewith, and be blameless?

"And they overcame him by the Spirit and Life of the Lamb, and by the word of their testimony ; and they loved not their" generative "lives unto the death" and destruction of their souls from true Jewish Christianity. "Therefore rejoice, ye heavens" (in the Spirit-world), "and ye that dwell in them." But, "woe to the inhabitants of the earth,"—the Christ Church yet in the scattered wilderness state,—"and to the inhabitants of the sea,"—the people, nations, kindreds, and tongues, where the Whore sitteth,—the world ; "for the Devil hath come down unto you, having great wrath, because he knoweth that he hath but a short time" before the witnesses on earth will ascend into the Church of Christ's Second Appearing, where they will be out of his reach and power, as are those who are in the Spirit-world.

"And when the dragon saw that he was cast unto the earth, he persecuted the woman" (by means of his Church - and - State Governments — the sword) "which had brought forth the man-child," to prevent her bringing forth any more such offspring.

The English government persecuted Ann Lee, so that she fled, as "with the wings of a great *eagle* (the ensign of the ship which bore her), "into the wilderness" of America, where a place was prepared near Niskauna, for three and half years, — "time, times, and a half time,"—"from the face of the serpent." For the separation between the English Church and America was not yet effected by the successful termination of the revolution.

The serpent cast a flood of lies out of his mouth after the woman to carry her away with it. But, as Ann Lee predicted, the war was successful; an Infidel Government was established, so that "the earth opened *its mouth*," and declared it to be the right of all men and women to worship God as they pleased, according to the dictates of their own conscience; thus "swallowing up the flood" of lies and slanders, by rendering them powerless—taking the sword into its own hands, away from the dragon Catholic and Protestant Churches.

Still, the dragon is not destroyed; but is "wroth with the Woman"—the *Christ Order*—that has now brought forth the woman-Child, Ann Christ (as she previously brought forth the man-child, Jesus Christ, eighteen-hundred years before), and "went to make war with the remnant of her seed,"—the Shakers,— "who keep the commandments of God, and have the testimony of Jesus Christ."

Chap. xiii.—A beast comes up out of the sea—the Pagan world—with seven heads, ten horns, and ten crowns; and upon all the heads the name of Blasphemy. Is like a leopard, with feet like a bear, mouth as a lion's; and the dragon gave him his power, and seat, and great authority.

Is not that a horrid compound figure?

The Gentile Christian Church arose out of the Pagan world, and, when Constantine became a Christian, the dragon gave him his power—war—and all the authority of the Pagan Roman empire.

All the world wondered after the beast, and worshipped the dragon, which gave him his power,—sword,—saying, "Who is like the beast?"—Catholic Church—"Who is able to make war with him?" by argumentative reasoning. For, when logic fails, he will apply the Inquisition, and use blows and torture upon the body.

"He had a mouth speaking great things"—blasphemies—the power to continue twelve hundred and sixty years. He "made war with the saints"—witnesses—heretics—"and overcame them," as Delilah overcame and conquered the strong man, Sampson, by introducing *marriage* into the` Church. And his power extended over "all kindreds, tongues, and nations, that dwell upon the earth"—the children of this world, who marry and give in marriage,—live in the generative life,—and *they* "worship him." But not those whose names—characters—are written in the book of the life of the Lamb, slain—*cut off*, by the cross of Christ,—celibacy,—from *the foundation of the world*"—marriage. Is not *marriage the foundation* of the world, of the State, and of the Church?

"He that leadeth" souls "into captivity" through lust, "shall go into captivity." He that killeth—"will hurt them"—with the *external* "sword, must be killed with the fire and two-edged sword" of the Spirit, which "proceedeth out of the mouth of the non-resisting witnesses—overcoming evil with good. "Here is the *patience*" and faith "of the saints," as all their enemies must, "in *this manner*, be killed."

"And another beast came up out of the earth," the heretics, rationalists, and witnesses, with two lambs' horns, Luther and Calvin—" and spake like a dragon; and exercised all the power of the first beast," doing great wonders in religion, making "fire come down from heaven,"—priestly revivals, to fill up the churches, and so multiply marriages—"and deceiveth men, which he hath power to do, by those miracles."

He makes to the beast an image, and gives life to it; and kills those (as did Henry the Eighth) who do not worship it. It causes all to be marked in the hand or forehead. "Count the number of the beast: for it is the number of the" generative Christian; "and his number is six hundred, three score and six," * "And no man might buy or sell" private,

---

* The ancient Greeks and Romans used the characters of their alphabets, instead of figures, to express numbers. Thus:

The first character, χ (in the letters of our alphabet, Ch) is, in number - - - - - - - - - - 600

The second character, ξ (in the letters of our alphabet, xi) is, in number - - - - - - - - - - 60

The third character, ς (in the letters of our alphabet, st) is, in number - - - - - - - - - - 6

By putting the Roman letters together, they form the word *Chxist*, a very specious but false resemblance of the true word *Christ*.

By adding together the numbers, they make 666.

Thus we see that Chxist is the *name* of the *beast*, or animal man, and 666 is the *number* of his name.

" Let him that hath understanding " to compute his pernicious doctrines, horrid blasphemies, and abominable cruelties, make the application. Here we see that man (Gentile Christians included), under the dominion of the beast, is reckoned by *sixes*. The five physical senses, seeing, hearing, tasting, smelling, and feeling, together with language, make the six natural powers that form the organization of all animal subsistences. In this respect, " man has no pre-eminence above a beast."

The sacred number *seven* being left out, shows that the natural man is

selfish property, "save he that had the mark, or name of the beast." For to hold *private* property is one of the marks of the beast. This is the great Protestant Reformation.

Chap. xiv.—Then comes a vision of the work of God again in the Spirit-world. " I go," said Jesus (into the Spirit-world, where there are many mansions — spheres), " to prepare a place — organise a Church—for you." And now, at the end of the reign of the beast and his image, the twelve hundred and sixty years, we are presented with the result of the centuries of travel of the twelve thousand from each of the twelve tribes of Israel, as described in Chapter vii., who were then converted, and sealed unto God, gathered into a Christian Church, to take up their cross, as though in the body, and work out a pure *virgin* character.

" I looked, and lo, a Lamb stood on the Mount Zion—in the Spirit-world—and with him a hundred and forty and four thousand, having his and his Father's name — character — written in their foreheads." (It is an Eastern custom, to put a mark of the idol they worship in the forehead.) There was " a voice from heaven, as of many waters, and of thunder, and of harpers. And they sang a new song —testimony—before the throne and the four beasts —Dispensations—and the elders ; and no man could

---

not governed by his *intelligent understanding*, which is the seventh and highest property of his nature, the only recipient of revelation, and that which distinguishes him from a beast. Therefore, until he overcomes his beastly propensities, by the power and gift of revelation within him, he must be numbered as is (and with) the beast—by *sixes*.

learn that song—testimony—but those who were virgins—not defiled with women," or men, by generative acts—even the hundred and forty-four thousand Israelites who were redeemed from the earth. For they were *not* born virgins any more than was Jesus born the Christ.

"These follow the Lamb—Jesus—in all respects, "whithersoever he goeth," being redeemed in their life from among men ; the first-fruits (of the Gospel) unto God and the Lamb. This was the glorified Church of Jewish Christianity, in the eternal spirit world, after twelve hundred and sixty years of travel. "And in their mouth was found no guile ; for they were without fault before the throne of God." And yet there was something better for them in the future, when Christ should have made his second appearing on the earth ; without which, their glory could not be complete.

Then John saw an angel with this *everlasting Gospel*, "to preach to them that dwell upon the *earth*, to every kindred, nation, tongue, and people ;" saying, "Fear God, and give Him glory ; for the hour of his judgment is come" (the day of judgment) ; and worship *not* the dragon—Paganism, nor the beast—Catholicism, nor the image of the beast—Protestantism, nor any of the "horns"—powers—growing out of them. But worship God, who made all things.

Then another angel said (as a result of the preaching), "Babylon is fallen, is fallen, that great and mighty city,—Christendom,—because she made all nations drink of the wine of the wrath of her fornication" (love philtres—Clarke).

7

Another angel said, All having the "mark of the beast" of Babylon—an external cross—"on the forehead, or in the hand,"—swearing by the Book,—"the same shall drink of the wine of the wrath of God, which is poured out without" being diluted, "into the cup of his indignation ; and shall be tormented with fire and brimstone," when in the presence of true Christians. "They have no rest, day nor night, who worship the beast or his image." And again it is said, "Here is the patience of the saints ;" for all these states are in themselves ; and against those evil things they must "keep the commandments of God, and the faith of Jesus ;" be true Christians— *Shakers*.

"And I heard a voice from heaven, saying, Blessed are the dead who die in the Lord from henceforth." Why? Because they rest from their labours on earth, in the Christ Church in the spirit world,—the place prepared for them ; "and *their works*," not their faith in an Atonement, "do follow them"—form their character.

THE SECOND APPEARING OF CHRIST.

"And I looked, and behold a white cloud, and upon the cloud sat *one like the Son of Man*, having on his (her) head a golden crown (of victory), and in his (her) hand a sharp sickle."

What is so like a man as a woman? Ann Lee was like the Son of Man, in that she was the Daughter of Man. The Eastern world was the *male* part of the earth ; and the Western world was the *female*.

In the East, the man was developed, in all of its

nations. Zoroaster, of Persia, Confucius, of China, Brahma, of India, etc., to Jesus, of Judea.

These men were the ultimated fruit of the progressive laws of *generative creation*, in a line of men and women who the most perfectly observed the law of Nature,—to cohabit only for propagation,—avoiding the unfruitful act of coition as a " work of darkness," and *damnation* to the race. Thus Abraham begat Isaac under the influence of angels in the generative Jewish heaven,—Paradise,—when Sarah was past age, and he "as good as dead." It was clearly supernatural : " the angel did unto Sarah as he had said."

It was the same all the way down to the Virgin Mary, who was visited by Gabriel ; and she said, " Be it unto me as thou hast spoken." For all of which there is a scientific law, which Spiritualism—the last and highest of the sciences—will yet unfold to the understanding of the truly learned.

The product of the Eastern world was Jesus ; and the product of the Western world, of the Eastern Hemisphere, was Ann Lee, who was born under the same generative laws, operating through the Gentile Christians and witnesses in the Western world, where women were always held in even superstitious veneration among the Celtic nations, more especially when they were *virgins ;* as see the Sybils, the vestal virgins, the female priesthood among the Druids, in Britain, the birth-place of Ann Lee ; and the priestesses in the Pagan temples, followed by the nunneries of the Catholic Church in the Monastic Orders.

The restraints of the Quaker Order upon the lust of generation were beyond anything theretofore on earth, because they had a dual government—male and female—who together understood human nature just as a dual Congress will know how to protect female virtue and rights ; to suppress licentiousness, and secure humanity from the horrid, depopulating practices of masturbation, fœticide and infanticide— the murder of the innocents ; as well as the obser- vance of Nature's *primordial law* by those who are now, under male laws, licensed by marriage to violate it, without even the rebuke that the Koran and a Turkish magistracy would surely and inevitably administer.

It was, then, from this modern Jewish community in Babylon—the Quakers—that "one like unto the Son of Man" came forth ; and being baptized, as Jesus was, in Jordan, by the "Lord from heaven, the quickening Spirit" from the Resurrection Christ Order, in the eternal world, she gathered around her a "cloud of witnesses," clothed in white raiment— righteousness—and now sits upon it as her throne of glory.

An angel cries to her, as she sits upon this white cloud, "to thrust in her sickle and reap : for the time is come for thee to reap ; for the harvest of the earth is ripe. And the earth was reaped." Many thou- sands have been reaped from the world—cut off from its rudiment, reproduction, as the grain is cut off from the earth. To them has come the end of the world.

"And the angel thrust in his sickle and gathered the vine of the earth"—men and women—and put them, as clusters of grapes, "into the great wine-press of the wrath of God" (Shaker Church), against all generative uncleannesses, "until" the life of the generative man and woman, "the blood, came out of the wine-press unto the horses' bridles"—the ruling powers of the human soul.

Chap. xv.—There were seven angels having the seven last plagues" (upon the seven perverted senses of humanity) ; "for in them is filled up the wrath of God" against sin. "And I saw," says John, "a sea of glass mingled with fire, and them that had gotten the victory over the beast and his image, and over his mark and number, stand upon this (transparent) sea of glass." No more "fig-leaf" coverings of sin and shame ; no more "unfruitful works of darkness." But with "harps" of joy "they sing the song of Moses, the servant of God"—Salvation of body from all disease and sickness ; "and the song of the Lamb "— Salvation from all the unrighteousness of soul against which the "wrath of God from heaven" hath been revealed in them.

"Who shall not fear thee, O Lord, and glorify thy name ? All nations shall come and worship before thee ; for thy judgments are made manifest," not against the wicked worldlings who do not yet believe, but against the righteous saints of the old generative heavens and Churches : the witnesses first ; then each class in its order. For judgment begins with the people of God ; and scarcely are the righteous saved from the wrath and displeasure of God against sin, so close and searching is the work. For the war is against all wrong-doing, all evil imaginations and vile thoughts, until purity of heart is attained : as Jesus said : " Blessed are the pure in heart ; for they shall see God."

The Lamb was first slain ; and if we be slain as he was, and become " baptized into his death, we shall be raised in the likeness of his Resurrection " Christ Spirit. Here, again, is the " patience of the saints."

" And the seven angels came out of the temple— Church — with the seven plagues." They were " clothed with pure white linen," unspotted by the flesh ; and the " testimony in heaven was opened " to the world ; but " no man " who received it " was able to enter into the temple until the seven plagues," upon his seven perverted senses, " were fulfilled " in him or her.

Chap. xvi.—After the Church of Christ's Second Appearing—the temple—was established, judgment unto salvation was executed upon those called into it : " Whom I love, I chasten."

There was a great voice came out of the temple, saying, to the same seven angels, Now " go your ways, and pour out your vials of the wrath of God upon the earth." The first vial, poured upon the earth, pro- duced a noisome and grievous sore—sickness and diseases—the result of physical sin and ignorance, supporting an army of doctors.

" The second vial was poured upon the sea—all nations, kindreds, tongues, and people "—the world : " and every living soul in the sea died ; it was as the blood of a dead man : " no spiritual life.

" The third vial was poured upon the rivers and fountains of waters, and they became blood." War had become the life of all the ruling powers of the nations. They had taken the sword to persecute the "saints and prophets," and kill them. And now, the seats of learning, and even the *Churches*, no less than the army and navy, *are war powers*. Literature, commerce, and religion, all drink blood. They took the "bible and the rifle," and the sword,—the war principle,—and with it spiritually perish.

The fourth vial was poured out upon the sun— Revelation. Its light was perverted, distorted, by the lenses—Churches—through which it passed ; so that religion became a power for evil controversy, and fiery contentions,—not Peace,—and this, too, among the ordained and consecrated mediums thereof, the priesthood themselves.

The fifth vial was poured out upon the seat of the beast—the social relation of the sexes—the sexual affections—the marriage order ; which is so utterly subverted, that divorces and adulterous connexions equal the marriages. And so full of darkness is this beastly kingdom, that "they gnawed their tongues for pain, and blasphemed the God of heaven, because of their pains and their sores," and repented not of their deeds. And whereas Jesus affirmed that neither himself nor his disciples were of the world, where they marry and give in marriage ; the professed Christians, while "hasting to the coming of the day of the Lord," and crying, "Lord, Lord Jesus Christ, come quickly, and bring the world to an end !" actually marry under the pretext of preventing "*the world* from running out."

Within the last half century, two new elements have been introduced into Christendom, making it a

little more Babylonish. Two extremes—*Mormonism*
and *Oneidaism*—Polygamy and " Male Continence."
The *first*, a revival, in part, of ancient Judaism, teaching, as did Moses, that " children are a heritage from
the Lord," and " the glory of their parents ;" and that
the law of Nature—the use of marriage only for offspring—should be sacredly observed. The *second*,
teaching the law of " *male continence*"—" complex
marriage" without issue.

The *Mormons* allow Polygamy, as did Moses both
it and Divorce ; not that it is right ; but *they* allow it,
as other Christians do marriage, thinking " it is
better" than to do worse, and for the time being ; and
that by it, they keep from their cities the " social evil"
of Christendom.

The " Association for Social Science" may be able
to determine whether " it be better" for their posterity, that the Eastern Christians should marry one
woman, with the certainty that the above-named law
of reproduction will be disregarded; or that the Western Christians shall marry a plurality of women, with
the certainty that the violation of the same law will be
in the inverse ratio to the number of a man's wives.

Also, that other phase of the sexual relation, introduced by Noyes,—" Complex Marriage,"—where each
man marries all the females in the community, and
where each woman marries all the men (is that polygamy ?) with " unfruitful works of" generation reduced
to a science, might well occupy some spare moments
of the above-named Boston Association.

The sixth angel poured out his vial upon the great
river Euphrates—generation itself—the source of

natural life,—upon which the race depends for its continuance, as Egypt does upon the Nile for its sustenance ; and, according to their own showing, they, instead of using *marriage*, as did the Jews and primitive Quakers, for the purpose of *increase only*, seek how to use it *ad libitum*, and still be " unfruitful ;" so that the most intelligent race in the world—the *Yankee*—is rapidly becoming extinct.

The "three unclean spirits (amphibious) like frogs," which came out of the mouths of the three powers, Paganism—the dragon, Catholicism—the beast, and Protestantism—the image of the beast, is disorderly Spiritualism, the parent of Free-loveism — unclean affections—being " the spirits of devils"—disembodied, unredeemed souls, working miracles before the kings of the earth ; as through Home, the typical medium, before the Emperor of Russia, the Emperor of the French, Queen Victoria, and others. All of which is ripening them up for the harvest, when they will be quickened and gathered together " to the battle of the great day of God Almighty," which will unexpectedly come upon them, as the Spirit saith : Behold, I come into the world as a thief into a house, in a way, manner, and time, the least expected and looked for by the inmates. The wise and prudent of to-day, as really as had those who lived eighteen hundred years ago, in the first advent, have it entirely hidden from them. " The world " (any more than the Bourbons) " never learn or forget anything." The high religious dignitaries will be wholly circumvented.

" Blessed is he that watcheth and keepeth his garments, lest he walk naked, and they see his shame."

[" The overseer of the mountain of the temple had authority if he found a Levite sleeping on his watch to burn his garments ; and the sleeper had to return home naked."—Dr. A. CLARKE.]

The seventh vial was poured upon the air—the breath of life. The very Spirit of Truth—religion— was turned into a lie ; and the grace of God into legalized licentiousness ; the "*man of sin*" sitting in the temple of God itself was fully developed : all was perverted : the apostacy was complete. And there came a great voice out of the temple of heaven—the Second Christian Church—saying, "It is done !" And, as at the end of each of the preceding six days of judgment, "there were voices, and thunderings, and lightnings, and a great and mighty earthquake" (so great as was not since men were upon the earth), and hailstones of truth, the size and weight of each man's talent or ability to sin.

Chap. xvii.—Judgment. Then one of the seven angels, who had poured out the vials of wrath, said, " I will now show thee the judgment of the great Whore—Babylon—that sitteth upon many waters— nations and peoples—with whom the kings of the earth have committed fornication," by mixing together the principles and elements of Paganism and Christi- anity—generation and regeneration—flesh and spirit —the Church and the world—" and the inhabitants of the earth have been made *drunk* with the wine "— wine philtres—" of her fornication,"—the ignorant multitude being seduced by " the doctrines of devils," the " blasphemies," and the high-sounding, pompous professions of a generating, fighting, private-property-loving, oath-taking, office-seeking, hireling, flock-shearing priesthood.

"So he carried me away in the spirit into the wilderness," where no Pentecostal Church organization had been for twelve hundred and sixty years ; and I saw what had usurped during all that time the name and place and power of the true Church, represented as "a woman sitting upon a scarlet-coloured" (blood be-dyed) "beast, full of names of blasphemy, having seven heads and ten horns,"—multitudes of sects and parties, and influential powers, "and she was arrayed in purple and scarlet colour, and decked with gold and precious stones and pearls, with a golden cup in her hand full of the abominations and filthiness of her fornication ;"—the antithesis of a true Church.

What a gorgeous and true description of Christendom ! *not*, indeed, of a sect or Church only, but of *all Christendom ;* the Catholic, Protestant, and Infidel Church and Powers, who are responsible for the doings of the State.

"And upon her forehead was a name written: MYSTERY," — in doctrine — " BABYLON THE GREAT "—the Roman Catholic and Greek Church —" THE MOTHER OF HARLOTS "—the Protestant sects and Churches, all of them, who marry and give in marriage—and " MOTHER " also " OF THE ABOMINATIONS OF THE EARTH "— War, Slavery, Riches, Poverty, Speculation, Usury, Physical Diseases, Lunatic Asylums, Poor-houses, Prisons, Fœticide, Infanticide, Murders, Suicides, Cities, Brothels and Barracks ; and all those Doctors,

Lawyers, and Priests who live upon the ignorance, labour, and sins of their victims. This MOTHER OF ABOMINATIONS was *drunk*, too, with the blood of Truth's martyrs.

At all this significant and appallingly-grand display the poor man John "wondered," as well he might, "with great admiration," or rather *astonishment*.

"The ten horns upon the beast hate the Whore" —Christendom—"and shall make her desolate and naked, and shall eat her flesh, and burn her with fire. For God hath put in their hearts to fulfill his will." These are, to Christendom, the servants of God, the Infidel Powers, as already stated. "And the waters where the Whore sitteth are peoples, and multitudes, and nations, and tongues."

Is there anything else, I ask, upon this earth that could supply the place, and time, and character of the present Christendom, as applied to these prophetic symbols?

We have now passed the period of Christ's Second Appearing (as described in chap. xiv. 14) *ninety-nine* years; and therefore we know—as mariners on the ocean of time, by the Revelation, our chart, and by instruments and calculations—just where we are.

Chap. xviii.—"I saw another angel come down from heaven, having great power, and the earth was lightened with his glory." This is (as before stated) *Spiritualism*, a powerful agent (and one of the Infidel horns) in the fall of Babylon; and yet adding another element to the mixture.

"And I heard another voice from heaven, saying,

Come out of her, my people, that ye be not partakers of her sins," for they have reached the heavens—the Churches—"and that ye receive not of her plagues. Here is an invitation to God's people—the witnesses —to come out of the world into the heavenly Order of Christ's Church in his Second Appearing—the Shaker Society—whose members have "all things in common;" and wherein is going on "the restitution of all those things which God hath promised, by the mouth of all his holy Prophets, since the world began."

Great was and is the fall of Babylon. In her was found the hellish principle of War, which has caused the shedding of the blood of multitudes of saints and prophets *in* the Church, and of all that have been slain upon earth *outside* of it.

Chap. xix.—Then there was "a great voice of much people in heaven," who had obeyed the call to come out of Babylon, "Saying, Alleluia! Salvation, and glory, and honour, and power unto the Lord our God : for true and righteous are his judgments ; for he hath judged the great Whore which did corrupt the earth with her fornication. And then the four and twenty elders, and the four Dispensations, worshipped God."

"And I heard as it were the voice of a great multitude, and as the voice of many waters, and as the voice of mighty thunderings, saying, Alleluia! for the Lord God Omnipotent"—not the beastly compound of Church and State—"reigneth. Let us be glad and rejoice, and give honour to him : for the marriage of the Lamb is come, and his wife hath made herself ready."

This was the union between the Church of Christ's
First Appearing (composed of Israelites in the spirit
world) and the Church of Christ's Second Appearing
(composed of progressed Gentiles on earth) effected
by and through the union of Jesus, the Head of the
Church in the spirit world, with Ann Lee, the Head
of the Church on earth. "And to her was granted
that she should be arrayed in fine linen, clean and
white," that is "the righteousness of saints."

"Blessed are they which are called to the marriage
supper of the Lamb," to confess and forsake sin, and
thus make themselves ready to wear the wedding
garment—*not* (as millions ignorantly imagine) of the
"*imputed* righteousness of Jesus Christ," but of the
righteousness—"*clean and white linen*"—that comes
by bearing the same cross that he bore against all
impurity and wicked suggestions of a carnal generative nature, as well as against the temptations to
wrong-*doing* by a sin-polluted world, "which lieth in
the arms of the wicked one ;" and by the perpetual
cultivation of the mind in whatsoever is pure, virtuous,
lovely and heavenly. "*These are the true sayings of
God.*"

Then John fell down the second time to worship
the angel under the impression that he was God.
But "he again said unto him, See thou do it not : I
am thy fellow-servant, and of thy brethren" in the
Church of the first-born, in the spirit world, "who
have the testimony of Jesus. Worship God ; for the
testimony of Jesus is the spirit of prophecy ;" that is,
it is of the Christ Spirit, that has been the Pattern in
the Mount of God, after which the saints and Pro-

phets of all ages have aimed to make all things as they have from time to time had occasional glimpses thereof, and towards which they were continually drawn to fashion themselves.

Then John had a view of the *Father* Church. Heaven was opened unto him; and upon a white horse sat him who was called "Faithful and True." He is clothed in righteousness—fine linen. He doth judge and make war against *evil* in human souls; but not against the poor soul itself. His eyes were as fire to sin; and upon his head were many crowns of the victories he had won in "the battles of the Lord"—"battles of shaking." His name—character— none knew fully, except such as had lived as he lived, and thereby formed the same character.

His vesture was dipped in blood—the life of genera- tion; and his name was "The Word of God." Out of his mouth proceeded a sharp sword—words of truth, *not* carnal weapons—with which he smote the nations; "and he shall rule them with a rod of iron." He treadeth the wine-press of the fierceness of the wrath of Almighty God, who is no respecter of persons, but of principles and character. "He hath on his vesture" of righteousness, "a name written, "KING OF KINGS, AND LORD OF LORDS;" "and on his thigh."

"On his vesture, and on his thigh," etc. It was the custom of all heathen nations to put inscriptions upon the images of the deities and heroes of antiquity. But this text has a deeper meaning.

Gen. xxiv. 2.—"Abraham said unto his eldest ser- vant, Put, I pray thee, thy hand under my *thigh;* and

I will make thee swear by the Lord God of heaven,
and the God of the earth," etc.

Adam Clarke says : " This form of swearing has
greatly puzzled the Commentators. But the simple
fact was, the hand was put upon the part that bore
the mark of circumcision, the sign of God's covenant ;
which is tantamount to our kissing the Book, or laying our hand upon the New Testament, or Covenant
of our Lord Jesus Christ," or making the sign of the
cross.

" Our ideas of delicacy," he adds, " may revolt from
the rite used on this occasion. But, when the
nature of the Covenant is considered, of which circumcision was the sign, we shall perceive that this rite
could not be used without producing sentiments of
godly fear and reverence ; for the God of this Covenant was a consuming fire " to the procreative powers
and life ; for he was the Christ Spirit, by influx, from
the seventh heaven ; and circumcision was the sign of
celibacy—a virgin life ; the *testimony of Jesus Christ*
being the knife of circumcision : this is the Covenant
of which it is said : " *Gather my saints together*, they
that have made a covenant with me by sacrifice " of
wife, and husband, and children, and houses, and
land ; for none but such may " gather themselves together" into a Pentecostal Community of " all things
common."

As Ephraim,—Israel,—when his spiritual eyes were
opened, and when (like Peter) converted *from* the
natural, generative Order (he was outwardly circumcised in the flesh, and yet was continually paying the
penalty of sin for every act of sensualism, however

legal) *to* the *soul* circumcision — the regenerative Order, exclaimed: " Surely, after that I was turned," —from natural to spiritual Israel,—" I repented ; and after that I was instructed, *I smote upon my thigh*,"— the mark of circumcision,—" I was ashamed" of my ignorance—" yea, even confounded," by the continual condemnation of this " accuser," not only of the professed " brethren" and sisters in Christ, but even of ancient Israel. " I did bear the reproach of my youth"—my natural, generative life.

And an angel standing in the sun,—the Church on earth,—cried with a loud voice to the unclean, carrion fowls of heaven, to come to the supper of the great God, to eat " *the flesh*" of kings, and captains, and mighty men, and " *the flesh*" of all men, both free and bond, and small and great ; for they would all be " *slain*" by the sword of his mouth—the testimony of Jesus Christ, which " crucifies the flesh, with all its affections and lusts." " I wound, and I heal ; I kill, and I make alive."

Chap. xx.—Then comes the *last* day of judgment ; for there have been already six judgment days, one for each of the previous six Cycles.

John now saw " great white thrones," like the white clouds composed of the saints—the Church—who are to judge the world ; and the old earth and the old heaven—the State and Church—fled away from the face of him and her who sat upon those thrones, "and there was no place found for them with their lusts, and wars, and fightings." And the "dead, small and great, stood before God; and the books were opened" —the book of memory, in which was recorded their

8

sins ; and the " book of life,"—the memory,—which contained the record of their good deeds : thus making a " resurrection of the just and also of the unjust," in each individual ; for all were judged out of, or by, the things written in those books of memory, "according to their works."

Thus fulfilling the declaration of Jesus, that " there is nothing hid," in a person's life that would not be discovered—found out ; and not one thing, however secret, done in darkness but that should be brought to light.

" And the sea "—world—" gave up the dead which were in it ; and death and hell gave up the souls which were in them ;" many of whom had died and gone to and been in hell for ages and ages. And they were all judged according to their works, whether at the time of dying they believed in Jesus or not, or in any other being, created or uncreated.

" And all the armies in heaven followed him on white horses, clothed in fine linen, white and clean." In this it is seen that Jesus, and all the members of the New (and spiritual) Jerusalem, — the Jewish Christian Church, in the spirit world, and Ann Lee, the Head of the Christ Church upon earth (until after the " marriage,") and the " armies that followed them," —rode upon white horses,—Divine revelation,—and were alike " clothed in fine linen, white and clean," which is always explained to be " the righteousness of saints "—salvation from sin.

This was the " wedding garment," not only of Jesus, " the Bridegroom," but of Ann, " the Bride," the Lamb's wife, or true counterpart ; and also of all

those who accepted the proffered invitation to the
" marriage supper of the Lamb," where they not only
eat and drink together, but also work and worship
God together, as brethren and sisters of one family
and Parentage.

" I saw Satan "—Lucifer—" as lightning fall from
heaven."

That David, " the sweet singer of Israel," was
inspired by a Christ Spirit, and saw the " Pattern," in
the *seventh* heaven, of the true Church, ages before
John's Revelation was given, is easily demonstrated,
simply by quotation from, or reference to, *Psalm* xlv.

" My heart is inditing a good matter. I speak of
the things touching (or respecting) the King. My
tongue is as the pen of a ready writer."

" Ride " the white horse—Revelation—" prosperously, because of truth, and meekness, and righteousness ; and thy right hand "—the Bride—" shall teach
thee terrible things. Thou lovest righteousness and
hatest iniquity ; therefore God, thy God (' the King
Eternal ') hath anointed thee with the oil of gladness
above thy fellows." " Thou and thy fellows that are
with thee are men to be wondered at." (Zech. iii.)

" Upon thy *right hand* did stand the Queen " of
Zion—Ann—" in gold of Ophir. Hearken, O Daughter " of God, " and consider and incline thine ear ;
forget also thine own people, and thy father's house ; "
—the house of *generation ;*—" so shall the King " of
Zion, Jesus, a Son of God, " greatly desire thy beauty ;
for he is thy Lord, and worship thou him."

" Ye shall be my sons and my daughters, saith the
Lord Almighty."

"The King's Daughter" of God—Ann—"is all glorious within ; her clothing is of wrought gold. She shall be brought unto the King, Jesus, in raiment of needle-work : the virgins," men and women together, "her companions"—Christians—*Shakers*—"that follow her, shall be brought unto thee, with gladness and rejoicing, worshipping God in the dances of them that make merry."

"Instead of thy father" Adam's generative children, "shall be *thy* children,"—virgin characters, by the second Adam—"whom thou mayest make princes" (and princesses) "in all the earth."

"I will make thy name"—Ann, as is that of Jesus, —"to be remembered in all *generations*. Therefore shall the people praise thee"—Ann Lee—"for ever and ever."

Love before Logic in Theology.

"How can ye believe"—understand—"that seek honour one of another, and not that honour that cometh from God only?"

John was *in the Spirit* when he wrote, in outward language and symbols, what he then saw and heard. Spiritually-interior ideas translated into images, words, and things of earth, with which other ideas are already associated in the minds of all natural men and women, render it *impossible* for them to understand or comprehend the primary ideas of the Vision, until their state becomes changed, and an interior degree in them is opened, corresponding to the heaven whence the ideas originated and proceeded.

In other words : Of all the Apostles, John was the

47676

most divine in his love of God *(in esse);* and in purity of heart he approximated, in his *soul* history, and spiritual ascension, the nearest to Jesus ; and, after the crucifixion, was, of all human beings, the most in rapport with him, and with the seventh Resurrection heaven, or sphere.

And it was not until the earth had produced a woman, the true correspondent and counterpart of the man Jesus, that another step of progress in *that direction* could be taken.

The two Orders, of Generation and Resurrection, being both of God and Nature, like the negative and positive poles, have acted and re-acted upon each other, like Jacob and Esau ; or, as Dr. Bellows expresses it, they are centripetal and centrifugal forces acting alternately. They alternated through seven Cycles, or Churches—each having its Saviour, each its rise and fall, from Adam the first to Jesus the last. Then they have alternated through seven Cycles, or Churches, each having its origin, rise, and fall, through seven Saviours, from Peter to Ann Lee.

Man is to Woman *her* God, in physical and intellectual power, as representing and revealing the Father in Deity—*Wisdom.* And Woman is to Man *his* God and Saviour in affectional power, and in Divine spiritual intuition, as representing the Mother in Deity—*Love.*

Woman rising out of Man is his superior, in the complexity and variety of her physical functions and powers, as also in the superior refinement of her organisation generally. She is the intuitional and spiritual Preceptor and Educator, and the "glory of the man." While Man is the originator and inventor, in the arts and sciences, and mechanics, and the Revelator of the heavens; and is the "glory of God."

History repeats itself; and therefore as, in a former Cycle, "they ceased in Israel;" so "they ceased in Israel, until that I," Ann Lee, "arose, that I arose a Mother in Israel."

After the "marriage of the Lamb and Bride," (in the Lord) as the respective heads of the Jesus Christ Church in the spirit world—(which, by reason of the eighteen hundred years of travel in the Divine life, was adorned with the gifts and graces of the Gospel testimony),—and of the Gentile Second Appearing Christ Church upon earth, these two Churches began to come gradually into rapport; so that there will be a perfect union effected in the course of the seven Cycles—"seven thunders"—through which the Shaker Gentile Church of Christ's Second Appearing—the second temple—will have to pass before the restitution of all that God has spoken and wrought through Moses, pertaining to this material world, can be fully accomplished; for the earth itself must, by true science, be subdued and redeemed unto God, as a new earth— New Jerusalem.

And as this comes down gradually from God, out of heaven, the tabernacle of God is with men, and He will dwell among them; and they become in truth his people. "And God shall wipe away all tears from their eyes; and there shall be no more death, neither sorrow, nor crying, neither shall there be any more pain; for the former things," as they now exist in Babylon, are, in the Shaker Order, fast passing away.

"And he that sat upon the throne said, Behold, I make all things new. Write; for these words are true and faithful."

And, while the *Mother* Church on earth is receiving, and will continue to receive, from the *Father* Church in the spirit world, the things of God and of Nature, in the material truths of Moses; the *Father* Church is being taught by this *right hand*—the Mother Church — "terrible things,"—truths pertaining to the final Resurrection, for which they have been waiting and crying to God continually. For, without the revelation of the Mother Spirit in Deity, through the earthly Bride, they could not be made perfect; and therefore John "saw them under the altar, crying, with a loud voice, How long, O Lord," shall we have to wait for the second Eve—the spiritual?—as Adam had to wait for the first Eve—the natural; that, by the operation of these truths, they might make themselves living sacrifices, giving to God their whole heart.

In Mexico they offered human sacrifices by placing the victim upon the sacrificial stone, and taking out the heart, and laying it all throbbing upon the altar of their god. This was a "terrible" external type of the living sacrifice of the innocent lamb of *generative nature*, made by faith spiritually. Also, the blood of the dead man was drank by the priests: to which reference is made, in "Thou hast given them blood to drink." Thus Christendom "became as the blood of a dead man: and every living *soul* in the sea"— world—Christendom—"died."

When we take into consideration the state of the religious world, as now existing in the whole of

Christendom, I do *not* consider the foregoing forms of expression *too strong*.

I cannot but contrast the economy, or system, of ideas and principles, and the varied manifestations of the living spirit attending the worship of God among the people called Shakers, with the whole system of incomprehensible, mysterious, irrational, and impractical ideas and principles, embodied in the formulas of words; the senseless ceremonies; the Psalms, a "Hundred" years "Old," sang by bands of paid singers, not even belonging to the Church—all together constituting the life, or blood of the Churches, whom the beast has overcome and killed; and may it not, with the greatest propriety, be truly said, that the spiritual ministrations of such "dead bodies" are as "the blood of a dead man, causing every spiritually-living soul to die?"

And now, Friend Fields, you will perhaps ask me, Is *this* biography? But, in the letter of invite, you said, "*and* the reasons of the faith that is in you, that the world may know exactly what the Shakers believe." Well, *here it is;* and, although it is lengthy (and might be trebled without at all exhausting the matter), I could not stop myself or my subject sooner, without leaving something *unsaid*. No one but myself is responsible for these utterances.

Your well-read Magazine is the vehicle of information to the *public* of what they have in their midst, in the form of a Shaker Order.

I will now close with the following, as the breathings of my own spirit.

" I, Jesus, have sent mine angel (messenger) to testify unto you these things in the Churches. And now the Spirit and the Bride *unitedly* say, *Come !* and let him that readeth say "—to those who are hungering and thirsting after righteousness — " *Come !* for all things are ready."

"Let not the eunuchs"—virgins—who have made themselves such for the kingdom of heaven's sake— "say, Behold I am a dry tree ! For, thus saith the Lord, I will give unto them who take hold of my covenant, a place and a name" in my Shaker Home, "and within my walls, better to them than sons and daughters" would be ; "even an everlasting name"— character—"that shall *not be cut off*" either in this world or in the world to come.

It is a matter of historic record, that Jesus was only one of some thirty men who arose about the same time, and out of the same elements, who each claimed to be the long-and-generally-looked-for Jewish *male* Messiah. And also that Jesus predicted that history would repeat itself in that particular ; and that, when the Gentile world should bring forth the long-looked - for and generally - expected "desire of all nations," — the *female* Messiah, — she would be one amongst many, male and female, preferring the same claim. And such is the fact.

By their fruits, not their theories, they were to be judged by the seekers after truth. "Where the body" —the Church — "is, there will the eagles " — truth-seekers—" be gathered together," in an Order, where

love of one another shall be the bond of their union,—
a Community,—in which each shall labour for all,
spiritually and physically ; and "those who will not
work, neither shall they eat ; " which was the law of
the primitive Church.

The last half-century has witnessed a host of Mes-
siahs ; some three hundred have been enumerated
among Spiritualists alone. But Miller concentrated
the Orthodox expectation of Christendom upon this
subject, and set not only the *year,* but the very *day,*
for the end of the world ; creating an excitement that
has no parallel in religious history; and is all material,
from Deity to earth :—the angel, the last trumpet, the
sounding, the resurrection, the throne, the Judge, the
books, the judgment, even to Jesus, with the blood
streaming from the wound in his side eighteen hundred years after it was made.

This is followed by Cumming, who approximated
a little nearer to the Shakers, both as to time and
manner. And lastly, Shimeall, whose time expired
in 1868, with that of Cumming's.

"And I, even I, only, am left a prophet in Israel,"
to testify that the Lord—the coming Messiah—was
not in the great and strong wind (of words, that was
raised by Miller) which broke the rocks—Churches—
in pieces before the Lord ; nor in the earthquake of
fear, which it finally created ; nor in the "high
mountains" of learning and learned men, as "lofty"
as Babel ; which were rent and divided, by the calcu-
lation of numbers, and interpreting of symbols.

And, although much rubbish and error was burnt
up by the consuming fire of religious zeal and fervour,

—often amounting to *fury*,—the Lord was not in the fire, and did not come, according to the Orthodox expectation, in either the wind, the earthquake, or the fire.

Yet, glory be to our Eternal Father and Mother,— the *Most* High God,—the *female Messiah has come*, in the "still small voice" of *Shakerism*, saying to all mankind, O do not any "abominable thing which I hate;" but break off your sins, by *doing right*, and all your iniquities, by turning to the Lord, in the *Church* of Christ's Second Appearing, which is built upon the rock of continual *Revelation* from the seventh or Resurrection heaven—the *Apocalypse*.

" It is done."

APPENDIX TO FIRST EDITION.

———

SINCE this "little book" was sent to press, a remarkable and interesting work has been published, entitled "*The Seers of the Ages.*" The author is a valued friend of mine. He has dedicated himself to the good of humanity—the cause of Truth in the outer court of the Temple—the Gentile Christian world. The Temple itself, and them that worship therein,—the latter-day Pentecostal Church,—may not be measured, except by revelation from above—the Christ Order.

I have permission from the author, J. M. Peebles, to make extracts from the work, for an Appendix ; and of this privilege I hasten to avail myself—it being too late to insert them in the body of the "little book," where they properly belong.

———

ANN LEE.

"ANN LEE," honoured by her admirers with the appellations, "Sainted Mother," and "Sister," over-shadowed by angels of purity, and enlightened by the descent of celestial influences, received her heavenly commission in 1770, in Manchester, England. Her visions were remarkable ; her prophecies, oracles.—

The physical manifestations, relating to herself and adherents, consisted of dancing, trembling, whirling, and speaking with tongues. These exercises and spiritual gifts called down upon them the hostility of the Church. Priests and magistrates, who have ever sought to gag the truth, dungeon conscience, and impeach the inductions of science, charged them with disorder and Sabbath-breaking. The religious authorities slandered, fined, and imprisoned them.

"In 1774, inspired by the 'Christ of the new Order,' she received a revelation to emigrate to America. A few pure-purposed loving souls clustered around her as a central teacher directed by angel ministers.

"This new Church—the '*Shakers*'—much resembles the Essenes of Philo's time. The Nazarene had but three hundred followers when martyred upon Calvary. The increase of the Shaker fraternity has not been rapid, but is permanent. Holding that God is dual, eternal, Father and Mother in deific manifestations, they practically teach the strict equality of the sexes. 'First *pure*, then peaceable,' they profess to live in the 'resurrection state,' and preach to those 'without'— the Gentiles—to raise few and better children. They all believe in spirit manifestations and revelations.

"Elder F. W. Evans wrote Robert Owen in 1856, that 'seven years previous to the advent of Spiritualism, the *Shakers* had predicted its rise and progress, precisely as they have occurred, and that the Shaker Order is the great medium betwixt this world and the world of spirits. Physical manifestations, visions, revelations, prophecies, and gifts of various kinds, of which voluminous records are kept, and indeed 'divers operations of the same Spirit,' were as common among us as gold in California.

"Elder J. S. Prescott, connected with the Community near Cleveland, Ohio, made a similar statement to us during the session of the Fourth National Convention of Spiritualists. Mr. Dixon, an English writer of

considerable note, visiting Elder Evans, of Mount
Lebanon, during his American tour, wrote thus of the
Shaker doctrines:—

" 'To this dogma of the existence of a world of
spirits—unseen by us, visible to them—the disciples
of Mother Ann most strictly hold. In this respect
they agree with the Spiritualists, indeed they pride
themselves on having foretold the advent of the
' Spiritual *disturbance* in the American mind.' Frederick tells me—from his angels—that the reign of the
Spiritualistic movement 'is only in its opening phase!
it will sweep through Europe, through the World, as
it is now sweeping through America ; it is based on
facts representing an active, though an unseen force.'

" 'These Shaker communities all claim to be of
spiritual origin! to have *spiritual* direction! to receive
spiritual protection! Hundreds of *spiritual mediums*
are developed throughout the eighteen Societies. In
truth, *all* the members, in greater or less degree, are
mediums.

" ' *Spiritualism,*' he continues, 'in its onward progress, will go through the same *three* degrees in the
world at large. As yet, it is only in the beginning of
the *first* degree, even in the United States. It will
continue until every man and woman upon the earth
is convinced that there is a God—an immortality—a
spiritual no less than a natural world ; and the possibility of a social, intelligent communication between
their inhabitants respectively,' &c., &c.

" Basing our opinions upon reliable testimony, these
Shaker communities constitute a body of the neatest,
healthiest, the most pure-minded and kind-hearted
souls of earth. Certainly they are the only people
on this continent who have successfully maintained,
for more than seventy years, a system of rational
living, one of the fundamental principles of which is
the Apostolic community of property."—pp. 182-184.

LOVE.

" Thus discourses Emerson :—' I know how delici-
ous is the cup of love—I existing for you, you existing
for me, but it is a child clinging to his toy, an attempt
to eternise the fireside and nuptial chamber ; to keep
the picture alphabet through which our first lessons
were prettily conveyed. Once abroad, we pity those
who can forego the magnificence of Nature's Eden,
for candle-light and cards. This early dream of love,
though beautiful, is only one scene in our life-play.
In the procession of the soul from within outward, it
enlarges its circles, like light proceeding from an orb.
It passes from loving one to loving all, and so this
one beautiful soul opens the Divine door through
which he enters to the society of all true and pure
souls. Thus, in our first years, are we put in training
for a love which knows neither *sex, person* nor *partial-
ity ;* but which seeks virtue and wisdom everywhere,
to the end of increasing virtue and wisdom.'—p. 346.

" The German Zschokke, says :—' If Jesus were to
come to-day among Christians, they would nail him
to the cross, as did the Jews.'

"Appearing, as of old, in some of our commercial
cities, he would not 'go on 'Change at twelve o'clock ;'
would not visit an eight o'clock prayer-meeting, to
make an oration to the Lord ; would not swing a cen-
ser in a Catholic cathedral, muttering Latin ; would
not swell in the Episcopal robes of Ritualism ; would
not conjure up a credal interpretation to a Univer-
salist confession of faith; but, with a toleration wide
as human wants, he would say, as of old—' By this
shall all men know that ye are my disciples, if ye
have love one for another.' Then, going about blessing children, seeking vagrants, eating with sinners to
reform them, healing the sick and teaching by the
way-side, till weary, he would retire for rest to some
Shaker community, Essenian-like, where love is pure,

free and fraternal. Sincerely do we believe in this Jesus of the Gospels—the *man* that *was*—the Christ-*spirit* that *is*."—p. 269.

> " 'For love is the theme that the seraph choirs
> Are now hymning through the stars,
> And we catch the strains from their golden lyres,
> When our souls let down their bars.'

" Love bears no more relation to lust, than Christ to the Adam—than heaven to the hells. Lust is perversity, and is no more love than light is darkness, or good is evil. How important clearly to comprehend the occult forces of life, to distinguish between use and abuse! The legitimate purpose of Combativeness is not pugilism, but a force-power acting in conjunction with benevolence and justice. So the primal purpose of Amativeness is not gratification nor pleasurable intoxication, but the 'replenishing of the earth.' All more than this is wasted expenditure; and Nature hurls terrible penalties at those who thus destroy their vital forces. The legitimacy of the generative plane, under the guidance of the wisdom principle, is admissible.

" On the earthly planes of life, reproductions are earthly ; in the spirit realm, spiritual ; in the celestial, celestial. Angels generate thoughts, ideas, redemptive reforms. It is beautiful to become angelic on earth. There should be a mount of ascension, a spiritual birth to each brain organ, a heavenly polarity, before physical death. Said Jesus, 'Ye must be born again!' Each faculty should be developed on the ascending line of Divine use. Desire should be gratified only when pure, normal, and subjected to the highest reason.

" The Apocalyptic John saw, in vision, ' a hundred and forty and four thousand, having his Father's name written in their foreheads.' And he heard the voice of these 'harpers harping with their harps.' They

sang, as it were a new song, and none could learn the
song but the redeemed. And the voice said, ' These
are they which were not defiled with women. They
enter through the gates into the city,'—city of the
' New Jerusalem,'— the Angelic Dispensation that
' cometh down from God out of heaven.'

" Starving souls cannot find supplies on the animal
plane. Physical commerce cannot satisfy *soul*-wants.
' That which is born of the flesh is flesh.' As the
beautiful vine in the filthy cellar, pale and sickly,
needs solar light—so the soul, satiated on the poisons
of sensuality, is emaciated and dying—dying for love
—for heart-love—for Divine love, the solar love of
angels.

" Hidden deep under soils and sloughs, are the
nuclei, the types and buds of unblown flowers, struggling to rise from their sedimental graves into the free,
fresh light of heaven. So are there mortals who, from
pre-natal conditions and debasing associations, live
and seemingly luxuriate down in the lower, back-
brain department of their being. Their condition is
deplorable ; their suffering must be intense ; their
struggles long and tearful. Far be it from us to
condemn them. Jesus did not condemn the woman
caught in sin ; but he *did* say, ' Go and sin no more !'
White-robed angels, standing upon the mountains of
the pure and beautiful, are saying to them—to all—
' Come up higher !'

" All the germinal forces of the soul are Divine ;
the wrong comes from their misdirections through
material forms ; the transgression, from the ignorant
or the wilful abuse of the good. Amativeness disrobed of earthliness, turned into higher channels,
resurrected and actualized, as in angelic life, may
not only originate, but may be considered the syn-
onym of emotional love—a love pure, free, and Divine
—working with and inspiring the moral excellence of
the immortalized in heaven. This love, so spontane-

9

ous and holy, flowing out in gushing fountains of purity from regenerate souls to all humanity, should be cramped by no chains, crushed by no 'law-corpse,' appropriated by no selfish parasite, nor hedged about by the cage-wires and conventionalities of custom.

"The tendency of the spiritually-minded is from grossness to refinement; from promiscuity to chastity; from chastity to holiness; from holiness to Divinity. The higher the moral ambition, the more complete and victorious the virtue! This Adamic battle-ground cleared, the kingdom of God has come with its new-ness of life—'not according to the flesh, but according to the Spirit.' The Apostle John declared that he had 'passed from death unto life, because he loved the brethren.' This love can never degenerate into license, nor its liberty into anarchy; for it is a prin-ciple, disrobed of earthly passion—a holy resurrection.

"During that precious Pentecostal hour, when the Divine afflatus streamed down in rivers of light from angelic abodes, not only 'many believed,' but they were so baptized into those unselfish loves of the spiritual world, that they resolved to 'have all things in common.' When these universal love-principles are made practical, the soil will be as free to all to cultivate as the air they breathe. Gardens will blos-som and bear fruitage for the poor, and orphans will find homes in all houses, there drawn by the music of tenderest sympathy; and the brows of toiling millions will be wreathed with white roses—symbols of per-petual peace."—pp. 347-352.

CYCLES.

" 'Through the harsh noises of our day,
   A low, sweet prelude finds its way;
   Through clouds of doubt, and creeds of fear,
   A light is breaking calm and clear.

That angel song, now low and far,
Ere long shall sound from star to star !
That light, the breaking day which tips
The golden-spired Apocalypse.' "

"Circles are the highest symbols. There are probably no straight-line motions in the universe. Those
seeming such are on a scale so vast the curve cannot
be perceived. Fragments are all parts of circular
bodies, as a piece of granite rock is a part of those
primitive formations that encircle the earth. Atoms
gyrate upon their axes, and follow the line of their
strongest attractions. Things move in spirals, and
generally with the sun, from left to right. Sea shells
are built up spirally. Vines ascend forest trees spirally. Particles of steel flying towards a magnet move
spirally. This law, with few exceptions, applies to
atoms, worlds, systems, civilizations, and all those
historic cycles of ever-recurring spiritual epochs and
eras that distinguish antiquity.

"Progress underlies all things ; and Spiritualism,
though ever majestic in its past windings, may be
compared to the ocean waves that rise and fall. It
has had its mornings and evenings of decline. Its
careers fleck the nights and days of earth's varied
revolutions with splendours unspeakable ; and its
heaven-illumined truths, voiced by angelic inspired
chieftains, have rolled in solemn grandeur all along
the sun-lit periods of the half-buried ages ; and its
musical echoes add to the glories of the nineteenth
century.

"Each spiritual wave, in accordance with the laws
of accelerated motion, rose above the preceding, bearing the masses higher up the altitudes of wisdom.
The impetus was greater ; the spray from the wave
more glittering ; the principles involved, coupled with
its holy teachings, were, during each succeeding period,
more widely diffused.

"Under some name, and in some form, Spiritualism, as herein demonstrated, has constituted the basic foundation, and been the motive force, of all religions in their incipient stages. The Spiritualism of to-day differs from that of five thousand years since, only in the better understanding of its philosophy, the general concession of its naturalness, and its wider dissemination through the different grades of society. It has been, and *is*, God's visible seal of love to all climes and ages.

"The spirit world is the world of causes; this, of effects. Objective entities are but the projections of etherealized spirit substances. Inventions relating to industrial activities, or the spiritual exaltation of the races, have their first birth in the inner life. All great projects for the moral redemption of humanity, primarily conceived in the upper deeps of infinity, are inflowed from immortal minds to receptive mortals by the law of influx. These mediumized souls, impressionally catching the shadowy, dim-defined plans, fashion them into forms; or perhaps partially constructing, push them out into the sensuous world. As spirit moulds and takes on form, so wisdom ceaselessly descends from the heavens.

"Cognizant of a rising spiritual wave, Congresses of Angels devised the noble project of laying the foundation-stone of this new Temple, majestic, cosmopolitan and strikingly sublime, in America—land of free thought, free speech, free press; land where the people, conscious of their God-given rights, and cringing before no cowled priests, feel themselves sovereigns—'kings and priests unto God.'

"Premonitions and prophecies are announcing heralds, breathing 'a mystical lore; And coming events cast their shadows before.' The record stands undisputed, that Swedenborg, just before his departure to spirit life, in 1772, prophesied that, in about eighty years, wonderful phenomena of a spiritual nature would occur on the earth. The fourscore years expired in 1852.

"A young man, residing in Western New York, (1836) and other individuals in different localities, examining the merits of Mesmerism, fell into trance conditions, disclosing the fact that, within twelve or fourteen years, a remarkable book would be published, the contents of which would be as startling as the source whence it originated. In about eleven years, ' Nature's Divine Revelations' was dictated by spirits through A. J. Davis, in his clairvoyant state, and issued from the press.

" In 1835, and several years thereafter, W. Miller and his adherents were impressed with great impending changes, denominated ' The End of the World, and the Second Coming of Christ to Judgment.' They interpreted the 'word' of the Scriptures literally ; thus confounding the personal with the spiritual coming. The blunder was fatal to the progress of the sect. The end of the theologic world of creeds and popish dogmas was approaching, and Christ was speedily coming as a spirit spiritually in 'the clouds of heaven, with all his holy angels with him.' [These clouds were then in process of formation, being the Shaker Societies.—ED.] These 'holy angels' were the ministering spirits with whom many of earth's inhabitants now hold converse.

"About this period, immortalized spirits originally from India, China, Persia, European countries, and American Indians, visited the various Shaker communities of the country, and controlling the more mediumistic members, 'spoke in tongues,' prophesied, and gave remarkable communications relative to the opening of the ' seals,' and the descent of spiritual powers and gifts to the 'world's people.' Earth and heaven abounded in signs of an approaching new era."—pp. 191-194.

RESURRECTION.

" The Greek *anastasis*, generally translated by the English word *resurrection*, does not necessarily signify that those to whom it refers should be physically dead. In the Scriptures and the classics, it is often applied to the living. Its best definition implies a *rising*, an *exaltation*, a being *lifted up higher* in regard to condition or circumstances."—p. 330.

DEATH.

" Death is the disengagement of the spiritual from the fleshly—the severance of the sympathetic copartnership between the spiritual and earthly bodies. The thinker will note the distinction between the soul and spirit. The old philosophers clearly perceived this distinction. Plato considered the soul to be ' the image of the spirit.' Paul prayed God to ' preserve body, soul, and spirit.' Professor Bush, of the New York University, said :—

" 'As it is through the gross material body that the soul manifests itself in the present world, so are we warranted in believing that it is through the soul that the spirit manifests itself in the other world ; in other words, it performs for the spirit the office of a body, and is consequently so termed.'

" Soul and spiritual body, often confounded with spirit, are synonymous. We employ the terms soul and spiritual body reciprocally : and, as constituting the man, use this formula—Physical body, Spiritual body, Spirit ; or body, soul, and spirit.

"As the butterfly's folded wing, in its rudimentary state, can be traced under the shell of the chrysalis, so the whole future resurrectional body is contained, or wrapped up, in the material form, during mortal life. Its release, termed death, is really birth. A modern seeress, writing upon the 'Philosophy of Life,' well says :—

" 'As the physical birth of the fœtus is death to its placenta envelope, so a spiritual birth is death to its physical casket—the body ; or, as the destruction of the casket in which the child is developed implies the birth of the physical system, so the destruction or death of the physical body implies the birth of its spiritual system.'

" Death, as a Divine appointment in harmony with natural law, and in its time beautiful, is equivalent to spiritual birth, giving enlarged freedom to the soul, and increased facilities to the spirit for manifestation and perfection. The buds swell into flowers wooed by the sunlight ; the birdlings burst from their shells for flight on joyous wing ; the child, maternally developed, gains its individual freedom in outer life through pain, effort, and crying ; so the spasms, throes, and pantings, sometimes beheld with sympathizing sorrow, are but the strugglings of the soul to release itself from the coffined walls of its earthly tabernacle. What seems agony to us may be pleasure to the emancipated."—pp. 335-6.

Jesus said, in reference to a new birth from the natural state into the Resurrection or Christ world, "Agonize to enter in at the strait gate." " If we be baptized into his death, we shall also be raised in the likeness of his resurrection."

This death awaits many millions of souls who are now in the natural or lower spiritual world.

APPENDIX TO NEW EDITION.

TESTIMONY OF THREE WITNESSES.*

TO ALL WHOM IT MAY CONCERN.

"Out of the mouths of two or three witnesses, every word shall be established."—JESUS.

THOUGH the "Autobiography of a Shaker," from its own intrinsic worth, needs not a further recommendation, still, out of respect and love to the author, with a desire that the public may be convinced of the truthfulness and sincerity of his life labours, these few lines are appended.

Having been acquainted with Elder F. W. Evans for nearly forty years, and intimately so for a quarter of a century (being connected in an official capacity), I can speak with confidence as to his personal integrity and excellence of character. Persons are known, in a good degree, by the company they keep; but they are better known by the principles they advocate and practically apply to use.

As a natural man, — physically speaking — Elder Frederic is strong and vigorous. This condition continuing at his advanced age, being now in his eightieth year, may be measurably attributed to his hygienic

* Written—October, 1887.

manner of living, and his regular and systematic habits.

"Whatsoever thy hand findeth to do, do it with thy might;" this, with the injunction that Mother Ann Lee gave to her children in her day, "Do your work as though you had a thousand years to live on earth, and as you would if you knew you must die to-morrow," is eminently demonstrated in his character.

Like all genuine Englishmen, Elder Frederick is slow to accept, without first calmly deliberating, and not until convinced of the truth or error of a claim will he decide. To attain unto the highest truth given, has been his aim through life; and though all the world were against him, he would maintain his position, did he thoroughly believe himself in the right.

His rather stern, commanding way is against him, and sometimes awes the stranger, until he gets to his heart; there he finds love, tenderness, and compassion. He frequently misrepresents and injures himself by abrupt and seemingly crude remarks, that come unexpected; at the same time, these are the very things that take hold of the individual and are remembered to their advantage. One instance:—Our friend and brother Dr. J. M. Peebles, when first he visited the North Family, Mount Lebanon, told with a relish how he was chided by the Elder, when eating a meal with him, because he left food on his plate—"James, clean off your plate; *we* eat up the crumbs that nothing be lost." This would be generally considered quite a peremptory command to a stranger. It was accepted in this instance, and was appreciated.

Socially, Elder Frederick is fond of genial, like-minded society. His characteristic remarks, and his kind, fatherly manner under such circumstances, does not fail to attract and win admiration.

Theoretically, the Autobiography speaks for itself.
Like all other theorists, he is certain that his theory
is right, because, as he claims, it is based upon Divine
Revelation ; and when he is properly understood,
others who are somewhat averse may possibly arrive
at the same conclusion.

As an inspirational, prophetic man, probably Elder
Frederick stands as high as any other one in the
estimation of his people.   Hear the last words of an
exalted, sainted sister who has recently ascended to
her spirit home — Eldress Antoinette Doolittle.
" Though Elder Frederick seems to some individuals to
be rather firm and radical in opinion, yet he is a man
of God ; yea, I can testify to this truth, he is a *noble*
and *upright* man of God!   Together we have travelled
the same way, bearing a heavy burden for forty-eight
years, and I now question whether any other two
individuals, with the same difference of organisation,
mentally and spiritually, could have worked more
harmoniously together."

Often when speaking under Divine Inspiration, we
have felt the presence and seen the unction of the
Holy Spirit descend upon him ; and so deeply is he
imbued with the subject of his discourse, and so
thoroughly baptized in the spirit, that he appears as
one on the Mount of Transfiguration, and the hearer
is convinced beyond a doubt, that as the Master
spake, so speaks he ; " My words they are spirit and
they are life."

Our greatest desire is, that his godly example and
practical experience, only partially set forth in his
" Autobiography," may incite others to " Come and
see what God hath wrought" among His people.

Witnesses :—

> ANNA WHITE.
> MARTHA J. ANDERSON.
> DANIEL OFFORD.

MOUNT LEBANON N.Y., U.S.A.,
Oct. 17, 1887.

ESTEEMED FRIEND,*

In speaking of the autobiography of Father
F. W. Evans, perhaps it will be well to say a few
words about myself.

I was born in Paisley, in the year 1804. Went to
England about the year 1829. I took an active part in
the movements of the first Reform Bill. After settling
down, I had my attention drawn to the British factory
system of labour ; and its horrors touched me deeply.
Public sentiment was being stirred up on that subject,
and a certain party published a kind of official statement, " That the present time was not auspicious for a
movement to reduce the number of hours of labour to
which minors were subjected in said factories." That
statement stirred me up, and I published a card in
the *Leeds Intelligencer* declaring " That the times *were*
auspicious." I drew up a set of resolutions, and a few
persons like-minded with myself had a public meeting
called. It was a success. We organised local com-
mittees, went to work legally, zealously and persis-
tently, and the times proved to be " auspicious." The
limitation of the hours of labour, in factories, to which
minors are *now* subjected, is the result, in some degree,
of our labours. There is not a mine, or factory, within
the limits of modern civilization, but that the workers
therein have been benefited by the labours of a few
persons who had no object in view but to do good.

I went to London on this business ; had an interview with the Duke of Sussex and others, desiring
their aid. When in London I saw for the first time

---

* Sent to the Editor of this work by Daniel Fraser, author of "Shaker
Hygiene," the dietetic troubles of the 1st and 19th centuries contrasted, and
"The Music of the Spheres," a 75 page work, the opening chapter of which
lays down these truths—Theology is *not*, and goodness *is* Religion —
Albany, N.Y., 1887.

Robert Owen and his son, Robert Dale Owen. Imbued with the sentiments of his communal ideas, I
landed in this country, fully satisfied that our civilization needed a higher form of economic, and also of
social life. At that early day, more than fifty years
ago, I saw the necessity of the wage-earners having
access to the land. When that is reached, free from
the taint, tax, and oppression of landlordism ; crime,
pauperism, and the number of the unemployed will be
reduced to their minimum. Some years after, when
I had joined the Shakers, Robert Owen visited Mount
Lebanon, and we had some pleasant interviews with
that venerable communist. The last words I remember hearing that lovable man speak, were : " I will
visit the Governor of the State of New York, to see
whether he is a man or a politician."

On my first visit to Mount Lebanon, I found Father
Evans. I have known him for more than fifty years.
He has pursued one undeviating course of unselfish
devotion to the elevation of all within his sphere. His
central idea, and the central idea of Shakerism, is—
" Man is capable of living a divine life." To the unfoldment of this idea, he and his associates have
devoted themselves. He maintains unflinchingly and
uncompromisingly, that Right Living—obedience to
Hygienic Law, and Right Doing—the fulfilment of
all Moral obligations, are the foundations of a divine
life. Divinity of life is, living to do good to others at
the expense of self. With that sentiment he visited
Glasgow and other places, the present season, with the
intent of turning the current of human thought in that
direction.

The outcome of a divine human life is, that all
should fare alike—have goods in common. Communities having only economic and personal advantages in view, have all been failures. Communities,
the members of which live for others, as we do, will
stand. That such a form of human social life should

find an abiding place in Scotland, was the object of Father Evans's mission. He thinks, and others think, that the time to inaugurate the Millennium—a new Heaven and a new Earth—in Great Britain, has come. We enjoy the conditions, and the fruit, of the "higher life" now. Why should not the more advanced of the inhabitants of the valley of the Clyde also enjoy them? "Whosoever wills" may do so ; and even fulfil the prophecy, "Greater things than these, ye will do." That is, we shall expect further unfoldments of the said central idea in Scotch communities.

Father Evans's autobiography is a true statement of but a small part of the experiences of that man of God.

I have the great happiness to be, affectionally, your friend,

DANIEL FRASER.

The following phrenological character was given by N. Sizer, at New York, 10th March, 1887 :—

F. W. E V A N S.

YOU have a strong frame, and good indications of vitality for the support of that frame, so that physically considered you ought to be a strong and substantial man.

Your brain is large enough, measuring as it does twenty-two and a-half inches by fourteen and a-half, to indicate an ample development of the brain ; the hair being fine, and the quality of the skin fine, there is an intensity as well as susceptibility in the constitution which gives along with power an intuitive sense of truth and a keen feeling in regard to that which is addressed to the affective faculties, consequently your life is not only intense and susceptible, but strong.

The head, from the opening of the ear forward, is long, showing that the intellectual development, along with the religious and moral, are the leading forces of your mental life ; when we measure the masses of brain development by anatomical indications, we find that the anterior lobe of brain is in you the major factor, while the middle lobe, in which the propensities and animal impulses are located is not so strongly marked ; the middle lobe is short, and the head is comparatively narrow through that region.   When we study the heads of men whose life is given to roughness and wickedness and animalism, we find that the anterior lobe of the brain is short and contracted, and that the middle lobe of the brain is not only long fore and aft, but the middle section of the head is broad and massive, so that the middle lobes of brain in which the selfish propensities are located is in them the master force in their mental life, and yet they might wear a hat the same size as yours, and have twice as much of the animal and not half as much of the intellectual.   The posterior lobe of your brain is not short, but it is not very broad or massive.

You have the friendly or fraternal spirit, and you have the home loving spirit, and the love of pets, children, that which is young and innocent and playful, and little folks believe in you and always have ; they don't know nor care why, only it seems comfortable to be where you are.

Your interest in woman has more of the sense of refinement and spirituality than of the physical ; you would admire delicacy and beauty, and modesty and refinement, but if you were not a Shaker you would dislike very much anything that bordered on vulgarity in woman ; it would make you feel uncomfortable to hear a stranger that you never expected to see again, use a coarse or vulgar expression or statement, while men that are differently organised that we meet in every day life, seem to enjoy the society of those whose plane of social sympathy is low and animal rather than that which is refined and high toned.

The intellectual development is uncommonly large in the lower range of faculties, which brings you into intimate harmony with the world of things, consequently you are a naturalist by nature ; you would be interested to study plants, minerals, insect life, and would know more about the characteristics of animals and insects which you had occasion to deal with than most men do ; people sometimes would think you were taking notes of little and unimportant things because you would understand all about the insects that destroy grass and fruits and infest vegetation ; they would think you studied a great many things besides their eating up the plant, and this quality of perception would enable you to become learned in many branches of information which are interesting and profitable for one to know. You are historical in your tendencies ; you like to trace facts back through generations and see where they begin, just as you would trace the Mississippi river to its nest among the peaks of the Western Rocky Mountains ; it is a rill no larger than your finger, but it has a relation to the swollen Mississippi, so you run historic facts to their ultimate or legitimate conclusions, and no fact to you in a chain of facts is unimportant; and though you sometimes have an elevation of thought which enables you to sail over the whole landscape of the subject, when you undertake to teach it you can come down and do by it as a man does who sails in a little boat down the river, you give your hearer a detailed account of all the facts that seem necessary to a conclusion, and you remember places as well as facts ; you remember persons and are a natural critic of people. You are impressed favourably or otherwise with each stranger whom you meet, and you are not often far wrong in your estimate of strangers. Sometimes you meet a person that you can't make out, so you leave him uncriticised, and wait for time to tell what should be thought of him.

You have Comparison large which gives you the tendency to see the difference and the resemblance existing between things, and thoughts, and purposes, that bring you into the domain of mental philosophy or theology.

You have a sense of character, hence you incline to read biography or to write biography. If a person has a development of character which is important, you like to trace out the motives, through actions and experiences, to a result, and you generally do it with pleasure and with correctness, and when you look at the world of matter you go through it as something full of interest ; but when you strike the human being, the highest created object, you feel a new interest, because of the wideness of his capacities and the immortality of his destiny ; as you sometimes say, " He is a son of God, and therefore the highest factor of life that we know," and you study this higher factor in his higher phases of life and purpose.

You have large Benevolence which gives you the philanthropic tendency, the desire to do good.

You have uncommonly strong Spirituality, and we should suppose that it had been cultivated; we should suppose, if we never had seen our subject, that you had been for many years cultivating the spiritual side of life, for that part of the brain in which the spiritual elements are supposed to reside seems to have been elevated and to have grown ; probably your head at that part is from a third to a half inch higher than it was 45 years ago, sometimes the regions through the base of the brain, as a man gets past the meridian of life, become less active ; courage begins to furl its sails and close its wings ; in like manner the spiritual, the intellectual, the æsthetical may be receiving larger culture, and the development will be enhanced accordingly, until a man is 75 years of age ; Veneration,

Spirituality, and Benevolence constitute the top region of your head, running towards the front, and in this region we see the evidences of continued recent growth; we mean that the growth must have been continuing for half a century, and we believe it is still improving, becoming more and more active, hence we say recent growth.

Your Conscientiousness is large, but the spiritual elements are still stronger.

Your Hope is well indicated, as if you were expecting life to rise and broaden as you proceed, as if you had anticipation of enriching future for men, as if you would say, in the language of the Scriptures, " In the morning sow thy seed, in the evening withhold not thy hand," looking forward for the great growing future, for the " bread cast upon the waters that shall come back after many days;" in other words, you have a faith of the future on earth, not for yourself merely, but for the work you can do, and that people may plant and water, but God is going to give the increase some time and in His own time, but you would believe that it would be done in the present time if those who worked together with God would work rightly; your life does not feel cramped, confined, and narrowed down to small results, even in common things; you would make reforms that might take twenty-five years to perfect; it would be natural to you to have faith in hygienic law, and sacrifice to-day something for the benefit of the long succeeding future; we say succeeding because we mean the day-by-day future that will last long enough in its benefits to pay for the original outlay. Citizens lay out millions to bring water to their city, and then other millions to get rid of the sewage, and a single generation does not get the value of the result; it is spread over all the future, so your faith takes hold of the to-morrow and then of all the to-morrows.

Your Firmness gives you persistency rather than

10

obstinacy ; people you come in conflict with will have
an idea that you are a man for a long pull, and a
strong pull, and a pull altogether, rather than for a
great rush just now, and then have it calm down ; we
do not call you obstinate, we call you persistent.   A
man in a boat sometimes strikes out with a boat-hook
and fastens it to the dock, and he can both push and
pull ; sometimes he throws a line ashore, and then can
only pull, that is like your Firmness; it does most of its
work in pulling, persisting, rather than in a contrary,
offensive, and oppugnant pushing.

Your Conscientiousness is strong ; it does not work
so much in your case towards the selfish faculties as
it does towards the moral faculties; consequently, you
don't do right to-day so that somebody will feel under
obligations to do right by you to-morrow.   It may
have that effect, but you sometimes study the right
and argue for the right, and that is to take effect in
moral ways and for the general good—not to-day
only, but for all time.   Hence you would do right on
principle, whether it was going to put money in your
pocket or temporarily take it out.

Your sense of approval is strong.   It hurts you to
have people think unfavourably of you, of your work,
even through ignorance ; and you sometimes feel
worked up and sorry and anxious to inform people,
even against their own will, that your purposes and
your suggestions really have not a selfish but a benign
purpose.   You want to be appreciated and associated
for good.   If people don't think you are wise, you
sometimes laugh and let them think otherwise ; if
people impugn your motives, and fancy that you
somehow have a selfish axe to grind, that worries you
when it is not true.

Self-esteem never was quite large enough, and the
self-confidence which you have acquired has come to
you little by little, in consequence of trying to work
out thoughts and plans and motives which you think

are right, and there is less of personality about your dictation than some people might be led to suppose. We direct children sometimes against their will for their good, and they think we are tyrants because we put our will up and make it dominate in a case. Older children sometimes will have similar notions, but yours is not a spirit of domination for the sake of domination. We pull a child away from the fire by force when it don't know any better than to be too near it, and we compel people to avoid doing wrong for their benefit, and they think we are tyrannical.

Your Cautiousness is active and influential; Secretiveness is not and has never been very large; you have a feeling that the honest truth, judiciously and properly spoken, is the best policy; it is sometimes said that "honesty is the best policy;" you would say if a man wants to use policy it is good policy to be honest, because it will ultimately turn out best.

The desire for gain in your case works towards intellectual and superior purposes; you are not so anxious to get money for its own sake and for your own use as you are to plan for the general good and the future good, and in business your skill and talent would lie in creating resources for income rather than in grasping and holding that which you had acquired; you can make business better than you can keep accounts and collect debts; it would be more in harmony with your spirit to find new resources of profit, to work up new individuals and widen the life of enterprise, than it would be to gather in and salt down and say: "Soul, thou hast much goods laid up for many years, take thine ease, eat, drink, and be merry." You are very likely to work in the direction of future prosperity so long as you are able to do anything, and when it comes to pass that you decide to sit down and do no more of work in any form, your friends may know that you are pretty nearly through.

SHAKER LITERATURE.

Extract from " Shaker Communism." *

RUDIMENTAL PRINCIPLES OF THE PATRIARCHAL ERA.

" For the Lord hath made all things for their uses."—
Ecclesiasticus xxxix. 21 v.

USE.

Man :—Is he the product of Nature, or of a Supreme Being? He is now in a *fallen* condition. Nature is either perfect or imperfect. If *Nature* be the author of man, and she be *imperfect*, then there is no rational hope that he will ever be raised from his present fallen condition. If *Nature* were the author of man, and she be *perfect*, then it may with propriety be asked how her child, *man*, became *imperfect;* also, how it happened that Nature, which possessed the power to bring man into existence a *perfect creature*, should ever have suffered him to become anything other than what she at first made him. And again : If she, *Nature*, lacked the ability to keep him perfect when he was so, how can she possess sufficient power to *restore* him to that condition, or to keep and pre-

---

* Shaker Communism ; or, Tests of Divine Inspiration. The Second Christian or Gentile Pentecostal Church, as Exemplified by Seventy Communities of Shakers in America. By F. W. Evans. Published in London, 1871.—pp. 185.

serve him in it, supposing him to be so restored? The product of Nature, man, could not have *fallen* unless Nature also fell, for he would not have been a free agent, as Nature could not bring a *free agent* into being ; for free agency pre-supposes the existence of two opposite powers, controlled and directed by two primary antagonistic Intelligences or Beings.

Therefore, none but a free agent could fall, or be again raised after it had fallen ; for to *rise* also pre-supposes the existence of a superior intelligent Power and Being, by whose agency the resurrection is effected. It is, therefore, clearly demonstrable that *Nature* was not the originator of the human race ; and that there is a *Supreme Being*— *God*, an invisible Power and Wisdom, the Author and Creator of man and of all good things (Gen. i. 31), as may be plainly seen by the visible creation. " For the invisible things of Him from the creation of the world, are clearly seen, being understood by the things that are made."

Creation consists of two parts ; the outward and visible, which may be denominated the *body ;* and the interior and invisible—spiritual—part, which may be designated the *soul*.

The outer visible body, with all its elements, must be directed and governed by the living power of the interior or spiritual part—the soul.

Man, male and female, was brought forth as the highest production of the elements of this world, and represents both parts : his *outward*, or animal being, the visible body—a microcosm of the outward earthly world ; and his *interior*, or soul, a microcosm — an organisation of the invisible or spiritual world.

The *order* of his creation was, for the *animal* organ-isation, which connected him with the external world, to be directed and governed by the powers of his superior part, or living soul ; and for the *spirit* to be under the guidance of the Divine laws of his being, through the medium of which he was rendered account-

able to his Creator for all his goings. All the faculties
of man were originally good and innocent, not excepting that of *procreation*.

These, through the insinuations of a foreign evil
influence, he was led to corrupt by *making* PLEASURE,
not USE, *the end of their action and exercise.* This is
lust.

Man, in his sphere, was *not* a machine, *but a free
agent* to choose between obedience and disobedience
to good or evil. For it is impossible for man to be a
living, rational being, without having sensible self-
acting life ; and the power of choice must be the
result.

The ability to receive, and the desire of, knowledge
in man, were necessary for the development of all the
faculties pertaining to his physical and spiritual organisation, and in themselves were perfectly innocent. By
these, he would have increased in his understanding of
the order of his creation, and of the will of God respecting him—how to subdue or govern the world, and
to keep it and himself in order.

But, under the instigation of evil, the innate love of
knowledge was used to " seek out many inventions "
—knowledge of evil things ; and it thus became the
medium through which the tempter inspired his own
principles of life, by which man, not waiting to be
appropriately developed, or to be guided by superior
wisdom into the appointed time and season for procreation, was *untimely* led into the work of generation.
And thus was implanted in man the principle of *lust*.

Without revelation from the Spirit-world, man is
ever liable to mistake the Divine agency, by which
all the operations of the visible worlds are effected,
and to ascribe them to some mysterious imaginary
power which he calls *Nature*, but respecting which
he can give no intelligent information. All effects,
whether they be natural or spiritual, are often thus
referred to this unknown and unintelligent cause ;

which yet leaves the mind of man in a state of doubt and uncertainty, and also with an undefined, dissatisfied feeling.

But the unchangeable nature of the constituent elements of the visible worlds, and the regularity and harmony of the laws by which they are governed, resulting, as they do, in nought but *useful ends* and purposes, clearly reveal to the rational mind a Supreme Intelligence, of omnipotent power and wisdom, possessed of a superior organisation to all other substances; for it is self-evident that no intelligent organisation could be derived where no intelligent organisation exists. "Understand, ye brutish; and ye fools, when will ye be wise? He that planted the ear, shall he not hear? and he that formed the eye, shall he not see? He that chastiseth the heathen, shall not he correct? He that teacheth man knowledge, shall not he know?" (Ps. xciv. 8-10.) As no visible thing has power to organise itself, of necessity all organisations are, by gradation, derived from an unoriginated primary intelligent Being or Organisation. And, as no derivative can equal the original, all visible organisations must be inferior to the original Supreme Organisation or Being.

In a recent "Treatise on Revelation,"* the object is to prove the existence of a communication between the natural and spiritual worlds, continuously, from the creation of man to the present time; whilst the object of the *present* treatise is to establish a standard, or rules, by which all men may judge or discriminate between the true and false, the good and evil, in all such communications.

In order the better to attend to this principal object, certain points will now be assumed *as true*, as that there is a God; a Spirit-world, which to the natural man is the prototype and a transcript of this; and

---

* By Elder William Leonard, of Harvard.

that in all ages there have been intelligent communications, from one to the other, which have been both
true and false, good and bad, and sometimes a compound of all ; and that the Bible contains the most
authentic record of such spiritual intercourse—especially of that which has come in the most direct line of
the Divine order, but not the ten-millionth part of all
the revelations that have been made to man, individually and collectively.   An Apostle declared that if all
that Jesus alone said and did had been written, "the
world could not have contained the books." How
much less, then, would it contain a record of *all* which
has passed between the natural and spiritual spheres !

No truth can be more certain than that God is a
God of order and not of confusion.   (See I Cor. xiv.
33.)   The external creation alone demonstrates it.
Astronomy, natural philosophy, and chemistry are
witnesses of it; as are all the sciences, which bring to
light the laws of God as they exist and are immutably
established in the physical world.   Everything, even
to the minutest particle of sand, derives its form from,
and is governed by, some law inherent in itself.   So
true is it that even the smallest atom, equally with
the most stupendous world, is embraced within the
circle of *cause and effect*, originating in the Divine
mind.

It is in this light that the very hairs of our head
are all numbered, and that not a sparrow falls to the
ground by chance.   "He" that "hath weighed the
world in a balance, by measure hath he measured the
times, and by number hath he numbered the times.
And he doth not move nor stir them until the said
measure be fulfilled." (2 Esdras, iv. 36, 37.) The
vegetable world shows forth order in all the infinite
variety of *its* productions.   There is not a plant so
vile as not to exhibit system and beauty in its organisation ; each branch, and twig, and leaf is but an
outward manifestation of an invisible and eternal law.

The *animal kingdom*, from the microscopic insect to the half-reasoning elephant, is also subject to, and governed by, laws, called *instinct*, far more enduring and unchangeable than the " laws of the *Medes and Persians*," and which lead them (in a state of original freedom) to do, in all respects, that which is for their best present good and future welfare. " This also cometh forth from the Lord of hosts, who is wonderful in counsel, and excellent in working." (Isa. xxviii. 29.) And of *man*, who is so " fearfully and wonderfully made," that, in his outward form, he is in truth a perfect organisation of all the principles of law, order, and beauty pertaining to our world, can we rationally believe that *he* was not designed to be governed and regulated by fixed and permanent laws in his moral and spiritual nature and experience ?

" God made man upright " (Eccles. vii. 29) throughout. And, while upright, he was obedient to the physical, moral, and spiritual laws of his being : every thought, word, and action was but the effect proceeding from these invisible causes, and tended towards the health and strength of his body, mind, and soul. The whole creation, while it abode in its original integrity, was justly pronounced " *very good.*" But how widely different from that is its present condition, let the general verdict of all classes—religious and irreligious—determine.

SUMMARY.

The natural creation, governed by fixed immutable laws, all of which tend towards some *useful end and purpose.*

Man the microcosm of the world, and the product of nature, under God.

By the insinuations of evil, operating upon his innate love of knowledge, man was induced to violate the great law of USE, the first law of creation, by *perpetrating a premature and* UNTIMELY *act of generation.*

Thus the fall of man was effected by his rejecting the teachings and influences of Divine ministering spirits, friends who would have kept him in subjection to all the physical and moral laws of his nature ; and by listening to and obeying the whisperings and suggestions of evil spirits, whereby in his actions he began to seek, as an end, *gratification*, and *not use.*

LAW.

BY dividing the spiritual history of the human race into four great Eras—the Patriarchal, the Mosaic, and the First and Second Christian—we can the more easily trace the creation, the fall, and the rise of man.

In the First Era, previous to the *fall*, man is represented, in the Scriptures, as enjoying easy and uninterrupted communion with spiritual beings. But since that event, angel visits have been "few and far between." And in what way, and by what means, man has fallen to his present degraded and deplorable state, is vividly pourtrayed and set forth by the Prophet Isaiah (xxiv. 5, 6): "The earth also is defiled under the inhabitants thereof, because they have transgressed the laws, changed the ordinances, and broken the everlasting covenant. Therefore hath the curse devoured the earth, and they that dwell therein are desolate."

Thus it was obedience to well-known laws and established ordinances, and the breaking of a solemn covenant which God made with all his creatures when he directed them to "multiply and replenish the earth," and which was pre-eminently designed to be an "everlasting covenant" for the regulation of MAN in the chief and most important operation of nature—*procreation* — that constituted him a fallen being.

This "everlasting covenant" which God made with his creatures, was, *that no animals should use their reproductive powers and organs for any other than the simple purpose of procreation,* and was the sole condition upon which God would impart to them the power to bring forth offspring in their own likeness and after their own kind, in the primitive Divine order of "*very good.*"

The violation of this covenant, which *man,* on his part, accepted by marriage, and to which he, as the head and lord of all creation, should have yielded the most implicit obedience, is the root of the transgression of every other law and ordinance that has ever been broken by man, and it was this act that originated and implanted the principle of lust in him ; and when lust was thus conceived, it brought forth sin ; and when sin was finished, it brought forth darkness of mind and soul, and *even death;* so that his intercourse with good spiritual friends was interrupted and confused by the evil spirits to whom he had hearkened and whose counsel he had followed ; and therefore " his servant he became unto whom he had yielded himself a servant to obey" (Rom. vi. 16); so that gradually he lost the knowledge of those laws and ordinances, and of the covenant that he had so shamefully broken.

" Because that, when they knew God, they glorified him not as God, neither were thankful ; but became vain in their imaginations, and their foolish heart was *darkened.* Wherefore, God gave them up to uncleanness, through the lusts of their own hearts, to dishonour their own bodies between themselves. God gave them up to vile affections. God gave them over to a reprobate mind. Being filled with all unrighteousness, wickedness, covetousness, maliciousness ; full of envy, murder, debate, deceit, malignity ; whisperers, backbiters, haters of God, despiteful, proud, boasters, inventors of evil things, covenant breakers," etc., etc. (Rom. i.)

These various evils, with very many others, are thus set forth as being the *necessary* effects of the human race having once broken and departed from the original law and design of God in creating them male and female *(i.e., that they should copulate for* PROCREATION ONLY, *and* NOT *for gratification);* and they found no stopping-place in their descent into the hell of lust, which is truly a bottomless pit.

And thus the human race in the First Era, having once entered upon a course of evil—that is, of making *sensual pleasure,* and *not use,* the end and object in their very action—did not cease in their insane career until they had " filled the earth with violence;" finally attained to that degree of lawlessness that " every imagination of their hearts was evil, and that continuously." (Gen. vi. 5.) " God was not in all their thoughts." *How then could man continue to exist while living in perpetual disobedience to the laws of his existence ?*

" For God made not death ; neither hath he pleasure in the destruction of the living. For he created all things, that they might have their being : and the generations of the world were healthful ; and there is no poison of destruction in them, nor the kingdom of death upon the earth. But ungodly men, with their works and words, called it to them ; for when they thought to have it their friend, they consumed to nought and made a covenant with it." (Wisdom of Solomon, i. 13-16.)

Thus man, who was originally good, and (so long as he was a law-keeper, in daily communion with the Spirit-world, and entirely under the Divine influence, when he broke the first and most important law pertaining to the propagation of his race, opened the way for evil of every name and nature ; and began to cut himself off from all spiritual intercourse, except that which was from an *evil* source—the lower spheres. " Darkness commenced to cover the earth, and gross darkness the people." (Is. lx. 2.) So that each succeeding generation came into being under increasingly perverted and corrupt influences, until they degenerated into a state of the most profound spiritual ignorance, even denying the existence of the spirits of evil that led and governed them daily; as they also denied the spirits of good by which alone they could have been saved from the destruction that awaited them.

SUMMARY.

Before man fell, he had easy and uninterrupted communion with good spirits.

God made an everlasting covenant with all animals, that they should not use their reproductive powers for any other than the simple purpose of procreation; and the laws of this covenant were primitively implanted in man as in all other animals.

This covenant man broke, and thus opened the way for the transgression of every other law that pertained to that Era; for man became a servant to those evil spirits unto whom he had yielded himself a servant to obey, until he was only evil. Then came the flood; for it was impossible for man to continue to exist in perpetual and entire *disobedience* to all the laws of his existence.

Man, when under Divine revelation, kept all the laws of his Era, and had happiness—*life.*

When under *false and evil revelations,* he broke all the laws of his Era, and had misery—*death.*

The flood, like the cholera, was an effect of violated laws.

TESTS.

To the present existing generations of men upon earth, upon whom the spiritual light of God has never yet shone, the assertions and denunciations contained in Romans i., etc., cannot in full be applied;

for *they* never "knew God" aright. In the earlier
ages, men possessed a knowledge of God *and of* HIS
LAWS *pertaining* to THEIR ORDER, but lost it by
wickedness. "They did not love to retain God in
their knowledge;" while the present generations must
be brought to a knowledge of God, and of *those laws*,
before they can be judged by them and reclaimed
from their wickedness.

The last and only hope of man is *revelation*—the
true science; for he finds himself born into a
deranged, disordered world, and possessed of an
inherent constitutional proclivity to evil; and that
himself has also inherited in *his own person*, from his
progenitors, its accumulated fruits.

Both the evil and its effects are, in the premises,
independent of his own volition and free agency.

It is, therefore, only through the medium of *revelation* that he can be brought to understand the *causes*
that have worked his ruin, and thus come to a knowledge of the primary fundamental laws of God and
Nature, by the continued violation of which he has
been reduced to his present deplorable condition ; for
the experience of thousands of years has proved that
Nature alone, or natural science, cannot impart that
knowledge.

Revelation, therefore, is the rock, the foundation,
upon which he must build, or never be saved from
the effects of the fall, and find eternal life. And here
is the trying point, for the prediction of Paul is fulfilled : " This know also, that, in the last days, perilous
times shall come. For men shall be lovers of their
own selves, covetous, boasters, proud, blasphemers,
disobedient to parents, unthankful, unholy, without
natural affection, truce-breakers, false accusers, incon-
tinent, fierce, despisers of those that are good, traitors,
heady, high-minded, lovers of pleasure more than
lovers of God," etc. (2 Tim. iii. 1-4.)

It is sin—such things as these—that separates

between the soul and good ministering spirits, and that unites the soul to and invites the ministrations of dark and evil spirits. Consequently, when the spiritual faculties in man (which have become dormant) are quickened and developed by the ministrations of *good* spirits, *evil* ones stand ready to occupy the avenue thus opened, and a mixture in their communications of truth and error, good and bad, is the result.

Hence the necessity for a higher standard of judgment, which was set up in the third Era, in which time mankind were brought into a nearer relation to a higher order of spirits than theretofore had ever had any direct access to them, and with whom they were henceforth to hold communion, and travel in that Gospel ("which the angels desire to look into") by which they expected to be judged with men, and, through obedience thereto, be participators with them of its salvation : these were the justified spirits of men which constituted "the Church of the first-born which are written in heaven," or first Christian Church existing in the Spirit-world.

And even *there* the spirit of error, or Antichrist, was also liable to work, though perhaps with less power than among those in the Church upon earth. Therefore, that faithful watchman, *Paul*, after saying to his brethren, "Ye are come unto Mount Zion, and unto the city of the living God, the heavenly (or rather *spiritual*) Jerusalem, and to an innumerable company of angels" (Heb. xii. 22), sounded the trumpet of alarm in the holy mount of Zion upon earth, when he, after referring them to the well-known Gospel doctrines of Christ, said, " Though we, or an ANGEL FROM HEAVEN, preach any other gospel unto you than that which we have preached unto you, let him be accursed. As we said before, so say I now again, If *any* man preach any other gospel unto you than that ye have received, let him be accursed."

Gal. i. 8, 9.) How imperatively essential, then, is it
that man should be possessed of some impeccable
rule or test by which to protect himself from the
shafts of evil thus projected from the spirit-spheres ;
and projected, too, through the operation of those
very faculties by which alone his resurrection can ever
be effected. To this end, must he not receive a
knowledge of the original laws of God as established
in nature, and of the great *fundamental law of animal
being in particular,* in the breach of which consisted
the very first transgression ?

This knowledge would operate as a key to the
human mind, by which to unlock the mysteries of
iniquity, whether they be of ancient and venerable
date, and covered over with the moss of antiquity, or
the product of more modern *spiritual manifestations ;*
and would thereby enable man to burst the bands of
darkness and death and to "cut the cords of sin"
that now hold and fasten him to the earth ; by causing him to return to *first principles,* and thus to
"discern between the righteous and the wicked,
between him that serveth God and him that serveth
him not" (Mal. iii., 18); and that he may not only
" *try* the spirits," and all their teachings and doctrines,
purporting to come from the invisible world, but also
be in possession of an infallible standard, or criterion,
by which he can judge them with a righteous
judgment.

Every cycle or dispensation of the work of God
commenced *in Divine revelation,* by which its *foundations* were laid. And, to support and perfect the work
of each dispensation, a continued revelation was also
indispensably requisite ; for whenever (from whatever
cause) the gifts of the Divine Spirit ceased, a "falling
away" among the professors of that order was the
inevitable result. "Where there is no vision, the
people" soon "perish." (Prov. xxix., 18.) Such a
"*falling away*" and "*perishing*" have befallen the

Church of each of the three first great Cycles, Epochs, or Eras.

But, although a continued revelation was always needful, by which to know the then present will of God, yet an all-important principle has ever been paramount to all others, in every age of the world ; and that is, AN UNERRING RULE, by *which to judge, distinguish, and know divinely-inspired revelations from those which are spurious and false.* And such rule has been given in the established principles which formed the foundation of each dispensation.

For all revelation, however high its pretensions, that did not conform to, and was not in accordance with, those permanent rudimental principles, was, by reason as well as by Divine appointment, to be utterly rejected ; and in all ages, the blessings and cursings or judgments of God upon the children of men were in proportion to their obedience or disobedience to this rule.

In the Dispensation of the Patriarchs, the well-defined principles of the *moral law of nature* (as already set forth) formed the foundation of that Dispensation, and became the rule by which to try all future revelations or principles in that Era, through whatever spirit or from whatever source they might come. Hence, all who conformed to this law and rule were blessed of God, in their day and *generation.*

The line of the Patriarchs was noticed and blessed of God for their obedience thereto. Enoch and Noah were particularly distinguished therein, especially with regard to the law of procreation ; they "walked with God."

" Noah was a just man and perfect in his generations." And for this cause God's covenant was established with him, and he was preserved from "perishing with the world of the ungodly." (2 Pet. ii. 5.) It is therefore evident that whatever revelations he received were in conformity with the fixed foundation principles of that dispensation.

11

On the contrary, the posterity of Cain (who was the seed of lust, and appears to have been the first fruit of transgression), designated "the *sons and daughters of men*," and also the apostates from the Patriarchal order, who violated the Moral Law, and would not hearken to the revelations enjoining obedience thereto, incurred the Divine displeasure, and were overwhelmed by the destroying Deluge.

SUMMARY.

Men gradually lost the *knowledge* of those *laws of life* that they would not keep.

The present generations are begotten, born, and brought up in ignorance of the essential laws of their own order—the *generative*.

They have lost the true Divine revelation that they would not obey, and are now in gross darkness.

Sin is the cause of the universal spiritual ignorance which now prevails on the earth among all people; and mankind universally are so lost, ignorant, and wicked, that when *good* spirits open a communication, *evil* ones also use it.

Therefore man needs tests, or unerring rules, by which to "discern between the righteous and the wicked" spirits.

For this purpose, he must have a knowledge of the laws of God and of Nature as pertaining to each of the Four Eras; and especially of the great fundamental law of animal being, that permits sexual union for procreation only.

This is the key to, and root of, the whole "mystery of iniquity"—all the wickedness among mankind.

"Where there is no vision" — revelation, — "the people perish."

The rudimental *laws* of each Dispensation were the rules, or *tests*, by which to judge all spiritual communications. If any spirits taught disobedience to them, it was "because there was no light in them"—*they were evil.*

In the *First* Era, those who stood in the Divine revelation were such as obeyed the laws of that Era. Thus, in and while fulfilling the great innate law of animal being (for every species to multiply and replenish the earth with its kind), they "*walked with God,*" because they were perfect in their generations, —the work of generation — the central impulsive object of that Era.

ESTABLISHED LAWS AND RULES OF THE SECOND OR MOSAIC ERA, AND MEDIUMS OF TRUE REVELATION.

THE next great Revelation of God, constituting the Second Era, commenced in *Abraham ;* the object of which was to renew, enter into, and ratify the original covenant pertaining to *generation*, which had not only been broken, but even the knowledge thereof was lost from among the children of men. Of this covenant Abraham received the seal—*circumcision*—which was also the sign of the covenant pertaining to *regeneration*, or virgin purity, that God would make with the "Everlasting Father" of the new creation in the Third Era, or first Christian Dispensation. Therefore, Abraham is *termed* the "father of the faithful," in both the typical and spiritual Israel.

This twofold object of the covenant with Abraham was also expressed in the Mosaic law, that was added (first) "because of transgression" by man, to teach him what the original law of the preceding dispensation was that he had transgressed, and to restrain him within certain bounds in future.

"By the law was the knowledge of sin " (see Rom. iii. 20), and of what was sinful. And from its requirements (see Lev. xv. 16, 18) men learned the depravity of their nature, *and that they could not cohabit, even in the* MARRIAGE *state, though* SIMPLY TO PROPAGATE THEIR SPECIES, *without* COMMITTING SIN AT THE SAME TIME; and that for every child, however legally brought into existence, a sin-offering was required to be made before the Lord as an atonement. (Lev. xii. 6, 8.)

Again, another object of the law was to prepare men for the work of Christ in the Third Dispensation. " The law was a schoolmaster to bring souls to Christ." (Gal. iii. 24.) This was done by types and figures, which were but shadows of good things to come. By circumcision, or the cutting off a portion of the organ of generation in man, and the days of separation from the camp of the saints required of the female (see Lev. xii. 1 - 5) were foreshown *the cutting off and separation of the work of propagation from all that are in Christ.*

If man could not, even under the restraints and purifications of the Mosaic law, and that after he was circumcised, generate offspring without committing sin, then Christ certainly could not save him from his sin, without, at the same time, cutting him off and severing him from the work of generation. For if " Christ came to fulfil the law, and not to destroy it," both himself and his followers must needs abstain and cease from all those things that the law of Moses condemns as sinful, and for which it requires a sin-offering.

Now, although Moses was ministered unto by angels, and the people obeyed him as an inspired leader, yet be it observed that his revelations formed a complete system of laws, statutes, and judgments, all of which were recorded ; that the ten commandments were written upon tables of stone ; and that these laws were taught to all the people, old and young ; so that every one knew what to depend upon. And, be it

further observed, no human governments are so unjust as not to publish their laws, that the people may
know what they must do to live.

Yet Moses did not claim the exclusive right to
inspiration, for he said that "he would that *all* the
Lord's people were prophets;" knowing that, if they
were all *true* "prophets," there would be no clash or
confusion.

Yet it was said to them, "If there arise among you
a prophet, or a dreamer of dreams, and giveth thee a
sign or a wonder, and that sign or wonder come to
pass whereof he spake unto thee, saying" (let us do
so and so, anything contrary to the laws and statutes
of Moses, with which everyone was acquainted), "they
should kill him." For the injunction was, "Thou
shalt not hearken unto the words of that prophet, or
that dreamer of dreams; for the Lord your God
proveth you to know whether ye love the Lord your
God with all your heart and with all your soul."
(Deut. xiii. 1, 5, and 9.) From these passages it is
evident that a *false* prophet might have as real a
spiritual ministration to him as a *true* one, as in the
case of Balaam; *but a criterion had been given* by
which he could be known; and that was, "To the law
and to the testimony; if they" (the spirits) "speak not
according to this word, it is because there is no light
in them." (Is. viii. 19, 20.)

And when they were desired to seek unto them
that had "familiar spirits, and unto wizards that peep
and that mutter," this was their answer: "*Should not
a people seek unto their God,*" *in the order of his appointment?* "for there were false prophets among the
people" (2 Pet. ii. 1), who taught them to go after
and serve other gods and forsake the true God, and
who had access to spirits that were not within or
under Divine influence.

And although God raised up a succession of prophets, whose revelations were in full accordance with

the established principles of the law, and who proved the truth of their missions by the godliness of their requirements and the fulfilment of their predictions, yet such was the influence of the *false* prophets, and their spurious revelations, upon the people, that oft-times they refused to hearken to and obey the *true* messengers of God, whose revelations were invariably crossing to their natural and corrupt propensities.

Witness the numerous prophets of Baal, and the false prophets, Hananiah, Ahab, Zedekiah, and She-maiah, and the judgments which followed them.— (See 1 Kings xviii. and xxii., and Jer. xxviii. and xxxix.)

SUMMARY.

The revelations of this era were designed to effect two objects.

First : To *re*-reveal the laws of the First Era, which had been broken and were lost ; and,

Secondly : To foreshadow, by types and figures, the laws of the Third Era.

Thus the confessions to the priests, exclusion from the camp, washings, &c., consequent upon all genera-tive works, were, for the time being, effectual restraints under the law of Moses.

And circumcision was the sign that *generation itself* would, in the next Era, be cut off by Christ the Messiah.

And the Jews learned that, even under the cloak and sanction of *marriage*, they could not cohabit, though simply to procreate, without committing sin at the same time. For a sin-offering was required for the very *act* and *fact* of begetting and bringing forth a child.

"Christ was the end of the law," by fulfilling it ; for it was made for those who break, *not* those who *keep* it ; and he could not keep—fulfil—it without refraining from the work of generation.

The Law pointed out the sins that Christ would *save his people from.*

The laws, statutes, and judgments were recorded on parchment or stone, and taught to *all* the people.

These were the Tests of Revelation in that Era, and were in every man's possession.

Any "dreamer of dreams," or prophet, whose teachings and requirements conflicted with them, was, by all the people, judged, condemned, and " killed."

The whole nation was to seek unto God in the order of his appointment, *i.e.,* from "between the cherubims"—two golden images of male and female. These were the mediums of all Divine spiritual manifestations to Israel. All other mediums must be in subjection to and in union with them.

THE CONSEQUENCES OF RECEIVING AND BEING GUIDED BY FALSE REVELATIONS.

THE *false* gods of the heathen were worshipped almost universally by acts of sensuality, in some form or other; *this was the true reason of the continual tendency of the Israelites to idolatry.* It was not the dumb idol, nor the stupid and foolish teachings of the idol-priests, that thus attracted them, but the *worship,* that allowed and encouraged a full gratification of their sensual appetites.

The people often went after false gods, and became corrupted with all manner of abominations, until they brought destruction upon themselves, which carried off thousands of them at a time (see Num. xxv. 6-9 ; and 1 Cor. x. 8) ; for God said unto them, "You of all the people of the earth have I known ; therefore I will punish you for all your iniquities." (Amos iii. 2.)

The violation of the law, in the abuse of the functions of reproduction, as it was the first, so has it ever been, and is now, the most universally seducing and besetting sin of the human race.

God is a God of order, and not of such confusion as has been the result of man's seeking *gratification by corrupting the fountain of his existence.*

Therefore Moses pronounced the following curses upon the Israelites, which should result as a consequence of their disobedience to the rudimental and focal law of their Dispensation :—

" The Lord shall send upon thee cursing, vexation, and rebuke, in all thou settest thine hand unto for to do, until thou be destroyed, and until thou perish quickly, because of the wickedness of thy doings.

" The Lord shall smite thee with madness, and blindness, and astonishment of heart ; and the heaven that is over thy head shall be brass, and the earth that is under thee shall be iron.

" The Lord shall make thy plagues wonderful, and the plagues of thy seed, even great plagues, and of long continuance, and sore sicknesses.   He will bring upon thee all the diseases of Egypt which thou wast afraid of ; and they shall cleave unto thee.   Also every sickness and every plague which is not written in the book of this law, them will the Lord bring upon thee, until thou be destroyed.

"And the Lord shall scatter thee among all people, from the one end of the earth even unto the other ; and thou shalt become an astonishment, a proverb, and a byword among all nations." (Deut. xxviii.)

These are the terrible consequences of forsaking God, transgressing the law of Moses, changing the ordinances, and breaking the *" everlasting covenant."* And how literally and perfectly these threatened curses and judgments have been executed and fulfilled, the past history and present condition of the Jewish nation and people furnish irrefragable evidence.

SUMMARY.

Divine revelation always taught fallen man *self-denial*, and tended towards perfect purity, justice, and love.

But the false revelations of the heathen led them to worship their gods by acts of sensuality and self-indulgence. Idol worship is devil or demon worship. (1 Cor. x. 20.)

This was the true cause of the dereliction of Israel from their own religion to idolatry.

All revelations from evil spirits—false religions—terminate in the violation of the law, and the abuse of the functions of reproduction. As this was the first, so is it the most bewitching, deceptive, and universally besetting sin of the human race.

The destruction of Jerusalem, and the scattering of the Jews over all the face of the earth, resulted from their hearkening to, and obeying the insinuations of wicked ministering spirits.

Physical diseases are the results of violated natural laws.

THE LAW OF CHRIST, CONTAINING THE RULES OF THE FIRST CHRISTIAN ERA.

THE most general influx of demons or disorderly spirits, in every Dispensation, was always at the latter end of it.

Thus, at the time of Christ's first appearing, an almost universal state of communion between the visible and invisible worlds existed ; so that it was quite common in Judea for individuals to be obcessed, and even possessed with spirits, both good and bad.*

In reading the New Testament, one cannot but be

---

* See Lightfoot.

struck with the frequency and familiarity with which spirits and spiritual things are spoken of. It appears that, for any one to be possessed of spirits, improperly called *devils*,* was as common an occurrence in those days as in our days it is for a person to have a fever : from which it is evident that the evil predominated. Hence, it became an important part of Christ's mission to close the door of that Dispensation, by casting out such spirits, and prohibiting their return. This power he not only exercised himself, but he also delegated the same to his disciples. (Mark xvi. 17.)

All spirits, in every Dispensation, should be subject to the established order of God—that is, to the true Church of that Dispensation.

In each Dispensation there was an increasing development of the eternal principles of *truth*, produced by greater displays of the Divine Spirit and Power ; and also, a further manifestation of purity, justice, and holiness, in the character of its recipients : each one not only confirming the truth of the revelation of its predecessor, but also preparing the way for, and becoming a stepping stone to, its *successor*. (Matt. v. 17-20.)

It was *Jesus* who *closed* the door to the *Second*, and *opened* the door to the *Third* Dispensation, in which the spiritual influx far exceeded what had yet been upon earth. Good spirits had the lead and ascendancy for a season : the dead were raised to life ; the blind were restored to sight ; the sick were healed ; the lepers were cleansed ; and, better than all, the poor had the Gospel preached to them (see Matt. xi. 4, 5): and finally, so great was the outpouring of the spiritual elements, that many really began to love one another in deed and in truth ; and this love they exhibited by selling all they possessed, and forming a united interest in temporal things (see Acts ii. 44, 45). Thus

---

* H. W. Beecher.

REVELATION WAS THE FOUNDATION, LOVE THE
LIFE, AND COMMUNITY OF PROPERTY THE OUT-
WARD FORM OF THE CHURCH OF CHRIST IN THE
BEGINNING OF THE THIRD DISPENSATION.

SUMMARY.

All spirits should be in subjection to the scientific
and spiritual principles of the Church of their Era or
Cycle.

The Mosaic Church fell, and thus lost the power to
regulate or cast out evil spirits. Therefore, at the end
of the Second Era there was a great influx of spirits
in Judea, over whom no one had any control.

Jesus opened the door to the Third Era, by which
hosts of better and higher spirits were admitted to
earth. It was by their assistance that he and his
disciples cast out evil and ignorant spirits; and by
their power it was that the blind saw, the lame walked,
the dumb spake, the dead were raised, and that "even
devils were subject unto them."

Thus, a further Divine revelation was the foundation
of the *Third* Era. Love was its soul, or life; and
community of property its body, or outward form.

ANTICHRIST.

WHEN Jesus was ushered into the world, the *testimony* that he was the true Messiah — the Divine
Teacher sent of God, to reveal His will to man in
a far higher order than had yet existed on earth—
formed the basis upon which rested the whole super-
structure of principles, precepts, and practice of that
Dispensation.

As these were inspirations from the Christ Spirit,
"who gave him commandment what he should do and
what he should speak" (John xii. 49), this system of

faith, principles, precepts, and practices, as first exhibited in his own person, and then embodied in the
Church, brought forth by the Holy Spirit, the Com-
forter, sent to guide them into all truth—temporal
and spiritual—formed the standard (or rule) by which
to judge and "try" all succeeding revelations, as well
as the teachings and influence of every spirit, whether
in or out of the body, throughout all the ages of that
Dispensation, down to the time of Christ's second
appearing.

And any spirit, or angel, or man that taught or
teaches any other gospel, or principle, or practice than
what had its foundation in that Church, was and is
antichrist. (See Gal. i. 8.)   John says, "Little children,
it is the last time : and as ye have heard that antichrist shall come, even now are there many antichrists."
(1 John ii. 18.)   "For many deceivers are entered into
the world, who confess not that Christ is come in the
flesh."   (2 John i. 7.)   He also exhorted his brethren
to "Believe not every spirit ; but try the spirits,
whether they are of God ; because many false spirits
are gone out into the world." (1 John iv. 1.)   Thus,
every spirit must be judged and tried by the standard
and rules appropriate to each particular Era.

All who confessed, by a life conformable thereto,
that Christ had come into the world through the man
Jesus, and that he taught the true principles of godliness for the salvation of men, were of God.   But those
who denied this, in word or works, were "deceivers
and antichrist."

Christ declared himself to be "the way, the truth,
and the life," and said, "No man cometh to the Father
but by me."   (John xiv. 6.)   THEREFORE CHRIST—
i.e., HIS ACTUAL LIFE AND DOCTRINES, ARE THE ONLY
INFALLIBLE RULE—THE STRAIGHT EDGE—BY WHICH
THE CROOKS AND TURNS OF ALL AND EVERY SPIRIT,
IN OR OUT OF THE BODY, MAY BE DISCOVERED.   All
in the primitive Church who walked by this rule were

blessed and protected of God: and if it cost them their lives, "white robes were given them" as the reward of their faithfulness.

Not many, however, could endure the cross necessary to walk by this rule, and to obey the spirits that testified of these principles of true godliness; but, after running well for a season, they listened to the *false* spirits that were "gone out into the world," and, through false teachers (whom Peter and other of the Apostles foretold would arise), had been led to believe that they could be saved by a *profession*, without actually living out the pure and self-denying principles of the Gospel which Jesus had declared.

This being agreeable to their corrupt propensities, they followed those false spirits and their revelations, and rejected the *true*. And, in a short time, to rid themselves of annoyance by those teachers who brought forth true revelations, enforcing Jesus as an example, and faithfully preaching his word of self-denying power and life, the ecclesiastical councils under the great antichrist *Constantine* decreed that all revelations ceased with the Apostles; and that thenceforth they must depend solely upon the *letter*, which, Paul said, "*killeth;*" and which did accordingly kill the Christ Spirit in them, and "afresh crucify and put him to open shame" before all the heathen nations of earth for the last thirteen or fourteen centuries.

SUMMARY.

It was the faith of Jesus and his followers, "not to believe every spirit, but to try the spirits."

The grand test by which to try them was, that they should believe and confess that "*Christ* had come in the flesh," or in Jesus of Nazareth and in his true disciples. Every spirit that could stand this test was of God. But every spirit that denied this truth, either did not know, and therefore was ignorant; or did know it, but was false. *All such spirits were antichrist.*

The principles, doctrines, precepts, practice, and actual life of Christ Jesus, together with the principles and laws (or tests) of the two preceding Eras, formed the *infallible criterion and test* of all doctrines, creeds, and religious systems, whether purporting to come through spiritual communications, or emanating from councils and ecclesiastical bodies.

When the first Christian Church, or Church of the Third Era, fell, and the antichristian kingdom of the Beast was fully set up under Constantine, then every great principle, doctrine, and test of the First Two Eras was entirely abrogated, denied, and denounced by the NICENE and other subsequent councils.

They first destroyed the foundation of the Church by voting and decreeing that revelation had ceased, and that the canon of Scripture was closed, and then they decided that thereafter nothing but the "letter" *(bible)*, that "killeth," should remain as "the rule and guide of faith and practice" to Christendom. And thenceforth "they would no more endure sound" *spiritual* "doctrine."

Thus the Church was cut off from all Divine communication, and was prepared to enter upon a course and to enact scenes of persecution and bloodshed against all who should not conform to its orthodoxy.

The "*man of sin*" was now in the temple of God, or Church, or people. Concupiscence, or the *lust of the flesh*, is the "man of sin," that sitteth in the heart of every professor of Christianity in all the various sects and denominations of the so-called Christian world; and is the "*abomination of desolation*" that occupies the heart of each individual heathen and every heathen temple.

From this time they would no more "endure sound doctrine; but, having itching ears, began to heap to

themselves teachers after their own lusts" (2 Tim.
iv. 3), by establishing theological institutions, to
qualify, by a vain and false philosophy, carnal young
men to interpret the Scriptures by human wisdom, in
a way pleasing to the basest passions of man's fallen
nature ; and both Catholic and Protestant entirely
doing away and making the cross of Christ of no
effect by their traditions, creeds, and dogmas, and by
their comments and commentaries on Holy Writ.

And, inasmuch as the great body of professed
Christians followed the "pernicious ways" of those
"false prophets and teachers" to whom Peter alludes
(2 Peter ii. 1, 2), the Church lost the true spirit of
revelation, and cut itself off from all communion with
Christ its Head, by rejecting the ministrations of all
those spirits who were sent forth to "minister," individually and collectively, to all them who should be
called to be the "heirs of salvation." (Heb. i. 14.)

Thus was consummated the "*falling away*," spoken
of by the Apostle, that should certainly precede the
second coming of Christ, in which should be revealed
"*the man of sin*, the son of perdition, who opposeth
and exalteth himself above all that is called God, or
that is worshipped ; so that he, as God, sitteth in the
temple of *God*, showing himself that he is God." (2
Thes. ii. 3, 4.) "Know ye not that ye are the temple
of God? and if any man defile the temple of God,
him shall God destroy; for the temple of God is holy,
which temple ye are." (1 Cor. iii. 16, 17.) "Your
body is the temple of the Holy Spirit." (*Ib*. vi. 19.)

Therefore, as man individually, and the Church
collectively, under the Gospel, is that temple, it is
thus incontrovertibly proved that the "man of sin"
is something in the *very heart* of the professors of
Christianity that *they* highly esteem "above God,'
although it "is an abomination in his sight."

And, notwithstanding that such persons may "just-
ify themselves before men, God knoweth their hearts'"

lust. (Luke xvi. 15.) "For the bed is shorter than a man can stretch himself on, and the covering narrower than he can wrap himself in" (Is. xxviii. 20) and hide from the All-seeing Eye. "For though thou wash thee with nitre, and take thee much soap, yet thine iniquity is marked before me, saith the Lord" (Jer. ii. 22), "neither is thine iniquity hid from my eyes" (*Ib.* xvi. 17).

It is therefore as plain as the sun at noonday, that concupiscence, or the *lust of the flesh,* is the god—"the man of sin"—which all Christendom has bowed down to and worshipped, in preference to worshipping the true and living God of purity, And this, too, is the same influence, or power, or goddess of lust—*Venus* —that is and always has been so potent in the heathen temples, whose worship ofttimes attracted the figurative Israel, to their shame, confusion, and final destruction.

This was also alluded to by Jesus in his parable of a king going to a far country, and returning again, and finding his kingdom in the hands of his enemies, who, in the interim, had killed his son, and then given themselves up to a riotous, self-indulging life, until the king suddenly returned, and executed upon them a work of judgment. (See Luke xix. 12—27.) Also the prophecies of Daniel and of John, both of whom not only agree in the great event of supplanting the Church of Christ by an opposite power, under different names and symbols, as "a beast that made war with the saints, and overcame them"—"the abomination of desolation standing where it ought not"—"the whore of Babylon, which would reign over the kings of the earth," &c., &c.; but they also agree that the time or duration of the reign of this antichristian power—in which there would be no true Church of Christ upon earth—would be 1260 years. At the expiration of which period, the sanctuary, or temple, or Church, "should be" progressively "cleansed, and an end

made of sin, and everlasting righteousness brought
in ;" or, in other words, Christ, who had been all that
period absent, would "make his second appearance"
on earth, "to those who look for him, without sin
unto salvation." (Heb. ix. 23.)

THE DIVINE LAWS OF CHRIST,

As Definitive Rules of Judgment, Perfected in the Second Christian Era, or Fourth and Last Dispensation.

" As the times of the Highest have plain beginnings in
wonders and powerful works, and ending in effect and
signs " (2 Esdras ix. 6), so, at the close of the Third
Dispensation, Jesus informs us there would be a
general rush of spirits—both true and false, and good
and bad—upon earth ; and that near the close of the
First Christian Era, and about the time of his *second
coming*, or the opening of the Fourth and last Dispensation or Era, "many false Christs and false prophets
would arise, who would show great signs and wonders,
insomuch, that if it were possible they would deceive
even the very elect" (Matt. xxiv. 24) ; that is, they
would draw them away from those purifying principles which constituted the foundation of his first
Church, and upon which also would be built the
Church of his second coming.

Consequently, however high might be the professions, or marvellous the wonders and signs of these
false Christians, to *those* who would hearken to the
good and the true spirits—the ministers of the shining
light that would be the harbinger (see Mal. iii. 1) of
Christ's second appearing — the *warning word* is,
" *Believe them not* " — " *Go not after them.*" (Matt.
xxiv. 23 ; and Luke xvii. 23.) " By their fruits ye
12

shall know them, for every good tree bringeth forth
good fruit; but a corrupt tree bringeth forth evil fruit.
A good tree cannot bring forth evil fruit ; neither can
a corrupt tree bring forth good fruit." (Matt. vii. 17,
18, 20.)

Again, the Revelator says, "And the sixth angel
poured out his vial, and I saw three unclean spirits,
like frogs, come out of the mouth of the dragon, and
out of the mouth of the beast, and out of the mouth
of the false prophet. They are the spirits of devils
working *miracles*, which go forth unto the kings" (or
leading minds) "of the earth, and to the whole world,
to gather them to the battle of that great day of God
Almighty." (Rev. xvi. 12—14.)

This will be the last tremendous struggle between
the powers of antichrist and all other corrupt powers
of the world, and those powers or principles that are
preparing the way for, and will have a place in, the
kingdom of God upon earth, in which a final separation between the elements of good and evil, and
between true and false revelation proceeding from
these two sources, will be effected.

And is it not manifest that in our day there is an
unexampled influx of spirits from the spirit-world to
earth ? evidently betokening that it is the end of the
Third Dispensation and the beginning of the Fourth ;
and that a condition of things precisely similar to
what existed at the close of the Second Dispensation,
when Christ made his first appearing, is the order (or
rather *dis*order) of the day.

When men or women, in any age, invited the presence and familiaries of spirits, and tampered with
them for worldly gain or from sinister motives, and
out of the *Church's order*, they were liable to be
obsessed ; and it often happened that thus the spirits
gained possession of persons who could not disengage
themselves from them.

And as the Church of each Dispensation, while

standing in its true order, possessed the power to cast out these spirits, and thereby release such souls, it followed that by this power or test the true Church of each Era could be known.

The heathen and false religionists attracted spirits by their sorceries and incantations, but had no power to expel them. The superior alone could govern the inferior.

There was a class of persons in the Jewish Church, called *exorcists*, whose profession was to cast out spirits. Adam Clarke says, " They were termed *Masters of the Name*—that is, the name of *Jehovah*, by a certain pronunciation of which they believed the most wonderful miracles could be wrought. And when they could not deny the miracles of our Lord, they attributed them to his knowledge of the true pronunciation of this most sacred name."

When the Jewish Church lost its Divine character, these also lost the power of exorcism.

This power was again revealed in, and possessed by, the first Christian Church. The same author says :—

"*Exorcisms*, or *adjurations* of evil spirits, were frequent in the primitive Church ; the name of Jesus was that alone which was used. The primitive fathers speak strong and decisive words concerning the power of this *name ;* and how demons were tormented, and expelled by it, not only from individuals, but from the temples themselves. Exorcists formed a distinct class in the Church ; hence we read of Presbyters, Deacons, Exorcists, Lectors, and Door-keepers."— (Comment. Acts xix. 14 and 17.)

When "certain of the vagabond Jews, exorcists, took upon them to call over them which had evil spirits the name of the Lord Jesus, saying, We adjure you by Jesus whom Paul preacheth—

" There were seven sons of one Sceva, a Jew, and chief of the priests, which did so. And the evil spirit

answered and said, Jesus I know, and Paul I know;
but who are ye ?

"And the man in whom the evil spirit was, leaped
on them, and overcame them, and prevailed against
them, so that they fled out of that house, naked and
wounded.

"And this was known to all the Jews, and Greeks
also, dwelling at Ephesus ; and fear fell on them all ;
and the name of the Lord Jesus was magnified.

" *And many that believed came and confessed, and
showed their deeds.* Many also of them which used
curious arts brought their books together, and burned
them before all men : and they counted the price of
them, and found it fifty thousand pieces of silver."
(Acts xix. 13—19.)

Thus it appears that the power of casting out spirits
had departed from the Jewish Church, and had passed
over to, and rested upon, the Church of the Third Era.

And the people were convinced that that which had
been glorious in its day, " was no longer glorious, by
reason of the glory which excelleth."

It is by no means improbable that again, in the
progress of the work of the present spiritual manifestations, men and women will become obsessed by
spirits, from whom they will not be able to free themselves. And should that be the case, it is very certain
that neither Catholic nor Protestant Churches possess
the power to cast out such spirits or demons.

Of the world-renowned physical demonstrations at
the house of Dr. Phelps, in Stratford, Conn., the
author was himself an eye-witness, having been one of
a committee of Shakers that proved to be the medium
through whom a superior class of spirits " cast out "
the former mischievous and destructive spirits, of
which the boy Henry was the medium.

Dr. Phelps informed the author that previous to the
arrival of the Shakers' committee, the retired clergy-
men, who, with their families, composed the population

of Stratford, had held a meeting, having the boy
Henry present, for the purpose of exorcising the spirits.

The result was, that when they were assembled, with
prayer, each with a Bible on his lap as a talisman, the
Bible—Word of God, as they term it—of one priest
flew across the room, and hit another priest on the
head ; and then another and another, until the meeting was broken up in confusion ; leaving the boy, his
father, and the spirits, in possession of the field of
battle.

This was a type of Babylon—Christendom—and of
what will occur therein through the instrumentality
of Spiritualism and Shakerism. There will be "battles
of shaking."

After the above occurrence, while a company of
Shaker brethren and sisters were visiting at Dr.
Phelps's house, the following incident took place.
Jane Knight, while in the sitting-room on a Sabbath
morning, thought to herself that she would like to
have a Bible to read; immediately one dropped at her
feet. Upon opening it, she found the print rather
small, and wished that, as the spirits were so kind,
they had given her one with larger type ; directly,
another Bible dropped gently into her lap, which,
upon opening, she found to be just right.

Therefore, if the power to cast out spirits be needed,
it must be sought, not in the mere record of bygone
Divine revelation, but in the Church of the Fourth
Era, which originated in, is based upon, and stands by,
the power of Divine revelation itself.

ALL NATIONS BLESSED THROUGH THE CHURCH OF THEIR ERA.

Now, although between the destruction of the first
Gospel temple, or Church, and the rebuilding of the
second Gospel temple, or Church (of which the two

temples of Solomon and Zerubbabel were striking figures), there was evidently no place for a true Christian Church; yet Revelation, notwithstanding it was denied and rejected by the false·Church, was *not entirely* driven from the earth. " The spirits of the heavens " (Zach. vi. 5) caused the " two witnesses," in a suffering state, to prophesy of the Church which had been, and of the Church which was to come ; *nothing more*, except to testify against that which then existed as antichrist. And however bright and shining might have been the light in which they rejoiced, it could only be for a season, for there was no basis for them to build upon, neither would any Government composed of Church and State have permitted such organisation, the foundations of the first Gospel temple having been raised, and those of the second not being yet laid. Therefore, " if the foundations be destroyed, what can the righteous do ? " (Ps. xi. 3.)

And in this day, any sect or body of people, however much of the Spirit and truth they may possess, who are not prepared to claim that they are in the Fourth and last Dispensation, and that Christ has made his second appearing in them, must needs be content with the character of " witnesses," who pray for the kingdom of God " to come." And all such may rest assured that something better awaits them in the future than anything yet in their possession ; for every degree of goodness and truth in any people is of God, and leads towards Him.

Revelation is the " rock " upon which the true Church of Christ is built. And this Church is the most direct emanation from God that has yet been upon earth. It is the " kingdom " which the God of heaven has " set up " (see Dan. ii. 44, and vii. 27), and which will finally supplant all human systems, " not " indeed " by might or power" *(carnal* weapons), but by " God's Spirit." In it, " righteousness and peace have met together, and mercy and truth have kissed each

other " (Ps. lxxxv. 10) ; and from it goes forth the law
of the inherent rights of man to all parts of the world ;
and the living Word of the Lord from thence is the
Angel that is enlightening the earth. (See Rev. xiv. 6).

This, " the new creation," is the most beautiful and
perfect system of principles and order, in both temporal and spiritual things, that has been witnessed by
man since the world began. A *new earthly order*, for
the supply of his physical wants ; and a *new spiritual
order*, for the satisfying of his spiritual nature—a
Millennium. Therefore, it is a system of which the
natural creation, with all its laws and principles, and
its immutable and unchangeable order, is the most
direct and perfect type.

And although, as has been observed, the Church
originated from, is based upon, and sustained by,
Divine revelation, in a much higher sense than was
the Mosaic one ; yet, like it, there are certain *first*
principles in it which are clearly understood by every
individual member of the body, " from the greatest of
them even unto the least," as was promised of the
Lord, when he said He would " make a *new covenant*
with the house of Israel ; not according to the old
covenant " (which he made with the natural man, in
the earthly order of the first Adam, and renewed
under the Mosaic economy, respecting the work of
procreation), " which my covenant they brake, saith
the Lord. For I will put my law into their *inward*
parts and write it in their *hearts ;* and will be their
God, and they shall be my people. For I will forgive
their iniquity, and I will remember their sin no more."
(Jer. xxxi. 31—34.)

And " if there should arise a prophet, or a dreamer
of dreams," who should show signs and wonders,
which should even come to pass, or one that should
have visions, or revelations, which tend to cause any
soul to violate the least of these well-known principles ; *then*, although it should be the highest member

of the body, spiritual death and separation would be the inevitable consequence. For the true " elect " cannot be deceived by either evil or seducing spirits, because they are the children of Revelation, and are familiar with spirits and " *spiritual manifestations,*" in all their forms.

How, then, can dark, ignorant, or evil spirits deceive those who are always accompanied by angels of light, and by the spirits of those who, while on earth, were made perfect by the cross of Christ ? (See Heb. xii. 22, 23.) Herein is seen the fulfilment of the ancient prophecy : " And Saviours shall come up on Mount Zion, to judge the mount of Esau ; and the kingdom shall be the Lord's." (Obad. 21.) It is thus that " judgment shall be given to the saints of the Most High ; " and that " the saints shall judge the world ; " yea, and " judge *angels* " in the generative heavens— that is, every spirit that speaks to or through man. (See Dan. vii. 22 ; and 1 Cor. vi. 2, 3.)

And herein is the oracle of the " Urim and Thummim " restored in its true spiritual order, by which judgment can be rendered in righteousness and truth.

But no individual can possess this, except he be in union with the Church of the living God, as established in this " latter day of glory."

URIM AND THUMMIM.

JESUS CHRIST testified, " I am not come to destroy the law, but to fulfil it "—that is, the spirit and right-eous principles of the law ; and to advance them to far higher degrees of perfection, by a fuller display of Divine revelations and power. Thus also, in this Dis-pensation, his Divine Spirit embraces all the righteous principles of the three former Eras; and, by increasing the inspired revelations, and giving a superior flow of

Divine light and power, he carries them out in their perfected order; thus completing the foundation and work which God began in him in his first appearing. (See Eph. ii. 20.)

The *leading* principle of this foundation is—"Christ *has* appeared the second time, without sin, unto salvation;" and the *seal of judgment* is—"the Lord knoweth them that are his," and "Let every one that nameth the name of Christ *depart from all iniquity*" (2 Tim. ii. 19). All professed revelation or inspiration, whatever its source, must be judged by this rule. And any revelation that sanctions the *violation of the law of nature*, as already set forth, is not of God, but is from false or ignorant spirits, who are still in the lost and benighted elements of the world.

For it is the breach of this law that produces those 'fleshly *lusts* which war against the soul" (1 Peter ii. 11); which *lusts* led to the destruction of the old world, and to the overthrow of the cities of Sodom and Gomorrah, and lie at the bottom of all the abominations of the heathen nations. It was a "generation who had eyes full of *adultery*, and that could not cease from sin" (2 Peter ii. 14), that "killed the Prince of Life" (Acts iii. 15); and from this foul source, according to the Apostle James (iv. 1), "proceed all wars and fightings," private and public.

This it was that caused the fall of the primitive Church, as is evident from the reproofs given by the Spirit to the "seven Churches in Asia" (See Rev. ii. and iii.); and *this* it is which, ever since that event, has been, day and night, *accusing* the servants of God before him. (See Rev. xii. 10.) And how frequently it brings even the professed "ministers of Christ" in the kingdom of the beast into public disgrace, let the daily prints declare. Therefore, any person bringing forth a revelation teaching that a *true Christian* can still follow the first Adam in the work of generation is either deceived or is a deceiver; as also is he who teaches that he can indulge in ambition, pride, or the vain glory of the world.

For in the Church of Christ there is a revelation of meekness, humility, and of mortification to the proud and lofty nature of man; also to the self-exalting principles of a false *philosophy*, which no doubt is often derived from a class of spirits in the lower spheres of the spiritual world, who have never found a relation to the true resurrection work of God; but are some of "the dead," who have not yet believed in Christ, nor have ever heard "the voice of the Son of God." "Marvel not at this; for the hour is coming, in the which all that are in the graves" (in the spirit-world) "shall hear his voice, and shall come forth; they that have done" and continue to do "good, unto the resurrection of life; and they that have done" and continue to do "evil, unto the resurrection of damnation." (John v. 28, 29.) Thus showing that the probationary state extends into the world of spirits.

Therefore, when Jesus was "put to death in the flesh, he was quickened by the Spirit; by which also he went and preached to the spirits in prison who were disobedient to Noah's righteous preaching." (1 Peter iii. 18, 19.) From which fact it appears that the wicked antediluvians, "every imagination of whose heart was only evil," and who had been tormented for centuries by their own ungodly lusts and wicked passions, raging within and among them "like unquenchable fires," were yet in a *salvable* condition; as it is certain that our Saviour would not have preached to them had it not been possible for them to obey his preaching.

As saith Isaiah (chap. ix. 2), "The people that walked in darkness have seen a great light; and they that dwell in the land of the shadow of *death*, upon them hath the light shined." And "for this cause was the Gospel preached also to them that are *dead*, that they might be judged according to" (or in the

same manner as) "men in the flesh," but "live according to God in the spirit" (1 Peter iv. 6) ; *that was the
object.*

But what ministers of *error* and *evil* such lost,
degraded spirits can be to those who are accessible
to them, it is needless to expatiate upon. Who is it
that is not in danger of being led astray by some of
them? None but the "*elect*" are safe, who, "lest"
even "*they* enter into temptation," must "watch and
pray" to "make their calling and election sure."
(2 Pet. i. 10.)

For the false philosophy emanating from these
boasting spirits is "after the rudiments of the world,
and not after Christ" (Col. ii. 8), which philosophy
leads souls into a labyrinth of darkness ; and, under
the sanction of a pretended Divine inspiration, teaches
that there is no *evil* spirit, nor *evil* of *any kind*, except
such as has been created by God and man ; and that
after death all will be immediately happy, without
any reference to, or being made partakers of, a work
of true repentance (which leads souls to confess and
forsake all sin) ; without suffering with Jesus, and
dying to a sinful nature, as he died to it ; and without
finding salvation as *the effects of their own true travail
of soul:* forgetting that "into the holy city nothing
can enter which worketh abomination, or that loveth
or maketh a lie." (Rev. xxi. 27.)

The doctrine that "*there is no evil*" entirely abro-
gates the teaching of Jesus Christ, which was exemplified by his life, sufferings, and *violent death*, and
which showed that *both good and evil had a veritable
eternal existence ;* and that as the elements of good
concentrate in and proceed from an absolutely good
Being, so do the elements of evil concentrate in and
proceed from a being absolutely evil. And it was
equally impossible for the good Being to create or
originate (directly or indirectly) an antagonist being
or element, as it was for that antagonistic being or

element to create the Author and element of all good.
For the same fountain can *not* send forth sweet water
and bitter. And Jesus affirmed that "men do not
gather grapes of thorns or figs of thistles," for the
simple, though cogent, reason that "an evil tree cannot bring forth good fruit, any more than can a good
tree bring forth evil fruit." As also in his parable of
the earth, which he represents as a field, in which
good seed was sowed, but in which tares, or evil seed,
was also sowed *by an enemy*. Thus arguing that, if
there had been no foreign enemy to God in existence,
no such evil seed would or could have been found in
the earth ; nor, indeed, would the idea of evil, had
there been no antitype thereof, ever have entered the
human soul.

A writer, recently, in attempting to prove that there
is no such thing as evil in or out of this world, ob-
serves, " If we admit the existence of evil at all, we
must admit that God is the author of it," and that
"what is called evil is comparatively good, or good in
its incipient, incompleted, and undeveloped forms."
These remarks he grounds upon the fact that mankind can and may progress from bad to better, and
so onward.

But if that which does not possess an acrid quality
cannot impart or transmit it, so neither can God, who
is essential, absolute, and unadulterated good, ever
exhibit outwardly, in his creation, that which is opposite to, and has no existence in, Himself—*evil*.

Again, good cannot be evil, nor can evil be good,
even in an incipient state ; nor can good change to
and become evil, or evil change to and become good ;
any more than darkness can become light, or than light
can become darkness. Darkness may give place to
light, and evil may be removed and give place to
good, but cannot possibly mix therewith. For the
principles or elements of good and evil are always
necessarily distinct and antagonistic, being never in

union or assistant of each other, any more than are light and darkness, truth and error, ease and pain, or life and death.

Man having been originally created "very good," if he had *never yielded* to the evil suggestions of a *foreign enemy*, and thus become a subject of moral and spiritual darkness and evil—sin, sorrow, and sickness, sighing and tears, war and slavery, and famine and pestilence, together with all the thousands of secondary sources of human misery, would have been as far from mankind as they ever will be in the consummation of the work of redemption—the *Millennium*.

Many minds, well-intentioned, have conceived the idea that if mankind had been created entirely and positively good, they could not have progressed.— Everything in nature testifies against this error; and the unlimited faculties of the human soul especially bear witness to the truthfulness of this position. Good may be good without any mixture of evil, and yet be eternally expansive and progressive in its nature and growth.

And shall we say, that because good can expand, increase, and continue its augmentations, it therefore is or was incipient evil?

Good is *good* in all the different stages and processes through which it may pass; as is proved by its happifying effects upon all sensuous existences, from the embryo to the highest state of physical, intellectual, and spiritual development. So also is evil, *evil* in all the different stages through which *it* may pass; as is evidenced by the pain, suffering, and unhappiness to which all things and persons are subject, in proportion as they are under its influence.

The practical effects of charging upon God the *creation of evil*, or (which is tantamount) disbelieving in and denying the existence thereof, must be to throw souls off their guard in relation to its pernicious influences and wily machinations.

If a disease that is *well known* is thereby *half* cured, then the converse of this proposition is also true ; and so dreadful a disease as *evil* being *totally unknown*, and even mistaken for positive *good*, by intelligent souls, must be tenfold more dangerous to them, as free agents, who are really placed between, and subject to, the suggestions and drawings of intelligent agents in both elements—good and evil—than it would be to such as are *fully enlightened* in regard to their *true position.*

It is a question whether the doctrine of *no evil* be not one of the most radically dangerous that has ever been broached to or by the human mind. It certainly is the antipodes of what Jesus and his Apostles taught upon that subject.

Jesus said, "What I say unto you I say unto all, Watch and pray, that ye enter not into temptation ; " and "Except a man deny himself, and take up his cross daily," and even "hate his own life also, he cannot be my disciple." To the Jews he said, "Ye are of your father the devil ; and the lusts of your father ye will do." The Apostle exhorts, "Be sober, be vigilant ; for your adversary the devil goeth about as a roaring lion, seeking whom he may devour." "To him that *overcometh*," said Jesus Christ, "will I give to eat of the tree of life." These, and many other texts of similar import, possess no sense or meaning at all except upon the assumption that two opposite powers and principles do exist ; and that man is not merely a non-progressed being in good, but that he is a *bona fide free agent*, standing between, subject to, and continually operated upon, by two antagonistic elements and powers therein—*good and evil.*

It is not possible to conceive of a greater insult being offered to the human understanding than the attempt that is now so sedulously, ingeniously, and extensively being made to convince and satisfy it that

all the evil of lying, robbery, murder, and rapine—
all the perfidy and oppression — all the gluttony,
drunkenness, and lechery—the riches and poverty,
the luxury and starvation, and the impiety and
ungodliness that the past and present history of
mankind unfold, are, and always have been, from a
perfectly good source ; or that they are merely the
result of non-development in good—a necessary state
and stage in the process of *progression* Godward ; and
are, therefore, the seed—the germinal sources and
incipient stages—of peace, purity, righteousness, and
love—*true religion.* The logical conclusion of this
doctrine of no evil is, that " whatever is, is right."

This is really commingling and confounding opposite and contrary qualities and things, if not over-
turning the foundations of sanity in the human mind.

Good and evil exist abstractly, and also mani-
festly. There are principles of good and evil ; and
these are reduced to actions—facts—by intelligent
beings. There is the same amount and kind of evidence in proof of the existence of the one that there
is by which to prove the existence of the other. Love
and hatred, peace and war, forgiveness and revenge,
benevolence and cupidity, chastity and lust, etc., etc.,
have each and all an equally positive and tangible
existence. Persons subject to these passions and
principles are real entities.

Upon the hypothesis that *either one* of these had a
beginning, the *other* must have created it out of
nothing ; for it is equally as absurd to suppose that
real evil could be made out of real good, as it is to
suppose that real good could be made out of real evil.

Also, it is not a whit less illogical to assume that
the evil principles and elements do exist, but that
there is no unoriginated *evil being* in them, than it
would be to suppose that the good principles and
elements exist, but that there is no unoriginated
good Being therein, who directs and controls them.

To attempt to *evade* the absurdity of the proposition that either of these principles or beings created its own opposite out of nothing, by saying they first produced good or evil beings, and that these created their own opposites, is unreasonable and disingenuous.

If evil *be evil*, then it was an *evil thought* and design *in the mind of the Creator—God*—out of which He created it, and first brought it into existence ; whether He himself did it directly, or whether He did it by producing another being—man—to do it for Him.

An acorn could just as easily develop itself into an apple tree (if no independent principle and being of evil have any existence) as can man progress or develop himself into a being, the germinal principles of whose character God had not thought of nor planted in him.

Thus "saith the Lord : they have built the high places of Tophet, which is in the valley of the son of Hinnom, to burn their sons and their daughters in the fire ; which I commanded them not, neither *came it into my heart.*" (Jer. vii. 30, 31.) *He never thought of it.*

But upon the hypothesis, or fact, that the principles, elements, and unoriginated beings (good and evil) exist, there is no contradiction, confusion, or absurdity, that necessarily follows. For as "God is of purer *eyes* than to *behold* iniquity," so also is He too pure in *heart* to *think* iniquity.

Just so far as man is in evil is he actually out of God and Christ. "He that sinneth hath not seen Christ, neither known him." "Then will he say unto them, Depart from me, ye workers of iniquity ; I *never knew* you."

God exists only in his own elements. Yet He could create beings with a capacity for receiving evil influences, as easily as a man can make a vessel out of the most pure material, capable of holding the most noisome and poisonous fluids.

It is very problematical whether a being thus "made upright" and "very good" in all his faculties and capacities, who, in the exercise of his free agency, prostitutes them under and to the influences of evil, is not *more unhappy* than one whose very being is *only evil;* of whom a figure is seen in the snake, tiger, hyena, vulture, etc., etc. For misery is the result of a creature getting out of its own—its native —element.

SUMMARY.

The Fourth Era, again, and the Church pertaining to it, like all the preceding ones, had its origin in *Divine Revelation,* and is the second revelation and manifestation of Christ, in the *female* order, as the *first* was in the *male* order.

As *Jesus* was anointed and filled with the Christ-Spirit, *so was* ANN LEE. Neither of them, however, is an object of *worship,* any more than are those who follow them (who are also baptised with the anointing or Christ-Spirit) objects of worship. "Know ye not that, except *Christ be in you*" all, "*ye are reprobates?*" (See 2 Cor. xiii. 5.)

Thus, in each succeeding Dispensation, the revelation is more directly from God—that is, the mediums or messengers thereof sent to earth are of a *higher* order. But in all cases it is a man or woman that receives the revelation from the messenger.

The *First* Era commenced in *Adam;* the *Second* in *Abraham;* the *Third* in *Jesus;* the *Fourth* in *Ann Lee.*

In this Fourth Dispensation is established the final Church and kingdom of Christ, which possesses the "Urim and Thummim;" and therefore it cannot be deceived or overthrown by evil or ignorant spirits ; for its communicants are familiar with spirits and spiritual manifestations in all their phases and forms.

This Church has its laws, statutes, and rules, as had the Adamic, Mosaic, and first Christian.

13

And these laws, with the "*new covenant*" *of re-generation*—virgin purity—are put into the heart of every individual, and form the touchstone or test of all revelation.

The faithful persons, therefore, who compose this Church, are the "very elect," who cannot be deceived.

Thus, all the righteous laws of the Four Dispensations culminate in this Church of the Fourth Era, uniting in a concentration of spiritual light; and form the "Urim and Thummim," which all the dark spirits in existence, on earth or in the spirit-world, cannot either dim or becloud.

The practical fruit of this Church is the entire banishment of poverty and want, and sin and misery; and a full supply of physical and spiritual necessaries for the body and soul of every one of its members.

He who teaches that Christ and generation can coalesce, is deceived, or is a deceiver.

No law of any previous Era must be violated. The Mosaic law was from God; and Jesus said, "Heaven and earth should pass away; but not in anywise should one jot or tittle of the law pass therefrom, until it be all fulfilled," or kept (see Matt. v. 18); *then it will cease and pass away*, for it was made only for sinners, or transgressors. And, therefore, if the professed Christian sin, he must pay the Mosaic penalty; as, in sinning, he breaks or transgresses the law of Moses; for "sin is the transgression of the law" (1 John iii. 4). Every spirit that denieth this is *false*.

The *lust of generation* is the one great evil that marred all the designs and works of God in the first three Eras. But it is utterly destroyed in the Fourth by the cutting off of the work of generation itself.

Lust caused the flood. By it the primitive Church fell. It has accused and condemned the "two witnesses," day and night before God, during the last eighteen centuries; and has caused the stars (priests and teachers) of the old heavens (Christendom) to fall to the earth, and wallow in the filth of sexuality. And from it have proceeded all "wars and fightings," Heathen and Christian.

The Gospel, or law of the Fourth Dispensation, will be preached to all peoples, nations, kindreds, and tongues, on earth and in the spirit-world.

Jesus preached it to the antediluvians. (See 1 Pet. iii. 18—20.) But there is a class of spirits who assume *great* names and who speak *great* swelling words of vanity—advocates of a vain and false philosophy—who find many willing proselytes, unto whom they minister, and teach that there are no evil spirits nor any evil, and that after death *all* will be happy ; that in the beginning there was nothing but God, and that there will be nothing but God in the end.

But it is hoped that these Tests will prove a sufficient guard, to every soul who will abide by them, against the machinations of all kinds and classes of spirits, and also from all error and false doctrine.

LOVE OF GOD IN MAN.

THIS is the first principle of goodness in man, from which every virtue and all truth and righteousness proceed and grow, as from their proper root. Hence the *first* commandment from God to man is, " Thou shalt love the Lord thy God with all thy heart, thy mind, thy soul, and thy strength." (Deut. vi. 5 ; and Mark xii. 30.) And again, " Thou shalt have no other gods (idols) before me." Nothing upon which man's affections can be placed should be otherwise than *secondary* to the love of God in the human soul; or that they would not sacrifice to do the will of God —" Love is the fulfilling of the law." (Rom. xiii. 10.)

To the wicked Jews, Jesus said, " I know you that

ye have *not* the *love of God* in you." (Mark v. 42.)
In Jesus was the love of God *perfected*, for the *first
time* in any human being. "This is the love of God,
that ye keep his commandments." (1 John v. 3.) "I
came not to do my own will, but the will of him that
sent me." (John vi. 38.) Again, Jesus affirmed, "Therefore doth my Father love me, because I *do* always
those things that please him." (John viii. 29.) And
he continued to *prove* his love to God by his "obedience unto death, even the death of the cross." (Phil.
ii. 8.) And greater love to God cannot be, than that
a being lay down his life in obedience to him.

It is plain, then, that God loves his creature man,
and seeks, through the influence of many means, to do
him good, by inducing man himself to become un-
selfishly good. And therefore this is one test of
revelation, as to whether it be of evil or Divine origin.

LOVE OF MAN TO MAN.

"THOU shalt love thy neighbour as thyself." (Mark
xii. 31.) "By this shall all men know that ye are my
disciples, if ye have love one for another." (John
xiii. 35.) "If a man love not his brother whom he
hath seen, how can he love God whom he hath not
seen?" (1 John iv. 20.) Again, "Let us not love in
word, but in deed." (1 John iii. 18.) Now, how can
any soul consistently profess to have the love of God,
and to love his neighbour as himself, when he is not
willing to give him an equal inheritance with himself
in even those things that perish with the using—the
temporary things of earth?

Therefore, whenever men see a body of people,
comprising the high and low, rich and poor, bond
and free, white or coloured, male and female, of all
classes and nations, who are all enjoying one united

interest in things spiritual and temporal, as brethren and sisters in Christ, and who have proved themselves in these principles for a goodly period of time, they may know that *it* is the *true* Church or body of Christ—the Zion of God to which "*all peoples*" may freely "flow," as to an ark of safety, a fountain of love, and work of salvation.

This order of the kingdom of God upon earth is inimitable by all the wisdom and powers of natural man; as was shown to the prophet in his visions of God of the spiritual building of the "*latter day*," when he was commanded to go into the field where no foundation of any building was, and it was said unto him, "In the place where the Highest beginneth to show his city, there can no man's building be able to stand." (2 Esdras x. 53, 54.)

The time when the Highest began to show his spiritual city was at the day of Pentecost, by the operative influencè and teachings of his Spirit, which resulted in a perfect oneness of feeling *internally*, and a community of all their earthly goods *externally*. This was effected *not* as an *ultimatum* to which they had deliberately set out to attain, but it was un-expected and unlooked for, though a necessary consequence of their own individual spiritual state and condition.

It was the labour of Jesus to root up and destroy in his disciples all the principles of sin, and, in pursu-ance of this object, he thus attacked their selfishness and distrust of God: "Lay not up for yourselves treasures upon earth, where moth and rust do corrupt, and where thieves break through and steal." (Matt. vi. 19.) And again: "Therefore I say unto you, Take no thought for your life, what ye shall eat, or what ye shall drink; nor yet for your body, what ye shall put on. Is not the life more than meat, and the body than raiment? Behold the fowls of the air; for they sow not, neither do they reap, nor gather

into barns ; yet your Heavenly Father feedeth them.
Are ye not much better than they ? Which of you
by taking thought can add one cubit unto his stature?
And why take ye thought for raiment ? Consider the
lilies of the field, how they grow ; they toil not, neither
do they spin ; and yet I say unto you, that even
Solomon in all his glory was not arrayed like one of
these. Wherefore, if God so clothe the grass of the
field, which to-day is, and to-morrow is cast into the
oven, shall he not much more clothe you, O ye of
little faith ? Therefore take no thought, saying, What
shall we eat? or, What shall we drink? or, Where-
withal shall we be clothed ? (for after all these things
do the Gentiles seek) ; for your Heavenly Father
knoweth that ye have need of all these things. But
seek ye first the kingdom of God and his righteousness, and all these things shall be added unto you."
(Matt. vi. 25—33.)

Thus did Jesus strive to detach their minds entirely
from this world, to cut them off from the cares of
supplying even the necessaries of life, thereby leaving
them to depend and trust entirely upon Divine
Providence for the supply of all their bodily wants ;
even as David prayed, " From my *necessities*, O Lord,
deliver me." " For after all these things do the
Gentiles seek." And when he sent them out to
preach the Gospel, "he commanded them that they
should take nothing for their journey save a staff
only, no scrip, no bread, no money in their purse, but
be shod with sandals, and not put on two coats."
(Mark vi. 8, 9.)

It was thus that he would have them *practically*
" seek first the kingdom of heaven and its righteousness," by actually leaving the *temporal* entirely out of
the question for the *present*, and as a preparation for
that which was to follow. For Jesus designed, in and
through them, to create new heavens and a new earth,
and by creating the " *new heavens*," the *spiritual* or

soul first, *that* would bring forth the "*new earth*," or its *body* in temporal things. And in this way God would indeed "*add* unto them all those things" that he knew they would have need of. "Their strength was to sit still" (Is. xxx. 17), and let God work by his Spirit to will and to do according to his own wisdom.

It is therefore evident that a community was not only not anticipated, and unexpected, but also unthought of, and, of course, undesigned by the Apostles ; but they, after having been together in one place, in deep tribulation of soul and fervent prayers to God, were baptised with the Christ-Spirit to such a degree as wrought them up to, and induced in them, the highest state of spirituality of which they were susceptible. This caused them to feel the strongest conviction and deepest abhorence of sin and of the nature of sin, by opening to their view their own actual state of soul, as contrasted with the infinite purity and perfection of the Divine Spirit and presence, with which they were thus temporarily baptised for that very purpose. Under this influence many began to cry out in very agony of soul, " Men and brethren, what shall we do to be saved ? " (Acts ii. 37.)

Then it was, and not before, that God could " begin to show his city," for he had now suitable materials with which to commence to build. He could now work to the establishing of that order in temporal things by which to supply the physical wants of his people, which he had designed from the beginning.

For the people received that conviction for sin that led them to show their deeds to the Apostles. In other words, they confessed and forsook their sins ; and, as a consequence thereof, became so " kindly affectioned one towards another," and experienced for each other such a depth of brotherly love, that it was soon found that the highest delight and happiness of everyone was best promoted by administering to the comfort and consolation of every other member of the body of Christ *in all things*—temporal as well as spiritual.

It was in this manner that the love of God and of man burned up and destroyed the love of sin and self, and COMMUNITY was the necessary result; so that ":all these things" were added to the "one thing needful," which they had sought and found. Here, then, was the place where the Lord God *began* to "show the city" which he would build in Christ's Second Appearing, as a permanent city of peace, love, and plenty. And although this order was seemingly lost in the fall and final overthrow of the primitive Church, yet man, seeing the temporal advantages to be derived from such a system, has never ceased the attempt, in any age, to build upon the foundation then laid by the Spirit. But no such "building" of man's has ever yet been "able to stand." These buildings—these efforts at social structures—lacked a religious basis, ay, the corner-stone itself—*celibacy*. Where there are husbands and wives and private property, there will be "fightings," and these necessarily lead to disintegration and dissolution. The Shakers alone, 'mid wars, revolutions, and the wreck of empires, have stood, solving the problem—the practicability of "holding all things in common."

In a thousand ways and forms, this principle of unity of purpose and effort has been adopted and applied, amongst men, to nearly all the common pursuits of life—from a cotton factory to a Fourier's association, or an Owen's community. In all these, however, the object aimed at has been the antipodes of that sought by the disciples on the day of Pentecost. It has been either naked and direct self-aggrandise-ment, as in companies or corporations, or else to form a community as an *object* merely for the supply of physical wants and comforts; exclusively seeking

what and how they should eat, and drink, and be
clothed, and how they should " lay up treasures upon
earth " to the greatest amount and extent ; and this
as the sole and main end of their being, either by
putting the kingdom and its righteousness *last*, or
omitting it altogether, thereby exactly *reversing the
counsel of Jesus to his followers.*

It may be objected that the condition of the
followers of Jesus, when having " all things common,"
where every want was easily and quickly supplied,
was widely different from that state set forth in the
Scriptures above quoted of " Take 'no thought," etc.
This is granted. So was the state of Israel, when
compelled by outward circumstances to depend from
day to day wholly upon God for their daily bread
while on their way to the promised land, different
from what it was when they reached that "glory of
all lands, flowing with milk and honey," and fertile
beyond anything now known upon earth ; yet it was
the one state that prepared them for the other. They
learned in the wilderness dependence, faith, obedience,
all of which they needed to enable them to make a
right use of the good things that they were afterwards
entrusted with in the promised land ; and thus, when
Jesus led his disciples about or sent them off on a
journey without any visible means of support, they
were often fed in a miraculous manner ; but *even then*
he *promised a different* order " *now in this life*," in the
future, where, as Israel did in Canaan, they must live
by the labour of their " own hands."

The true Spiritualist (Christian), in seeking God
and salvation, finds the kingdom of heaven to be
where love produces community ; while the natural
man, attracted by his earthly selfish instincts, seeks
to build upon God's foundation that which is not
" able to stand." It is as those who followed Jesus
for the loaves and fishes which were the results of his
miracles ; whereas, others followed him through love,

and to *witness* his miracles, who therefore rightly and justly partook of the fruits thereof, as *for them* it was that the miracles were wrought.

SUMMARY.

By this " we know that we have passed from death unto life, because we love the brethren."

The *absence* of true fraternal love amongst men has produced the present evil condition of human society, in all its relations, internal and external. By love, therefore, the inhabitants of the new heavens and earth were to be pre-eminently distinguished.

If a man really loves his neighbour as himself, it will *first* as the outward and inferior be *visible* to " all men," by their equal participation between them of all earthly goods and substances ; yet this is but the fruit and evidence of their equal participation in spiritual treasures pertaining to salvation.

If communion of earthly goods be sought as an *end*, it is of man ; but if it follow as a consequence of an *inward principle*—love—it is of God.

A baptism of the Holy Christ-Spirit from the resurrection heaven effected it in a short time, within the first century of the Christian Era, by withdrawing man's affections from things below and placing them on things above. They became transformed.

Jesus taught men to " take no thought " as to what they should eat, drink, or wear, as a *first* object, but to " seek *first* the kingdom of heaven and its righteousness," and promised that inferior necessary things " *should be added*."

A strong desire for salvation *from sin*—the sin of selfishness—is the best preparation that a soul can have for community of interest in earthly things.

Sin and self, produce *private* property.

Innocence and self-denial, produce *community* of property.

The first Christian Church set before men an example of love—a oneness of interest in all things ; and although the order was lost to the external view with the fall of the Church, yet men have never ceased to admire and try to imitate it, for the sake of temporal advantage—the *loaves and fishes.*

In all ages, and in a thousand ways and forms, the principle has been adopted and applied among men, but especially in our own day, and by our own generation. Yet the object aimed at has invariably been diametrically opposite to that of *the men of Galilee*—loving souls baptised of Christ. They have sought *first* what they should eat and drink and how they should be clothed.

The kingdom of heaven is where *love produces community ;* but when man, from a selfish motive, seeks to build upon the foundation of " all things common," his building is a " man's building, and it is not able to stand."

Love to man is therefore a sure and certain criterion of all Divine Revelation. Anything contrary to, or short of, this test—love to man—emanating from the spirit-world of angelic life, is proof that it comes from an order of spirits that is *not* joined to the Church of Christ in that world, and who therefore are not proper ministers to " the heirs of salvation " who belong to the Church of Christ upon earth.

THE SPIRITUAL MAN.

AND, finally, the greatest evidence that can ever be given to a man of the eternal truth and unchangeable principles of godliness, is realised when he finds in his *own* soul that abiding *revelation* by which he is freed from all doubts and uncertainties as to his present and future state, and of the duty which God requires of him. And when he experiences the operation of that Spirit, which enables him to live a perfect life, so that he can stand in justification, "having a conscience void of offence towards both God and man," according to the pattern exhibited in Jesus Christ, "the Captain of our salvation."

Thus, being "not conformed to the world, but transformed" therefrom into the image of Christ, he will be in possession of the infallible standard of revelation, which, when uprightly applied, will never fail; for herein are the words of Jesus Christ verified : "If any man will do my Father's will, he shall know of the doctrine, whether it be of God, or whether I speak of myself." (John vii. 17.)

And everything in any soul short of *this* point— "*As Christ is, so are we in this world*" (1 John iv. 17) —will not only fail to give boldness and confidence in the great "day of judgment," but it will also leave such soul in a state of spiritual darkness that will utterly disqualify it to "try the spirits."

As Jesus was a prophet, so also are his followers prophets, for "As he is, so are we *in this world*" (1 John iv. 17); and the glory which the Father gave to him he gives to his followers. (See John xvii. 22.) All other prophets and spirits must be subject to these true and genuine prophets; for "the spirits of the prophets are subject to the prophets." (1 Cor. xiv. 32.) For Jesus Christ left as a legacy to his brethren the "*Spirit of Truth*," which should not only "call past things to their remembrance," but also show them things to come." (See John xiv. 26, and xvii. 13.)

Thus did Jesus permanently endue his followers with the spirit of prophecy, which constituted them emphatically "the prophets," and they became so initiated into the very spirit, and so grounded and established in the constituent principles of his spiritual kingdom, that they could intuitively perceive "things to come" from the ground of their knowledge of first causes, which must of necessity and inevitably produce their legitimate effects. These were a kind of first fruits of the spirit and principles of Christianity, or of the "testimony of Jesus." But *true Christians* (in the proper acceptation of the term) are those who have received Christ in his second advent upon earth, in and through the order of the female, and are now standing in the "testimony of Jesus," loving not their carnal generative lives unto the spiritual death of their souls.

These are the "first ripe fruits" of the *Four* great Dispensations of God's grace to man ; and they are only created and brought forth by the Fourth and last of these Eras, unto which the prophets and Apostles of the preceding Dispensations must all find a true relation, and be subject in the spirit of true obedience to its light and order, or never be "made perfect."

Thus is fulfilled the saying of Jesus, "The first shall be last and the last first"; proving the truth of the Angel's words to Esdras, that God's judgments and works are like a ring. "And that as there is no swiftness to the first, so there shall be no slackness to the last." (2 Esdras v. 42.)

MODE OF WORSHIP.*

1. IT is pretty generally known that the Shakers serve God by singing and dancing ; but *why* they practise this mode of worship is not so generally understood.

2. It should be recollected that "God is a Spirit," and can be worshipped only "in spirit and in truth."

---

* Ann Lee (the Founder of the Shakers), a Biography, with Memoirs of William Lee, James Whittaker, J. Hocknell, J. Meacham, and Lucy Wright ; also a Compendium of the Origin, History, Principles, Rules and Regulations, Government, and Doctrines, of the United Society of Believers in Christ's Second Appearing. By F. W. Evans. Fourth Edition. 1858.

Without the presence of the Spirit there can be no true worship. Conviction of sin, godly sorrow, and repentance, are the first effects of the Spirit of God upon the conscience of a sinner. And when sin is fully removed, by confessing and forsaking it, the *cause* of heaviness, gloom, and sorrow, is gone; and joy and rejoicing, and thanksgiving and praise, are then the spontaneous effects of a true spirit of devotion. And whatever *manner* the Spirit may dictate, or whatever the *form* into which the Spirit may lead, it is acceptable to Him from whom the Spirit proceeds.

3. All the *Sabbaths* among the Jews, as hereafter set forth, were joyous festivals—times for men to do good to each other, by feeding the hungry, clothing the naked, etc.; for all to make each other happy, and thus rejoice before the Lord, "with music and dancing."

4. Dancing was a national custom among the Hebrews upon all extraordinary occasions of some great good, as a victory, etc. They expressed their satisfaction and happiness by *dancing*, as the Americans do by the abnegation of temperance and the explosion of gunpowder.

5. When Israel had escaped the Egyptians, "all the women went after Miriam with timbrels and with dances." The virgins of Israel held a yearly feast at Shiloh, with dances. When David killed Goliath there was dancing. "And David danced with all his might before the ark of the Lord."

6. Dancing is often mentioned by the seers, prophets, and prophetesses. "Thou hast turned my mourning into dancing." "Praise his name in the dance." "Praise him with the timbrel and dance." When the prophets spoke of the Millennial period and Church, it was with expressions such as,—"Then shall the *virgin* rejoice in the dance, both old men and young together." "O virgin of Israel, thou shalt

go forth in the dances of them that make merry."
And Jesus, in speaking of the return of the prodigal
son, included music and dancing as a part of the
proceedings and rejoicing.

7. But so plain and simple a subject does not require much extension or amplification. Suffice it to
say, that the Shakers believe the great "*Sabbatical
year*" of the world has come, wherein the long captive
sinner is released; "the poor have the Gospel preached
to them, without money and without price;" perpetual and universal brotherhood is established and
proclaimed, each one (as Jesus said) going back to his
inheritance in the earth; "Blessed are the meek, for
they shall inherit the earth," and all things else, *in
common*, as an everlasting Jubilee of jubilees, where
the rich and the poor, the high and the low, the bond
and the free, male and female, all become *one* in Christ
Jesus; and *love* is the bond of their union.

THE BIBLE.

THE Shakers hold the Bible to be a record of the
most Divine Angelic ministrations to man, and more
or less an imperfect record of the spiritual and religious experience and history of the most highly progressed portion or branch of the human family.

They also believe that the state and condition of
the seers, prophets, and prophetesses, or mediums,
determined the quantity, and affected the quality, of
every Divine revelation. The same may be said of
the translators and translations of the Bible.

It is thought by the Shakers that the book of the
"*Revelation*" has suffered less from interpolations and
mistranslations than any other; partly by reason of
the anathema it contains against all who should add
to, or take from, its contents; but still more because

the Spirit has clothed it with such a complexity of tropes, symbols, and figures, that it is utterly unintelligible to the generative man, and could not be comprehended until the central event — the *second appearing of Christ*—had transpired ; that being the only key by which to unlock its mysteries, break its seals, and unfold its treasures of wisdom and truth, by baptizing souls with the Spirit that dictated it, and forming in them the character of the " Lion of the tribe of Judah ; " during which process, all the events described in *that book* would be accomplished in them as individuals. And, indeed, it is a chart of ecclesiastical history.

SHAKER LECTURES.

RELIGIOUS COMMUNISM:*

A LECTURE BY

ELDER FREDERICK W. EVANS.

" Can we come to any other conclusion than that this Pentecostal day is to lead to the coming of a *Second Messiah!* He is not yet in our midst; we are only listening to the voices crying in the wilderness. These voices have come to us in the form of a spiritual *science*. But I do know that the *baptism of fire* is yet awaiting us, when we shall be found worthy. Fire consumes, but it does not annihilate. It changes, but does not destroy."— EMMA HARDINGE.

INTRODUCTORY REMARKS BY THE CHAIRMAN OF THE MEETING, MR. HEPWORTH DIXON.

I HAVE been requested to attend here to-night to introduce to an audience of my countrymen, Elder Frederick, of Mount Lebanon, in America. I have been asked to do this, I presume, because I am perhaps the only Englishman in this assembly who has actually slept under a Shaker roof, who has seen with his own eyes that beautiful Eden which the order to which he belongs has created, and who has lived amongst the people even for a short time, and seen the outward and visible beauty of their lives. Of course, a gentleman who is known to have a wife and a houseful of rosy children need not say that he is not a Shaker; but none of us, I take it, need to be so much with the world as not now and then to have some sense that

* Lecture delivered in St. George's Hall, London, on the evening of Sunday, 6th August, 1871.

14

there are concentric circles of fraternal and spiritual life about us, which it may be for our good that we should sometimes try to penetrate and understand. One such circle has sent to the old country, from which it originally sprang, a representative in Elder Frederick. A most interesting, and strange, and mystical circle that undoubtedly is. With its mystical side, I, at this moment at least, have no concern whatever ; but as regards its human side, I have seen enough of it to show that it presents phases and results of human endeavour, on a great and very high plane, so lovely to all seekers after a better set of things for mankind, that I am confident that I am doing what is a service to everyone, if I invite them a little to look into and see how those beautiful results are brought about. No war, no violence, no professional life of any kind, no lawyers, no doctors are to be found in that enchant- ing circle. The people have contrived a form of life eminently sober, orderly, beautiful, good in a thousand ways, which even all the world's people can thoroughly appreciate. We see the child there growing up in innocence, and we see that when he is grown up he is still innocent of the thousand evils which the unfortu- nate children of great cities in this country are too familiar with. We see the men and women living a strange life which many of us would find very difficult —some of us, myself amongst the number, quite impos- sible ; but we see human beings actuated by spiritual motives attaining to a degree of human perfection on this earth that is perfectly astonishing. How these results are brought about, of course I cannot explain ; Elder Frederick, I have no doubt, will give us some glimpses—will lift the curtain here and there, if not completely ; and will show us, at all events, a regula- tive, adequate cause for these extremely beautiful results, which everyone can see who will take the trouble to inspect them for himself. Elder Frederick, the gentleman who will now address us, has written his own autobiography, and it may be read by all of us. He has told us in that little sketch that he was at one time a very free thinker, indeed ; that he was a Materialist in opinion, that he was a philosopher; and he tells us how he travelled from this stage of thought into the higher region in which he now lives. Being materialistic and philosophical, he was seeking for a better state of moral human society, and in his search for a basis of a better social state, he fell upon that inner light which has led him to the position which he now occupies, and which he is about to explain to us. He has been forty years, or something like that, a leading member of this order ; he is its official exponent on the spot, and I presume that whatever he says we may take to be the official expression as regards their life. It only remains that I should ask Elder Frederick to address us upon the topic for which he has called us together to-night.

ELDER EVAN'S LECTURE.

Friends, I am much pleased and feel greatly obliged for the kind introduction that my friend Hepworth Dixon has given me. I stand before you this evening truly as a representative of the Shaker Order in America, the first that the order has sent out. From the life that we live, all of us working with our own hands—I presume I have averaged four hours a day, or very near that, of hand-labour for the forty years that I have been amongst the people called Shakers —of course you will not expect that I am a scholar, but a simple, plain working man.

MY FIRST INTRODUCTION TO THE SHAKERS.

I went out amongst that people, as has been re-marked, a stranger. We were searching for a location to start another community (for I was a Communist belonging to the Robert Owen school at that time), and having learned accidently of the existence of such a society as the Shakers, I called on them, was kindly received, made known the object of my visit, and stayed a few days. I became interested very greatly; first in the results that they had attained, which very much surprised me, because I had understood that they were, of all people in America, the most devoted to the religious idea, and I was destitute of that idea —a simple Materialist, not presuming to say there was no such thing as a spirit-world, or that man was not immortal, or that there was no God, but destitute of the evidence of these facts, if they were facts. I was always ready to receive instruction—to receive evidence. As such I appeared as a simple inquirer among the Shakers, which interested me at once in the community system and its operation as it existed there.

THE SHAKERS A RELIGIOUS COMMUNITY.

As I said, I was very much surprised ; for it was to me a wonder how a body of religionists could form a community ; but now I recur back to the words of Jesus, " If you will not believe in my words, yet believe me for the very works' sake." It was the works, the fruits produced in the Shaker Order—the manner in which I found the brethren and sisters living together, mingling with them at their labour for some ten days before I joined the society—it was these practical results, the social relation that they maintain to each other, that afforded the great evidence to my mind that there was some adequate cause at the back of it to produce those effects, and something, too, that we Materialists were not yet in possession of.

THE EXTENT OF THE ORDER.

I will here state that there are some seventy communities on the basis of Shaker principles in America.

Where several of these communities have lands adjoining, they form a society—some societies being composed of eight communities, others of three or four, and so on, there being in all about seventy small communities holding their property in common, in which the males and females enjoy equal rights and privileges —are equally represented in the government of the society or the community, all the offices being filled equally by males and females standing in correspondent relation.

A MALE AND FEMALE GOVERNMENT.

This is one peculiarity of the government of that society to which I would call your attention, for I think there is more in that than some of you may be aware of, as accounting for the success of the community system. I would also draw some inferences from that. When I look abroad over the nations of Christendom, and see what their social systems have come to—for instance, the condition of London to-day, taking all its population into consideration—I see a great lack ; there is something wanting ; the people are not all comfortable—they are not all well supplied with food, and clothing, and houses to live in. Why not ? Is there something in the foundation of your government to account for it ? Think of it. They are men governments—the woman element is not represented therein. True, you have a Queen ; but you all understand that she reigns more as a king than as a woman. Your Parliament, your House of Lords, your House of Commons, contains no females representing the population of the nation. How is this ? At least half of your population are females, possessed of the same faculties, the same senses, the same wants, with the other half—why are they subject to laws that they have had no voice in framing, and to penalties connected with those laws, and to taxation, where they have had no sort of representation? I merely refer to these ideas as something that occupies the minds of the simple Shakers occasionally when they are not attending to their orchards or fields, or mechanical labours. If you consider my views strange or unusual, you will pardon me, because I do not belong to the world. We believe, as a foundational idea, that Deity itself is dual—a Heavenly Father and a Heavenly Mother reigning over this world of ours, and that, therefore, all true normal government should be based upon the same foundation, recognising the existence of the two permanent elements in humanity —the male and the female. And I account for war and the social evil, and many other things that I might name in your social systems and organisation, in a great degree because of the want of normal government. Your Government, as I should express it, is abnormal, unnatural.

AN ARGUMENT IN FAVOUR OF CELIBACY.

I am aware that I am addressing an audience who all believe in the marriage relation, while I represent an order of celibates, both male and female; and I think I may safely say, having had forty years' experience with them, that they are quite as comfortable in their social relation one to the other, and enjoy—the male the female, and the female the male —fully as much as those who sit before me. I think so. I mention this as a subject of thought. You say if the celibate life is entirely abnormal, then the result ought to be entire unhappiness. How could we be comfortable, much less how could we enjoy ourselves as we do, satisfied and contented in the life we live, in the relation we bear one to the other, if it was contrary to nature, contrary to the Divine law, abnormal? I hold it could not be. Therefore I ask your attention to that point.

GOD IS MALE AND FEMALE.

Your Scriptures say, "In the beginning God created man in his own image, in the image of God created he him, male and female created he them." How could he do that if God himself was not in the order of male and female? How could man and woman, I ask, be in the image of God, if God himself has no element of the feminine in him? There is, you may depend, so far as my testimony can go, and that of my people, as truly in existence a Heavenly Divine Mother as there is a Heavenly Divine Father unto whom you pray. And indeed, my friends, how could there be a father where there is no mother? Is it not a little out of order to use the term father? Why do you not use the term "it"? Why do you not use a neutral word? Why use a word representing the male element, and which in itself implies the existence of a counterpart?

THE SHAKERS NOT OPPOSED TO MARRIAGE.

Then, my friends, if God made man male and female, and said to them, "Multiply and replenish the earth," as He said to all the animals in creation, I take it that it was simply a law of nature that all the animal creation, as all the vegetable, should reproduce after their kind, and there is no objection to it. We take no ground against it; we grant you the order fully, freely. That which is spiritual is not first, but that which is natural, and afterwards that which is spiritual. How then is Shakerism opposed to the marriage relation? Not at all. "Why then," you say, "are you Shakers? If it is right for you to be celibates, is it not right for everybody?" I say nay; I say, in the words of Jesus when he was answering the question put to him by the Pharisees about the marriage relation and condemning divorce, that Moses allowed it, not because it was right, but because of the hardness of their hearts, because of their low conditions, just as Brigham Young states that one man and one woman is the order, but that he permits polygamy because of the conditions of the people ; taking precisely the ground that Moses took in that respect, as well as in some other very important points, which it would be well for some other people to look into a little. Then, my friends, we have a starting point. I take away your objections to the Shakers on this ground. I hope I take away misconception out of your minds. I come on a mission of love and nothing else. If anything I say can be of any use or benefit to even a few of this congregation, I shall feel well paid for my labour, and I earnestly desire and hope that I may not say anything that should be the least injurious to any individual. I would do good, but not harm if I know it.

THE SHAKERS ON THE FALL OF MAN.

Then, leaving our starting point, what do we have next ? What you call the Fall of Man—what was that ? Something that brought shame where there was no shame previously. Was it the eating of an apple ? Read the account yourself when you have a little leisure, and revise that opinion. It was not an apple, taking the Scriptures themselves ; for we have all sinned after the similitude of " Adam and Eve's transgression." Have we sinned eating apples? and if so, are we particularly ashamed when we eat an apple ? But something pertaining to the social relation—the social evil—does work shame and confusion. The curse that was pronounced upon Adam, and upon the ground that it should bring forth thorns and briars, and the curse that was pronounced upon the woman—" I will greatly multiply thy sorrows and thy conception "—are they not multiplied ? " Thy desire shall be to thy husband, and he shall rule over thee "—contrary to nature; for in all the animal creation the female governs and rules in the work of reproduction, except amongst the human race. Man rules over woman, to her loss and damage, and to his own confusion of face. There is room for improvement. The Fall of Man consists in disorderly social relationship. But there was a promise given; the serpent is mentioned. Adam Clarke says that the serpent, according to the original, was the sensuous nature of man—the passions—that was the serpent. What is it that tempts a man to drink? It is the sensuous nature—it is the serpent. What is it that tempts a person to become a glutton? It is the serpent—the sensuous nature—*nahash*, curious; prying, seeking. It is not a snake any more than the other was an apple.

JESUS WAS A SHAKER.

Now, there was a promise given at that time to the woman that while sorrow and affliction withered her, and a state of slavery, bondage, and degradation was hers, the seed of the woman should bruise the serpent's head.

If the serpent is the animal nature, the senses, then the head of that is the reproductive powers and functions; the generative life is the head of the serpent; he should be bruised by the seed of the woman in the latter days. Hence, when Jesus of Nazareth came forth, he came not as a husband, not as a father, not as a brother, for he owned not his own relatives, and when he was speaking to a multitude, and they notified him that his mother and his brethren and sisters were without and desired to speak to him, he said, " Who is my mother, who is my brother, my sister? They that know the will of God and do it, the same is my mother, my father, my brother, and my sister." He was a Shaker; he lived a celibate life—not as a bachelor, who is no better than the married, and often not so good, for the very best life a natural man and woman can live is that in the married relation—father and mother, brother and sister, house and lands, which a dual government, male and female, would soon provide for every family in the land. Your man-government takes possession of the land, as he takes possession of the woman.

COMING CHANGES.

There is something there that will not stand when God arises to shake terribly the earth, as he will certainly do. " In the days of these kings, the Spirit said the God of heaven should set up a kingdom that should never be destroyed; but it should break in pieces all other kingdoms ;" " Not by the sword, not by might, but by my spirit, saith the Lord," by the truth. You are feeling after something you have not got ; you are dissatisfied with your own governments in Christendom ; you are trying this, trying that ; the pillars of the State are ready almost for an upheaval like that which has so recently occurred in Paris. Looking unto God would be a source of wisdom to you that some of you little wot of. You are too material, too earthly, too forgetful of God. I know you have a State religion ; you pay a good price for it. I saw a book containing the list of the clergy in all England this morning ; it was interesting to me. Pretty costly establishment we should call it in a Shaker village. We should be disposed to take all of those followers of the meek and lowly Jesus, and set them to work ; we should be likely to remember the saying of the Apostle, that he who will not work, neither shall he eat.

THE CONSEQUENCES OF WAR.

I don't believe that war is an element of Christianity, therefore I think your standing armies, your navies, and all your governments supported by the sword,

will perish with the sword if you do not repent.
Mighty nations have existed before England ; great
cities have been on this earth before London—they
stood by the sword ; where are they to-day ? The
ruin of empires is their history. It will be the history
of England and London if she does not repent and
turn and seek God before it is too late. Like causes
will produce like effects for ever. Let us learn by the
past.

WE ARE SHAKERS.

It is a wise man, a wise woman, that will see their
faults, confess them, and forsake them. That is one
of the elements of Shakerism for the individual to
look into their own souls, look into their own habits,
look into their own passions and propensities, and
judge themselves impartially, and then work the work
of God and of truth ; reform, acknowledge the fault,
and shake it off. We are *SHAKERS.* We shake
off intemperance, we shake off the lusts of the flesh
and of the mind to the best of our ability, and we love
that work because we think it agreeable to the spirit
of God. It brings suffering, it brings mortification, it
brings humiliation ; it is very contrary to the pride of
the natural heart, to the love of power, the love of
display, the love of control one over another, to be in
an order where he that would be great must make
himself useful to every member of that order as the
only way to attain unto it. " He that would be great
among you," Jesus said, " let him be your minister."
That is a good way. We find it very pleasant.
Wisdom's ways are ways of pleasantness, and all her
paths are peace. What are we before God, any of us ?
No very great affairs. When we only count one of a
thousand million million, it is not worth while to
trouble ourselves to be very distinguished. We may
as well make ourselves as useful to those with whom
we are associated as we can, and depend upon that for

our honour and our comfort, I think, as take any course I have ever seen pursued.

THE REAL PURPOSE OF A RULER.

I told my people when I left home—" Now, brethren and sisters, when I return from England, if I find that the family have kept the government, if the temporal and the spiritual have gone on prosperously, that my place has been filled by the unfoldment of your care, your burden-bearing, your interest, and your doing as well without me as you do with me, then the object of my life's labour would be accomplished ; I should be happy to be received amongst you, and fill any place that you may allot to me." And that was the feeling of my soul. The real purpose of a ruler should be to create rulers, as the object of a schoolmaster—if he is a good one—is to create scholars equal to himself, and if they exceed him he rejoices in it. It is the fruit of his labour—he still appropriates it—for self is pretty close to us after all.

THE NATURAL ORDER AND THE SPIRITUAL ORDER.

That promise, then, that the serpent's head should be bruised, and that interpretation that the attraction of the sexes to each other in the field of nature that culminates in the marriage relation is the head, implied the cutting off of the work of reproduction— cutting off the process of generation, for that is the head of the serpent ; and if so, then let us look into the mind of Deity, and see if we may not have been mistaken—if in our being when first created there was not the germ of another order, a higher cycle. If there is, we lose nothing by it ; you lose nothing by it. You may enjoy the order you are in as long as you can, as long as you please ; for the word of Jesus to the people when the apostles asked him, " If the case of a man be so with his wife as you have said it to us, to these Pharisees, it is not good to marry," was,

"All men cannot receive that saying, save them unto whom it is given." He did not send them to hell; he did not condemn them; he says he came not into the world to condemn the world, but to do the work of God, that the world through him might be saved from something that made them unhappy. He did not denounce any judgment upon them—did not say if they married they should be lost; no such thing; he did not even go so far as the apostle, who, when he gave the Gentiles permission to marry, told them that they should have trouble in the flesh. Jesus did not go so far as that, but he said, " He that is able to receive it, to make himself an eunuch for the kingdom of heaven's sake, let him receive it." " The Spirit and the bride say Come, and let him that heareth say Come, and let all who will, let them partake of the water of life freely."

THE SECOND COMING OF CHRIST.

Rise above the earth unto the spiritual order, for that is the resurrection. It is not the resurrection of your physical bodies; you will wait a long while, as you have waited a great while already, to ever see that, Christian. Dust thou art, and unto dust thou shalt return. When the Adventists filled the civilized world with an expectation that at a certain time Christ would come, as the orthodox world—Catholic and Protestant—had determined, their predictions agreed exactly, for, being orthodox, they merely said the time had come. They expected the world to come to an end—the earth to be burnt up—the saints to be caught up into the air to meet the Lord—and a throne to be set in the heavens, and the great book to be opened, out of which every individual would have the history of their lives read to them—for it was there written—the trumpet would sound, and the dead would be raised, bones would come flying over all the heavens, and the earth gathering round the throne of judgment. Those are grand ideas. Milton has worked them out very poetically, and I apprehend he has made almost as much impression upon the imagination of the English people as many of their archbishops have ever done. These ideas are imaginary—they will never be realized. The kingdom of heaven cometh not in that way by observation of the natural senses. The orthodox are as much mistaken in that as the Jews, who were looking for the Messiah in the days of his first appearing. Human nature is always the same. History repeats itself over and over again. They looked for the Messiah to come to set up an outward kingdom, to make them the ruling nation of the earth, to bring all the others under their power; then they would be a glorious nation, and well-satisfied. But when the Messiah did come, how entirely different. After a few of them had recognised him, he said "My kingdom is not of this world; if it were, my servants would fight; but as my kingdom is not of this world, therefore my servants will not fight." And, for three hundred years, Christians, neither Jews nor Gentiles did fight.

THE PRIMITIVE CHURCH AND THE SHAKERS.

The early Church was evidently not only a community of goods, not only celibates like the Shakers, but they were non-resistants like the Shakers, and they were Spiritualists like the Shakers. On the day of Pentecost, after the house was shaken, cloven tongues appeared upon their heads and they were shaken; they were wonderfully wrought upon in their physical bodies; their material bodies were quickened by the Spirit, as I hope you will be some day, and you will be Shakers. The Quakers were thus exercised in a degree; they trembled, and you called them Quakers because they quaked. All right—very expressive. So with the term Shakers. It came in consequence of the moving of the Spirit upon the people. They did shake, and many times powerfully too, I assure you. I have seen a whole assembly shake, and shake to some purpose too. And we think there is a great deal in this house that might be shaken. "Yet once more, saith the Lord, and I shake not only the earth"—your earthly systems and earthly orders of government, "but the heavens also;" your theological systems will be shaken; they are being shaken; they are trembling to their foundations, and the present theological systems of Christendom are just as sure to pass away, even if it be with a great noise, as did the theological systems of Rome before Christianity. Then there was a change of system, and a similar change is now impending over Christendom, and if the change had been more complete when Constantine became converted to Christianity, if he had been better converted, I think it would have been better for posterity. But as Mosheim says, it was a question whether Christianity had been converted to heathenism, or heathenism had been converted to Christianity, and that question has never, I believe, yet been settled.

IS THIS A PAGAN OR A CHRISTIAN COUNTRY?

As my friend the chairman has stated, we are not very much converted yet to the system of Christianity as a scheme of life. We breathe our prayers and go to church on the Sabbath day; then we come back into the streets again and are very much as we were before: we return back to our Roman Pandects and our Code of Justinian, which came from the heathen people of Rome. This is our ruling law, even in England to-day, of more authority than the Bible. You can take your Roman codes of law into your courts of justice with better effect than you can your Scriptures. You call yourselves Christians? Now, my candid opinion is that there is not a Christian in this house. (Order.) Oh, take it quietly, you are not afraid of what a simple Shaker can say—it won't hurt any of you. A man that has been a Materialist is not easily disturbed. A thing has got to be proved before they accept it, and you lose nothing by listening. My proposition was, that taking this assembly as representing Great Britain, the use of the word "Christian" is a very loose one. I know it is fashionable. We are Christians; we have a Christian system, a Christian priesthood, and we are very nice, all very good ; but go back upon our history, and look the facts in the face.

THE SHAKER'S ESTIMATE OF JESUS.

Let us remember what Jesus said,—" Except a man take up his daily cross and follow my example, he is not a Christian." Remember that Jesus was a Jew, and that Jesus was born of the Jewish nation, born of a woman, made under the law, and that he was a man and not a god. (Sensation.) Shaker theology is what you have come here to learn, I suppose. You would be very foolish to hiss at it because I tell you what it is. You want to know what Shaker theology is that produces Shaker communities. Very well. Then, according to that theology, Jesus was the first-born of many brethren ; and if you have a dozen brethren born in a family they do not make such a great distinction between one and the other. The oldest is the first-born of the family, you say ; but they were all born of the same father and mother, and much after the same fashion. Very well. He was the first-begotten from the dead. How so ? We are all dead in trespasses and sins, and he was the first-begotten from a state of death in trespasses and in sin.

SALVATION REQUIRED.

John the Baptist came as a Jewish reformer, preaching repentance to Judea and all Jerusalem, and the region round about came to John repenting and

confessing their sins—their Jewish sins, their transgressions against the law of Moses, which law, if it
were kept intact, was in this wise—the God of Israel
said, the Lord your God in obedience shall take all
sickness away from the midst of ye—and that was a
tangible promise to the Jews, something better than
your priests make to you. They promise you salvation for your poor souls, and they need it bad enough
in all conscience ; but I think your bodies need saving
too, many of them from sickness, from disease, from
the "diseases of the Egyptians" which are upon you
Christians, and you have no right to them ; you have
stolen them, as the Israelites stole the jewels of the
Egyptians. You had better return them back to the
Egyptians and become good Jews, having salvation
of body, learning to sing the song of Moses, who
taught his people so to cultivate the land that they
did not raise insects, animalculæ, disease-producing
things at the same time they raised their crops.

MOSAIC COMMUNISM.

The Jews cultivated the land scientifically ; they
observed their Sabbaths : and did you ever think what
their Sabbaths were? It was not the unmeaning
thing that you make the seventh day here, my friends—
far from it. The Jews had four Sabbaths : the Sabbath of days, the Sabbath of months, the Sabbath of
years, and the Sabbath of Sabbaths. The Sabbath
of days they observed by remembering how they lived
in the wilderness, when they were under the direction
of their God, and their free agency was in a state of
suspense, so that they were dependent for their food
upon the manna that came down upon the ground
every morning ; and all the people, high and low,
learned and ignorant, must needs go out, and bend
down to the ground, and pick up their manna —
something to eat—or go without it. Did that mean
nothing? They were in the hands of the God of

15

Israel, and He was teaching them important principles
necessary to human association, that should result in
general happiness—the greatest good to the greatest
number.   And all the people of Israel, under the
direction of God in the wilderness, for forty years ate
one kind of food and drank one kind of drink.   True,
they remembered back, how they did live in Egypt—
the leeks and onions, and flesh-pots thereof, and they
hankered after them, and often rebelled against God
and against Moses to their own loss and damage, for
thousands of them would be destroyed in their rebellion.   But Moses had cured them of all the diseases
that they brought with them out of Egypt by the
dietary system that he established among them, by
the physiological condition that he placed them under,
the good air they breathed, living in tents—not like
smoky London—the good water they drank, and the
exercise that every one of them took, early in the
morning, before the sun was up to melt their manna—
all very good conditions for health.   They did not
turn night into day and day into night, as we Christians do.   These were equalising conditions, and was
there no meaning attached to them?   Depend upon
it, my friends, that God Almighty has his eye upon
the human race, and he will never withdraw his hand
till he has brought about, on this earth, a millennial
order corresponding to that which existed in the
wilderness, of which that was but a visionary view.
Israel was in a vision then for forty years—it was a
visionary state.   When they came into the land of
Canaan, they were not to forget that vision ; for the
law is, that where there is no vision the people perish.
Hence, while they took possession of the land of
Canaan, every family was apportioned their allotment
of that soil — it was their homestead — it was their
home.   Here was another principle, then—the right
of human beings to the soil of the country in which
they live.   That is God's law and nature's law, how

contrary soever it may be to the existing laws of
Christendom. But if things go wrong in Christendom,
are there not causes for the wrong? and will we shut
our eyes, and stop our ears, and harden our hearts,
so that we may not learn what the causes of our
troubles are? Let us examine,—that is what I would
do with you this evening.

THE GOD OF ISRAEL NOT GOD.

I take you down to the teaching of him that you
recognise as your God—the God of Israel. I consider
him a tutelary divinity, not the Almighty Creator of
the countless worlds that roll in space, but a created
being—a spiritual being adapted to the conditions of
the people, and the minister of God unto the people,
but not God himself, any more than the spiritual being
that John the Revelator bowed down to worship, when
he said to him,—" See thou do it not, for I am thy
fellow-servant, one of the prophets,"—nothing more.
The God of Israel was a tutelary divinity, and Moses
was made a god by him unto Pharaoh, and Aaron
was his prophet.

THE JEWISH SABBATHS.

When the children of Israel took possession of the
land of Canaan, their God said to them distinctly
that the land belonged to Him, and they should
not buy and sell it permanently for ever. They did
sell it, however, under the action of their selfish elements, their speculative principles. The Egyptian
nature that was in them—the heathen nature—would
work for six days; then came the Sabbath. The law
of God and his order in the wilderness was thus on
Saturday night—" Let you that have send presents
to those who have not, that to-morrow ye may all be
brothers and sisters, having plenty to eat and drink."
That was the way the Jews kept the Sabbath; it was
in remembrance of the order of God in the wilderness

—the universal supply of the wants of humanity.
Every Sabbath day was a remembrance of that practically, by those who had giving to those who had
not ; that on the Sabbath there might be no work, no
food cooked ; that in every house there should be
sufficient to supply the wants of the family during the
day, that they might give their minds to that degree
of spiritual life which they were blessed with. Then
when the seventh-month Sabbath came—that was
their harvest month—then the rich must remember
the poor, and let them glean in their wheat-fields ; see
that they were not too particular in raking up the
grain, but leave something for the poor to glean after,
remembering that they were their brethren and their
sisters. And when the seventh year came, and the
jubilee trumpet sounded, what did it do ? It paid all
the debts of all the people. Every man's debts were
discharged when the jubilee trumpet of the Sabbatical
year sounded, and all slaves were released and restored
to their freedom. That was something practical; that
was bringing them back again to the wilderness state
—back to their equality. And for one year those
people were to let the land enjoy its Sabbath.

SCIENTIFIC AGRICULTURE—BIBLE FARMING.

During that year they sowed no crops, and that
which grew of itself was common to all the people—
the grapes and pomegranates, and the grain that grew
on the fields spontaneously was for the owners and
for their servants, and for the beasts of the field. They
were back again in their wilderness equality—that
was good—debts paid, slaves released ; people went
back to their inheritance in the land, and Israel was
Israel again. And then when the jubilee—the great
Sabbath of Sabbaths—came, which it did immediately
after the forty-ninth or Sabbatical year, then, without
let or hindrance, everything was restored back per-

fectly as in the start when they first went into the
land of Canaan. That was good. For two years
they had a camp-meeting, for two years they were
trenching their land ; they did not let the land lie
idle, but every man was working, gathering up the
fertilising materials of the six preceding years, com-
posting those together and putting them in the trenches
of their land, beginning on one side and trenching the
field all the way across, two, three, or six feet deep, as
they found occasion, so that the seeds of weeds and
the germs of insects might be destroyed that waste
Christian crops grown according to heathen customs,
and while the heathen crops around them were eaten
up by mildew, and midge, and caterpillar, and canker-
worm, and palmerworm, and all such destroying influences, the crops of the true Israelites were exempt
from harm. That was scientific agriculture.

SCIENTIFIC RELIGION.

Let me say to you that true religion and true science
belong together. They are now divorced, and hence
it is that religion has been brought into disrepute, and
that many honest, well-meaning, sincere, truth-loving
souls are to-day adverse to all forms of religion, and
all theologies, because they have not that amount of
good, of truth, of science, of common sense in them
that suits the English people. The English mind loves
common sense, and you cannot feed it with nonsense.
They may put on a something outside, but down in
their hearts they will have their own thoughts ; and
many to-day of the Established Church priesthood
have no more faith in that system of theology than
the Shaker before you has. But it is their living, and
they buy and sell it in London as men buy and sell
Stocks on 'Change. I see them advertised. What
do you suppose I think ? I have to think very carefully, very cautiously.

THE FOUNDER OF THE SHAKERS.

When the founder of our order was baptised with the Christ-spirit, and came out with a testimony in Manchester to the clerical people around her, what was the result? She was thrown into a stone prison, and kept there for fourteen days, with the purpose of starving her to death. A little boy, whom she had brought up, inserted a pipe-stem through the key-hole, and poured wine and milk into the bowl, and kept her alive while in prison, with the help of the good Spirit, so that she came out in very good condition, when they expected to find her dead. I am sorry to say it, because I am an Englishman, and I am ashamed of it—I am ashamed that such a thing should have occurred in this country, and I hope that spirit is eradicated now. She went over to America, directed by vision, she and eight persons ; each one received a special vision to go to America, and there establish the Church of God on this earth.

THE "CHRIST" BAPTISM.

Christ's second appearing, she declared, had occurred in her person. "How is that?" you will say ; "Jesus is the Christ, is he not?" No, my friends, He is not the Christ, according to Shaker theology. Jesus, as I have said, was a Jew, a man, and he went to John the Baptist with the rest of the people who went to John confessing their sins, and when John had heard him, "Why," says he, "you have lived a better life than I have, and I have more need to confess my sins to you, and be baptised of you ; back into the camp." You must understand that every time a person sinned amongst the Jews, they were cut off from the camp of Israel, and had to confess and be brought back in again as a heathen would be. So with Jesus. John baptised him with water as a Jew, and then with the Christ-spirit—the Lord of heaven—the second Adam.

This quickening spirit descended and abode upon him in the form of a dove externally. Know then, my friends, that, according to our understanding, the Christ-spirit was that which was promised when man fell—that the seed of the woman should bruise the serpent's head. It was also with this Christ-spirit that Melchisedec baptised Abraham. The line of prophets continued this order down to John the Baptist, and John made Jesus a high priest after the order of Melchisedec, or the Christ order. That 'Christ" is a sphere surrounding deity—the seventh sphere—and stands in relation to all the globes in existence, with all the inhabitants of the countless worlds that roll in our astronomical universe, if they are inhabited, which we unquestionably believe.

SHAKER REMEDY FOR OVER POPULATION.

Remember Herschel's problem : he says, take the diameter of this earth as the base of a pyramid, and if Adam and Eve had propagated without any checks to population from war, famine, and disease, the inhabitants, standing upon one another's heads, would extend to the sun and twenty-seven times beyond. Giving them thirty years for their life, there is no globe in existence, however large, that could contain the product of its inhabitants under the law of population and increase unless there were some check or some remedy. Malthus provided you with a remedy; you have your remedies to-day ; you have your wars, you have your famines, your pestilences. Where are you ? Are these normal—are these according to God and to nature ? They are certainly not according to the millennial order of things, for the time was to come when war should cease to the ends of the earth, and the nations should learn war no more. As a Shaker, then, I ask you what is your remedy for this increase of population ? You have none, and the remedy, my friends, that I propose to you is the institution of the Christ order, the remedy that Jesus of Nazareth provided, that there should be so many Christians on this earth living a pure celibate life, so as to keep in check the populative principle, leaving the natural order far better off than it is now.

THE SOCIAL ADVANTAGES OF SHAKERISM.

We would have every man sit under his own vine and his own fig-tree, with none to make him afraid. We would have all mankind not of our order blessed in their household, their fathers, mothers, brothers and sisters, and their houses and their lands, and then have a sufficient number of those that Jesus said should be his disciples—such as forsake father, mother, wife and children, houses and lands, that they may enter the celibate order. " There is no man that hath forsaken father, mother, and wife and children, and houses and lands, for my sake and the Gospel, but he shall receive a hundred-fold of fathers and mothers, brothers and sisters, houses and lands," but not a hundred wives. How is it that he does not include the wife in his promise at all, nor yet the husband ? There are a hundred spiritual fathers and mothers, a hundred spiritual brothers and sisters, a hundred acres of land, and a hundred houses. Will you get that by joining the Episcopal Church, or the Methodist Church, or the Baptist Church ? But if you join the Shaker Church, you do get them—you get a hundred-fold of houses and lands in this world, and in the world to come eternal life.

SHAKERS AND QUAKERS.

It would take a dozen lectures to illustrate all the principles involved in the Shaker system. As you will perceive, I have touched one and another, but I have not illustrated clearly a single one, for any one of these would form the subject of a lecture by itself ;

and I assure you when I thought of addressing such a congregation as this—of intelligent men and women cultivated far beyond myself, as most of you are—I was exceedingly perplexed, as I have often been before. True, I could say to you that we are shaking Quakers—that we include all the elements and principles of the Quaker order. Those which the Quakers hold in common with Presbyterians and Swedenborgians—the marrying, and giving in marriage—we drop ; but that which constitutes them Quakers—the peace principles, the no poverty principle, the plainness of dress and of language, and the inflexible adherence to principle, the spiritual religious life that they are called to live—these are all included in the Shaker order.

WHAT THE QUAKERS HAVE DONE.

The Quakers have been a blessing to England. That order has done you more good, my friends, than you can well realise. The Quakers have developed great governing power : first, in their own order, then in Pennsylvania. Why, in America, to-day, the Government, after working for years and years with the Indian question, trying to settle those savages with the sword, have finally given it up in despair ; and General Grant has called upon the Quakers to go and settle the Indian trouble, and what is better, my friends, they are doing it, and doing it better than it has been done before.

George Fox reformed himself and people out of extravagance and superfluity of dress and speech, ignored the "Church and State," with its living system of tithes and dead theology ; abjured slavery, poverty, and war, vice, and crime, including the social evil, and reduced marriage to its normal use—simple procreation (as with other animals)—condemning "unfruitful works of darkness," thus filling the houses with "rosy children."

Let England, as a nation, do the same amongst nations that Fox did among men.

A CALL TO THE QUAKERS.

Let the Quakers "rise and stand upon their feet." There has been "silence in heaven for half an hour." Be re-baptised; become Spiritualists. Their government is dual—male and female; as such let them develop Platonic orders, putting the men into the House of Commons and the women into the House of Lords, excusing or relieving the present incumbents. Then England could and would commence to confess her sins, and to right her wrongs, and pay her just debts as a people, both towards her own self and other nations. The Church and State would be separate; the military system broken up—army and navy; poverty banished by a great jubilee, wherein the people would return to the soil, and thus might a practical millennium be inaugurated upon our then renewed earth, and the nation be protected by Spiritualism from its enemies, as was Israel from the Egyptians.

THE QUAKERS RECOMMENDED.

The Quakers marry and are given in marriage, and therefore I can safely recommend them to you. They will save that which is of great estimation in your lives. And they have reduced the matter to order as no other people have done. They teach their young people to do their courting in the day-time, with the consent of the respective families, and then, with the consent of the monthly meeting, the marriage is consummated. I can safely recommend that course to all of you, my friends.

This would constitute a new earth, wherein would dwell righteousness, and the Spiritual, or Shaker Order, as being not of this world, who "marry and are

given in marriage," would be the New Heavens, and
would be the Resurrection, just as Jesus was.

It would gather those who are "elected" to be
Christians in this life in sufficient numbers to balance
the population principle, as a substitute for all depopulating agencies. " I have heard from the utter-
most parts of the earth, glory to the righteous."

CONCLUDING REMARKS FROM THE CHAIR.

I am requested to express the very warm thanks of
this deputation from the Shakers for the kind and,
indeed, generous attention with which you have
received him. In speaking before he addressed us,
you observed with what serpentine judiciousness I
avoided altogether the mystical side of his argument.
I asked you to attend—as I am sure I was justified in
doing—to any detail that he gave you about the
results, social and human, and in the very strange tale
to which we have just been listening, there has been
abundant detail of that kind. We in England, whatever we may think about the special marriage dogma
proposed to us to-night, will always have a kindly
regard for a community which has made of a rugged
mountain-top a kind of garden, and has converted the
daily lives of men and women into a religious service.

SHAKERISM IN LONDON.*

INTRODUCTORY ADDRESS BY DR. PEEBLES.

DR. PEEBLES opened the meeting with a general discourse on the merits and advantages of Spiritualism.
It was an effective discourse. Few men know better

* Report of a meeting at Claremont Hall, Penton Street, N., 3rd July,
1887.

what Spiritualism is, and few speakers exercise a more incisive effect upon an audience. There were many strangers present, attracted by public advertisement, and some of them with but little knowledge of Spiritualism. Yet they were quite content to receive with every token of appreciation the remarks made by the speaker. He resumed his seat amidst a hearty expression of applause.

ADDRESS BY ELDER EVANS.

Elder Frederick Evans was then introduced. He commenced by giving a narrative of the history of Ann Lee, of Manchester, the founder of the Shaker Order; how she was persecuted in her native place, and went to America with a faithful band of followers over 100 years ago. They settled in the wild country (as it was then), and lived in a log hut for three years without any visible fulfilment of the prophecy that had brought them thither. During that time a revival had been active amongst the Baptists of New Lebanon, a rural district in the same region of New York State. The pastor, in search of members of his flock, found this solitary cabin in the wilderness. As he entered he found "Mother Ann" under spirit influence; through her a strong power was being manifested, which prophesied to the visitor, taking him greatly by surprise. He found a counterpart of what had been so deeply affecting them in their own revival; the same teachings, the same manifestations of the Spirit. A deputation then visited the little temple in the desert, and ultimately the Shaker Church was established at New Lebanon. The side of the mountain was inhabited by farmers, who followed their pastor, one of the most learned men in the district, and who was the first to confess his sins and be admitted. They all threw their property into one common centre, and, as a community, had all things in common, which they have continued to this day. The Elder said he had resided in that family for fifty-seven years, and there were seventeen societies in the States. Each candidate for admission confesses his sins and renounces the world. This Mother Ann did herself, after being sorely exercised with the conviction of sin, and she had required it of all candidates, and the custom had been continued. The conviction of sin, the renunciation of the same, and the living of the spiritual life were the bases of the system. All mankind were not prepared to be Shakers. There were the "people of the world," who procreated and lived after the ways of the world. The Shakers were a distinct Order, and lived on another plane. There would be a new heaven and a new earth. The Shakers represented a heavenly order, in which the strifes, lusts, and distinctions which characterised the people of the earth did not exist. The speaker then made a scathing analysis of the present conditions of Christendom : the monopoly of land, money usury, unbelief in and out of the Church, the lusts of the flesh, the struggle for wealth, the great army of soldiers and the great multitudes of prostitutes, filling the land with moral and physical evil. Against all these evils the Shakers protested, and they did so in a practical manner.

"A NEW EARTH."

"O earth, earth, hear the word of the Lord," which is to create a new government wherein right, not might, shall rule. Make women citizens, fill the "House" of civil and ecclesiastical land-"lords" with them. Parliament will then abolish land monopoly, and proclaim a grand Jubilee, in which each inhabitant will be restored to their inalienable inheritance in the earth. Repudiate all national war debts, and cancel private debts, as did Israel every seventh year Jubilee. Observe the law against usury, and then let a dual government legislate war out of existence by extinguishing the fires of lust, whence come all wars and fightings upon earth. The people will then worship God as a Heavenly Mother and a Heavenly Father. She was ever with Him. "When he laid the foundation of the earth I was there, I was ever with him." Love worketh no ill to his neighbour. When people love their neighbour as they love themselves, wars will cease to the ends of the earth, and poverty be no more, for each one will "seek another's wealth, and not his own." Will not that create a new earth, wherein dwelleth righteousness?

Shakers (who never had any relation with the Girlingites of this country) have solved the land problem that now agitates England, Ireland, and other portions of the world. Our lands are held in common. We are communities of brothers and sisters. We love one another ; being first "pure," it is very easy to be "peaceable." We are temperance people ; the most of us are vegetarians. Our meetings abound in inspirations, revelations, and spiritual songs. With us "Thy kingdom come" is practically realised, and we invite you to repent, turn from your evil, selfish ways, prepare yourselves, and then come and share with us the good things of the kingdom—the new earth—the promised Canaan of spiritual rest and peace.

He then, in continuation, went into their theological beliefs : Jesus as a manifestation of the Christ was succeeded by Ann Lee as the "Second Coming," but in the female form. Both were representatives of celibate orders, holding all things in common, and living after the Spirit. In their families all the trades worked together for the benefit of the whole, each member being sustained by all the rest. No community had been of a permanent character except the Shakers, because they had eliminated all that which gave rise to selfishness, and therefore contention and disruption. Spiritualism commenced amongst the Shakers ; they had all the manifestations before Modern Spiritualism began, and its coming had been foretold by their mediums. They had manifestations which had not yet occurred outside.

QUESTIONS.

Questions were asked for, and a few were put, some of them in a very eccentric and excited manner. These were really answered in the speeches which had been given, but Dr. Peebles and the Elder very kindly replied. The Doctor explained that the Elder was an Englishman, who went out to America as a disciple of Robert Owen. He had gained much experience of communistic life before he had joined the Shakers.

THE SHAKER SYSTEM.*

WHEN society evolves a class of men and women, as now in England, in whom, the *Westminster Review* declares, that the marrying instinct has died out, these should fill the houses of parliament and the halls of legislation ; these should enact natural laws of righteousness. First, a law relieving all who have private families from public burdens. Second, a law of citizenship, male and female. Third, a law of property, giving the land of the nation to the people of the nation, and securing its just distribution and possession by land limitation and inalienable homestead laws. Fourth, a law of population, setting forth the physiology of reproduction, its rule of right, with appropriate checks and restrictions, as did Mosaic

---

* Extract from a Lecture delivered at Randolph, Cattaraugus County, New York, by Elder F. W. Evans, 9th December, 1877.

Law—under which marriage was *used* for offspring only, and children were nursed three years, during which period the woman was free.—*Clarke's Commentaries.* Fifth, the law of digestion, or the assimilation of food—the kind, quantity, and quality that is scientifically right and best for the individual and the nation. Sixth, the law of arbitration, under which no one should live for himself or herself, in family, society, or nation—but each live for all. In each family or society there should be a throne of judgment, unconditionally deferred to by the unit or individual. This would end private feuds and strifes. Seventh, nations when organised upon these principles of righteousness, can recognize a natural law of nations that would be God's justice and right incarnate —a Supreme Court of arbitration—all the nations beginning to be rational by universal disarmament. War creates war ; it begins with warlike preparations. The girl with her doll-baby is learning the rudiments of maternity. The boy with his toy fife, drum, and gun, is a germinal warrior. Cease to think war. Learn to think peace, and nothing but peace. Let the decision of parent, the majority, of the court of arbitration for nations, be as the fiat of the Almighty —the Persian-Medo decree of humanity, that a nation should no more revolt from the decisions of the grand Supreme Court of nations, than the law - abiding Americans revolted from the revolting decision of the United States Supreme Court, that "The black man has no rights that the white man is bound to respect."

It is the Shaker idea that the whole system of civil government should be so purely secular and materialistic, that no sectarian of any of the world's religions could justly complain of their children being taught, in the public schools, any thing but pure science and pure morality.

The civil government should claim and exercise the right of educating all children up to fifteen years of age.

I should as thoroughly indoctrinate every American child into the principles of secular American republicanism, as the Roman Catholics indoctrinate their children into the faith and principles of Church and State government.

How is it possible for the American Republic to perpetuate itself, if all parents, who choose so to do, exercise the right to educate their children as enemies thereof?

As ignorance of scientific knowledge and morality lays the foundation of criminals, that the State has to take the whole charge of, and bear all the loss to life and property occasioned by their existence, is it unreasonable that it should " see the evil afar off," and forestall it by national schools, into which all parents should be obligated to place their children, or emigrate to some Church and State country.

Laws for the forced collection of debts should be repealed, and all debts become debts of honour. *They* are generally paid.

Let citizens settle their debts and theologies amongst themselves, and the national government keep the peace amongst them while so doing. Thus far, the new earth under the Shaker system. Shall we try it?

SHAKERS AS FARMERS.

A VISIT TO THE NORTH FAMILY AT MOUNT LEBANON.

ON invitation of Elder F. W. Evans, of the North Family of Shakers, we visited that community recently, to note what was interesting from an agricultural point of view. So many times have the religious and social aspects of Shakerism been written upon, that anything we could say would be but a repetition

16

of what has already been better said, hence we confine
our notes strictly to what was either directly or indirectly connected with the farming interest.

We met with a most cordial welcome from our
genial friend, Elder Evans, the leading mind and
chief head of the Shaker community in this country,
or, in fact, of any country where Shakerism has been
established. Busy as he always is, either with hand
or brain, he yet found time to show us about the
place, and call our attention to what would be of
interest for us to relate. Directing our steps to the
great stone barn, the Elder first called our attention
to the three huge silos, that have just been completed.
But first a word as to the barn itself. This was built
several years ago, of stone, five stories in height, 196
feet in length, by 50 feet in width. Its cost was about
20,000 dols. Below are the long lines of cattle stalls,
and on either side on the floor above, bays run from
the second to the third story, upon which the loaded
wagons are driven from the elevated ground in the
rear. From this floor the hay, or other crops, can be
pitched directly into the deep bays. On either side
of the broad entrance door, are situated the silos above
mentioned. The one on the right is 15 by 15 feet, and
37 feet high, and the two on the left are of the same
height, but each is only 7 by 15 feet in the other
dimensions, thus making two narrow silos, separated
by a cement and stone wall. These two were built
of Portland cement, used in about the proportion of
one to five, cement and gravel, and cost about 300
dols., the large one opposite being of Rosendale
cement, and costing about 200 dols. Openings about
four feet by six are made on the first and second
floors, through which the ensilage will be taken out
when fed. The clover and corn which they propose
to put in will be cut by an ensilage cutter, and carried
by elevator in at the top of the silo. On a scaffold
between the silos, a strong platform is being made,

upon which barrels of sand will be placed, which will be used as a weight when the silos are filled.

"What is your opinion," we asked, "as to the value of ensilage as fodder?"

"We should not judge as to the value of this fodder from the mere fact that cattle eat it well. I look upon this as an abnormal appetite which cattle form, quite similar to that which a person forms for tobacco, for instance, and it does not follow that the value of the fodder is in proportion to the avidity with which cows eat it. This must be judged by the condition of the stock in spring, after having been fed on it through the winter, by the quantity and quality of the milk, etc. Some claim that ensilage is a better fodder and more nutritious than was the original corn or clover, but we should be satisfied with it if it is as good. A chemical change may take place, and the fodder be improved thereby, but just to what extent such change is desirable, is not quite apparent. When we have six months winter, and when we can keep three or four times the number of cattle that we could on pasture and hay alone, it is certainly worth trying. I consider it an excellent thing for stock in spring; they will do well upon it; but if it is fermented, it should be fed alternately with hay, or, if in summer, with pasture. But as to its value taken all together, there is little doubt."

The Shakers take a pardonable pride in their fine cattle. The North Family now have about 100 head altogether, mostly a cross between the Holsteins and native stock. Besides these they have several fine, pure bred Holsteins, and also grade Durhams, Ayrshires, and Jerseys.

"You seem to prefer the Holsteins, and why?" we inquired.

"Because they combine the good qualities of various breeds. Their milk is rich enough; they give a good quantity; they are docile; possess great vitality;

make good beef, and the oxen are strong sturdy workers. We were fortunate in having good stock to cross upon, and we now have as good a herd of cattle as one could wish for. We have 33 cows, from which we manufacture 130 pounds of butter per week at present."

The creamery where the butter is made is a model of neatness, and being in charge of an experienced dairywoman—one of the sisters—there is no wonder good butter can be made. "We believe," said our host, "that in order to make butter that shall be free from every taint, we must begin with the cow-barns. These are perfectly ventilated, so that even when the doors and windows are closed in winter, there is sufficient ventilation to conduct away all offensive odours, which are so liable to taint the milk. Not only are our stables well cleaned, but they are perfectly ventilated." The milk is set in 20-inch cans in the creamery tanks, and the best appliances for churning and working the butter are used.

One important consideration for every farmer has been met by the North Family, in providing an adequate supply of water for the stock. They have recently built a large reservoir on the hill above their buildings, and from this the water is conducted through iron pipes to the horse and cattle barns, the poultry yard, and wherever pure running water is needed. Also, they provide motive power for running their barn machinery, their grain mill and laundry machinery, having a pressure of 65 pounds to the inch. Hydrants are built with which hose can be connected in case of fire, and each and every room in the dwellings can be flooded at short notice.

Any poultry fancier would be pleased to visit the spacious poultry yards where now about 600 fowls are kept. "Poultry keeping pays," said Elder Frederick, and from the care given the poultry, and the accommodations they here have, we were not prepared to dispute the point. One brother has sole charge of the poultry yard, and finds quite enough to do. Pure running water for the fowls is an essential to success, and this they have in abundance. Last winter eggs brought thirty-five cents. a dozen, and we saw at once why there was money in the business. Speaking of each department of farming as having some one in charge of it, the Elder said,—"Yes, that is advantageous. Each man does the work he likes best, hence it is well done."

The kitchen garden was quite worth visiting. The brother in charge was hoeing the tomatoes, and was suddenly made aware of our presence by the Elder's saying, — "Peter, don't touch those tomato plants when they are wet; they will wither very quickly;" so Peter touched them not, and we in our ignorance learned something about tomato culture. In the garden everything in the vegetable line necessary for the large family of seventy is cultivated, and besides there was a fine display of blackberry bushes, quince trees—the largest we had ever seen — and almost everything to tickle the palate and please the taste. The Shakers being quite strict vegetarians, find here much that supplies their tables with daily food.

But space will not permit us to go farther into detail. In conclusion, we may remark that the Shakers raise the various cereals, grasses, potatoes, in fact, all farm crops in large quantities, though much of their land is stony and mountainous. The benefits which accrue from their farming are shared in common, and they are, as Elder Evans remarked, "nothing but a large family." Industry is practical, not theoretical, with them; they have no room for idlers, and all are busy. They use the latest and most improved machinery, and their farm land gives evidence that progressive farming is thoroughly believed in, and advanced farm methods are practiced. Could our farms in general be tilled with the care

they use and with like industry, the products therefrom would aggregate much more, and labour would
be better remunerated. That we may not seem un-
grateful, we wish to say that our entertainment at
the dinner hour was most sumptuous, and was most
heartily appreciated, and we are under many obligations to our host, Elder Evans, for favours extended.
—*Chatham Courier.*

ENSILAGE.

IN connection with Report of Third Ensilage Congress, we desire to publish the latest views of the
most experienced ensilers. Will you please write
your present estimate of the merits or demerits of the
system, and any recent facts that you may have on
this subject?

J. B. BROWN, *Secretary.*

ELDER EVANS' REPLY.

RESPECTED FRIENDS,—Since attending the Ensilage Meeting, over which you so ably presided, we
have had some experience in feeding ensilage. We
built, in the east corner of our stone barn, which is
196 by 50 feet, two silos, 15 by 15 feet, and built a
cement partition through one of them, thus making
two 7 by 15 feet. They are all 37 feet deep. The
two small ones were filled with clover, cut three inches
long, and not quite sufficiently weighted. There was
too much fermentation. The barn, milk, cream, and
butter, were all affected by the odour generated by
the fermentation, so much so, that if we had not built
the third silo last spring, the whole ensilage business
would have been pronounced by the North Family as
decided a failure as any that has occurred, and a vote

of the members would have pronounced it a public nuisance. Yet the greater part of the ensilage in the two silos was in prime order, and the stock eat it with avidity.

About the first of January we opened the large silo. In filling that we had a trusty man to take charge. It was done thoroughly. We did it ourselves, whereas the other two were done by hired men.

The bottom of the silos, thirty-seven feet deep, is on a level with the stable floor. This is a grand arrangement. Having doors on the several floors, we cut a tunnel down from the top to the door on the middle floor, then drop the ensilage down through a trap door into a large box on wheels, which is rolled along the whole length of the cow stables. In this way seventy-five head of cattle are easily and quickly fed. We took off all the weight and covering at once. It has worked well. Take off about a foot at a time from the whole top and throw it down the tunnel. It is as nice as when we put it in. The barn, milk, cream, and butter, are all right, sweet and good. Not a word of complaint is heard, but much praise. We feed about seventy bushels per day. The cows give milk abundantly. The young stock are suited, and oxen are fat. Parties desiring to see for themselves are welcome to come and form their own opinions of the value of ensilage. When cut to quarter of an inch length, well packed in sides and corners, covered with hemlock plank, and most effectually weighted, the large quantity of hay, sufficient to feed twice the stock, shows for itself what is the economy of feeding ensilage.

F. W. EVANS.

NOTE.—Covered with hemlock, no mould. With oak plank ensilage on top moulded.

THE SHAKERS AND SPIRITUALISM.*

ELDER EVANS is an enthusiastic believer in materialisations, and says the time will come when the past and gone orators will materialise and come forth on platforms and address audiences.

As for the doings at Mount Lebanon they were certainly marvellous. The cabinet, as the Elder says, was prepared by the Shakers, and had no trap doors or secret closets and communications by which accessories could be "spirited" into it, and yet from that cabinet no less than *thirty-one* different materialised spirits issued during the seances, and were seen and heard by those present. One was a brother of the Elder, who has been dead twenty-five years ; two were brothers of Eldress Antoinette Doolittle ; one was recognised as a dead sister from the fact that she had but one eye ; another sister was known because one of her fingers was missing ; and still another was a departed sister who was a dwarf, hardly four feet high, and it is claimed that Eddy could not have personated these characters, because he did not know of their personal peculiarities. But we will let Elder Evans tell how the mediums happened to visit Lebanon. He also appends the results.

MOUNT LEBANON MATERIALISATIONS.

After the Albany expositions of the Eddy and co-mediums, in May last, we invited them to Mount Lebanon, to rest and recuperate, physically and mentally. They needed it. We agreed to receive them kindly, treat them hospitably, and protect them from annoying tests and the teasing of cavilling sceptics. They came, and for one whole week we held seances with them. We built a cabinet in a room that held between two and three hundred brethren and sisters,

---

* From the *Berkshire County* (Mass.) *Eagle*, July 4, 1878.

gathered from all the families of Mount Lebanon and Canaan, and from the Hancock Society, three miles distant.

Ten seances were held, one each evening, the remainder in forenoon, thus giving all, who desired, opportunity to attend. As the medium was in our own house, continually under our supervision, and had nothing to do in preparing either the room or cabinet, it was not possible for him to create the machinery, or secrete the clothing and ornamental fixings necessary to produce the great variety of costumes and adornments that were exhibited during the continuance of the ten seances. A pocket handkerchief could scarcely have gone into that cabinet without our knowledge.

The twenty-five men, women and children, who appeared, were either what they purported to be—spirit materialisations — or personifications of the medium. Of that fact, each person attending could be his or her own judge, according to the evidence presented to their senses and inner consciousness.

Some of the materialised forms spoke of the past, present, and future of humanity, with a power of oratory, a depth and breadth of views, and with a degree of spirituality entirely beyond the condition and capacity of William Eddy—*as we know him.*

William Eddy was the *nominal*—the *assembly*, the *real* medium. The unity and harmony of the brethren and sisters constituted them the very best of materialising mediums. The " Control" recognised this fact, and said,—"You can have the best materialisations on the earth."

For the remainder of this communication, we will extract from minutes kept of the seances, adding that, during the sittings over one hundred songs that had, on previous occasions, been given by the spirits, were sung for their and our edification.

F. W. EVANS.

EXTRACTS FROM MINUTES OF SEANCES.

William Eddy, medium, inside the cabinet ; Edward Brown and David Williams, outside, as guardians of the circle. Seance generally continued about one hour. By request of the managers, brethren and sisters sang continuously between the manifestations. One, whom they call Mother Eaton, claims to be the controlling spirit of the band on the female side ; and the one known as Father Brown the presiding spirit on the male side. As a rule, female spirits appear before the male, but it is not always the case.

SIZE AND APPEARANCE OF THE SPIRITS WHO PRESENTED THEMSELVES.

Mother Eaton, medium size, with white dress and thin, dark coloured shawl thrown over the shoulders, also white head dress. Father Brown, very tall and rather spare, dressed in citizen style, with black coat and pants ; very dignified in appearance and voice. Meta, Witch of the Mountain, rather above medium size, with white apron and dress trimmed with black. Maggie Brown, medium size, dressed in white, with bouquet in hand. John Devins, rather short and thick set, with gray suit. Mary Williams, medium size, dressed in white. Little Willie, child, two feet high. Sally Holeman, very tall, dressed in ancient costume, with cap. Jane Williams (coloured), rather tall, dressed in light coloured gown with dark coloured shawl.

INDIAN SPIRITS.

Wickachee, tall and thick set, complexion very dark, Indian features and port of Indian, attired with ornamental head-dress ; generally danced, never spoke. White Cap, exceedingly tall, with a white cap on his head. Santum, very tall and corpulent, never spoke or danced. Honto, medium size, long flowing black hair, beads around the neck, very thinly clad, usually danced and materialised shawls. Lady of the Lake, another squaw.

BELIEVER SPIRITS.

Elder Richard, appeared very much in size as while living, dark coloured suit and white kerchief around the neck, hair white. Nancy Crossman, Annie Crossman, Nancy Lockwood, medium size, with cap and neckerchief. Mary Jane Maffit, Melissa Soule, Margaret Pattison, Rhoda Offord, all four nearly the same in height and dress. Ellen Rayson, dwarf, dressed in white. Almira Hull, dwarf, dressed in white. Alice Barnum, about three feet high, dressed in white. William Offord, striking resemblance of his form while living, dressed in dark coloured suit.

Nancy Lockwood, with spectacles on, whispered a few words of love and blessing.

Annie Crossman also gave a few similar sentences in a low tone.

Almira Hull, recognised by her form as being the dwarf who deceased at Canaan. When her name was spoken she rapped loudly, as she could not speak.

Elder Richard whispered,—"God bless you," and retired.

William Offord just spoke in a whisper, "yea" and "nay" in reply to questions.

WORLD'S SPIRITS.

Stranger, not recognised ; dressed in black. G. H. Evans, rather indistinct in appearance. William Doolittle, about his size, and dressed in black. Edwin A. Doolittle, life-like in size and appearance. John C. White bore a strong resemblance to the "White' family. [Light in room resembling twilight.] Mother Eaton came forth and spoke as follows,—"I have long desired to be in your midst, in your beautiful home, and am thankful for this privilege, and glad to feel the good that is among you, whose lives are devoted to purity, and who are helping to uplift humanity to better conditions."

Meta stood with dignified bearing, and, in clear reverential tone, gave utterance to a beautiful invocation, and also expressed great satisfaction in being with those who have adopted true Christian principles, and are living in angelic purity, who are striving for and do attain unto the resurrection of Christ while on the earth. "Let us be patient and toil on, for in so doing we are helps to humanity. You can do us good and we can do you good."

Joseph Belshazzar, brother to Meta (the witch of the mountain), said with a strong, deep voice, clearly articulating every word,—"I am glad to meet with a people who sanctify their bodies for the good of the soul. Only through purification of flesh and spirit can souls arise to the divinity of Christ." He spoke about ten minutes. His sentiments were those of a travelled, resurrected believer. His language was rich in eloquence and inspired by truth.

SECOND SEANCE.

Meta said,—"The purity of the Gospel shall be preached to all people till they shall know the way of salvation ; the voice of not one only, but many shall acknowledge the truth. Woman has prophesied, but her prophecies have not been heeded. She has been crushed, and the truths she uttered trampled upon." Then waving her arm to and fro, and raising it high, she said,—"The time has come for woman to stretch forth her strong arm of power to the uplifting of souls from fallen conditions. She will arise and show her virtue, and will yet speak with a tongue that shall make holy the house of Israel. Thus the world will acknowledge her glory ; for saving truth in its divine unfolding shall be revealed through her. You live in spotless purity as no other people have power to live ; you are doing a great work for yourselves and others.

Stand firm, and you shall be remembered in your Father's house of many mansions." [Elder Frederick said,—" In our Mother's house, too."] She repeated,— "Yes, and the Mother's too."

Joseph Belshazzar said,—" Friends, the lady who has just spoken to you is my sister, the daughter of Belshazzar, king of Babylon, who lived some 2000 years ago. She was not only a prophetess, but a teacher of truth, that calls souls to come up higher. It was my hand that wrote upon the wall through her mediumship, and I rejoice that my hand can again write upon the walls of time the eternal truths of God. I am thankful we have chosen pure spirits for our band, whereby we have the power to act upon mankind for their elevation, and teach them that by their own good works they may be saved from sin, redeemed unto life that dieth not, but is everlasting."

THIRD SEANCE.

Meta's Invocation : " Friends, may we all be guided by the promptings of purity and peace. Breathe forth sanctifying power. Blessed angels among these quiet hills and valleys, where the feet of holy saints have trod, let them re-echo the voice of peace and love. Sustain all with thine arm of strength, O Father of light, and nourish all, O Mother, who cling to thy breast. Let the revelations of truth roll on and on, and lift, through purity of life, to higher spheres, where the songs of the redeemed echo from hill-top to valley, and where all the joys and sorrows of the past reflect their glory. Baptised with one faith may we all toil on, walking hand in hand, till we reach the perfect land of rest."

FOURTH SEANCE.

Meta delivered the following invocation : " Spirit of truth, of divine love and purity, draw near. Angel of mercy, with thy sheltering wings, brood over the

children of earth ; cause all to feel the resurrecting
power of thy divine outflowings, and the grandeur of
the principles of a higher life ; baptise them with
truth that will abide for ever.   O purify them by the
fire of God's Spirit, and by the unfoldment of his
progressive laws ; lead them up to the tabernacle of
righteousness that will endure eternally, that they
may go onward in the broad fields of progression,
into the glorious house of many mansions, where the
Divine presence illumes the Father's and Mother's
rest above."

Joseph Belshazzar, — " Friends and Brethren : to
many people of this age materialisation seems like a
strange thing, but in my age it was not so ; it was
then a common thing.   Samuel made his appearance
to Saul through the Witch of Endor, and openly con-
versed with him.   It is the privilege of all mankind
to commune with those out of the form who have
passed the Jordan of death and ascended upward,
born of the Spirit unto eternal life.   The reason there
is not the intermingling now as formerly, is not
because spirits cannot as easily come to earth as
then, but it is because the people on earth to-day are
not prepared to receive them, for they do not live
so much in accordance with the laws of God and
Mother Nature.   While living in the lusts of the flesh,
which destroy the body, darken the understanding,
and shut out spiritual influences from the soul, men
can't be approached and instructed by spirits from
higher spheres, who have purified their souls by first
purifying the body.   I hope to-night we may be able
to speak of the grand truths possessed by resurrected
souls in our beautiful country, and on the earth ; those
who have part in the first resurrection.   Let all be
true to God and his laws, then the angels of love and
harmony will guide all such to the ever green shores,
there to abide for ever."

Father Brown said,—" I have been in many parts

of the world, among sects and nations differing very much from each other in belief, and have found that all who live on holy food receive no harm. Let us hunger and thirst for this. I rejoice with those who have found the springs of life that will never fail, who are progressing to diviner spheres. Men and women belonging to the natural order, who practice the self-denial belonging to that order, rise into the superior of their being, and by degrees conquer the inferior ; thus they become prepared to enter into the resurrection, and will yet march through the fields of heaven with palms of victory. Good night, dear friends."

LIFE WITH THE SHAKERS.

LIFE with the Shakers is very simple and uneventful.

The " brothers " and " sisters " of each " family " live in the same great four story " family house." The brethren have their rooms on one side of the wide, clean halls, and the sisters theirs on the other side. Two, three, four, or five brethren occupy one room with as many single beds. Two, three, four, or five sisters also share their room with one another, and each has her single bed.

The rising bell rings at five o'clock in summer and half-past five in winter. Upon rising the brethren take off their bed clothes, fold them neatly, and lay them across the backs of two chairs. They then go out and do the morning chores.

The sisters likewise, after properly caring for their rooms, attend to their morning chores.

An hour after the rising bell the breakfast bell rings, and all repair to the big dining-room, which they enter in two files, one composed of the brethren, from the oldest in regular gradation of age down to the youngest, and led by the elders, the other composed of the sisters, from the oldest down to the youngest, and led by the eldresses.

In this order they enter the dining-hall, and march down the long, spotlessly clean, but clothless table, the brethren on one side of the house and the sisters on the other. Arrived at their places, they all kneel for a moment in silent thanksgiving and prayer.

Then all seat themselves and eat the meal with speechless assiduity.

The table is completely furnished with food at intervals of four plates, and waiting sisters, who take monthly turns at this work, replenish the food-plates as fast as emptied. At the end of the meal all, at a signal from the elders and eldresses, kneel again, and thereafter pass quietly out in two files, but inverse order from that in which they entered.

Breakfast over, the work of the day follows. The brethren disperse over the farm and to the shops. The sisters go to the laundry, the ironing-room, the shops, or about the house work. Those sisters detailed for that work make the beds and arrange the rooms for the brethren. Others sweep the halls and polish them with their curiously hooded brooms.

Others work in the kitchen. All have work assigned for them to do. The endeavour is to give to each that which he or she can do best, and for the best good of all. It has been remarked of the Shakers that special talent is speedily recognised and appropriately utilised.

At half-past eleven all are summoned from work, and just at noon sit down to a silent but bountiful dinner. After dinner all work till their assigned task is done, or until summoned from work at five or half-past five. At six o'clock supper brings all silently together again, and a couple of hours quiet in their room for reading, writing, or study, prepares for bed at nine.

Sunday is preceded by a special service of song and silent prayer on Saturday evening. The great meeting of the day is in the afternoon, and consists of singing, marching, silent prayer, and exhortation. This meeting is held in the meeting-house or in the meeting-room of the family house of the "centre" or "church" family, and all are expected to attend, if not ill. A song and prayer service in the evening closes the quiet day.—*Manifesto.*

SHAKER MISSION TO SCOTLAND AND ENGLAND.

RESULTS OF ELDER EVANS' VISIT TO GREAT BRITAIN.

A CORDIAL RECEPTION IN THE MOTHER COUNTRY— PROSPECTIVE EXTENSION OF THE ORDER.

From the New York Tribune, 8th August, 1887.

MOUNT LEBANON, N.Y., 5th August.—Frederick W. Evans, Elder in the Order of Shakers, and his companion, Dr. J. M. Peebles, have returned from their missionary tour in Great Britain, which was undertaken some months ago with a view to establishing there the doctrines of the Order. They speak with hearty satisfaction of their experience abroad. Their reception was most cordial, and they believe that their work will result in a great revival of interest in Shaker doctrine and practice in England and Scotland. Following are the reports which they make to
17

the members of the various families concerning their unique enterprise :—

To the Elder and Eldresses and Believers at Mount Lebanon :

Grace, Mercy and Peace be unto you and all the Zion of our God.

If stewards are required by the laws of churches to give an account of their stewardship, why should not missionaries voluntarily and gladly give an account of their missionary work in far away lands over the waters?

We are to-day, 23rd July, 1887, in Larne, an old fashioned town of that unfortunate yet ever-green isle of the ocean, Ireland ; but our principal labours have been in Scotland and England rather than Ireland. On our first mission in 1872, to what is termed the Old World, our work was confined alone, as you well know, to England. But this time it has been wider in extent and far more effective. Upon reaching Glasgow, weary with a rough sea voyage, we were met in the railway station, cordially received, and conveyed to the residence of a prominent Spiritualist, furnished a repast, and given a most hearty hearing. It seemed good to be there. The Scotch, though a little obstinate and strong headed, are a genial, warm hearted, and sympathetic people. The Spiritualists opened their hall for us, and our meetings were largely attended, calling out many inquirers, and eliciting many questions and some sharp discussion. If some seed here fell by the wayside, much more fell into good ground, as the sequel proved. From Glasgow we travelled through a country rather hilly, but very finely cultivated, to Manchester, where a flourishing Vegetarian Society gave Elder Evans a most graceful greeting in the form of an inviting vegetarian supper. The spacious tea-room was well filled, the vegetables were fresh, the fruits were choice, and the bread was such, the Elder said, "as a Christian could conscientiously eat." After the supper the hall rapidly filled, the meeting was organised, and after a preliminary speech or two, the Elder gave a very able address upon Vegetarianism, and the principles and practices of Shakerism, advising that in the formation of Shaker Societies in England, certain to come, animal flesh be utterly ignored. No well read physiologist or hygienist can doubt that grains and fruits growing in the sunshine are a cleaner, healthier, and higher type of food than the bodies and often diseased bodies of dead animals. At the close of the speeches questions were asked and ably answered by the Elder during the evening. All present were not only willing to hear, but they seemed thoughtful and really serious minded.

The second day succeeding the reception we left for London, passing through a country resembling a well cared for garden. The farms and fields were enclosed by hedges where farmers were cutting their grass or otherwise carefully tilling their lands. We passed through many manufacturing centres, but saw none or very few new buildings in process of erection; from which we concluded that England was finished.

Arriving in London, we were made glad in the railway station by the face and hand-clasp of James Burns, of *The Medium and Daybreak*, and conducted by him to a temperance hotel. It was no sooner noised about that we were again in London than friends and former acquaintances began to flock in to see us. The gospel seed sown on our first united visit had taken root. The leaven had been working. Many not satisfied with their past or present condition were asking,—"What shall we do to be saved?" We did what we could to show them the better way, the living way, even that Zion of peace, and love, and purity, found in the more spiritual resurrection order.

Though both the Jubilee and the "season" were against us in London, our private meetings and public gatherings were well attended, and there was manifest in the audiences earnestness and a stirring enthusiasm. The people seemed hungering and thirsting for the Gospel of glad tidings, that Gospel which gives a hundred-fold of Heavenly things. The Elder's addresses upon these occasions were not only clear and convincing, but they were at times powerful in inspiration, and in the revelation and demonstration of the Spirit. At the conclusion of one of these Jubilee meetings in the hall, Mr. James Burns bore a strong testimony in favour of the spirituality of Shakerism, frankly acknowledging the two orders, the Adamic or generative, and the diviner Christ-like order, in which they neither marry nor are given in marriage. Inquiries were propounded as usual during these meetings, exciting thought, and the kind of candid thought that must ultimate in deep conviction. London at present is a Babel, but out of confusion there comes harmony, something as lilies come from the mud, or as kosmos came originally out of chaos under the guidance of the Divine Mind.

Feeling that our work was measurably done in London and vicinity, we began to retrace our steps by way of Manchester toward Newcastle, a large and flourishing city. As in other localities, the Spiritualists received us very cordially, giving us the use of their hall, and freely entertaining us during the visit. Here we held four meetings, the interest increasing to the close, when, upon the last evening, the hall was densely packed. As the Spirit seemed to lead, I opened these lectures with a brief address each session upon Spiritualism in its higher aspects, a spiritual and religious Spiritualism in no way differing from the spiritual gifts, and doctrines, and precepts of the New Testament, and then turned the audience over to the

Elder to give, as he did, thrilling accounts of spiritual manifestations occurring for years among the Shakers before their appearance in Rochester, New York, and also to proclaim to them the duality of the Deity, the second coming, the resurrection order, the celibate life, the principles of peace and the community of goods. And, as in Jesus' time, "the people heard him gladly." The objections raised to the resurrection order with reference to population and the community of goods, as on the day of Pentecost, were easily, and, I trust, satisfactorily answered.

Personally called upon and invited by a prominent Spiritualist of Sunderland, a manufacturing city some twenty miles from Newcastle, we listened to the invitation, and held a most excellent meeting. These industrious working people seemed ready for the words of life. They were longing for something better than old Calvinistic theology, something better than land monopoly, better than armies, navies, and gilded soldiery, better than the sordid, selfish lusts of the flesh, and better than the popular vices, prevailing follies and dissipating fashions of the age. The Elder ministered to them powerfully. Some of his words were like two-edged swords, cutting, convicting, and converting. And yet, while reproving and rebuking, he at the same time showed them the green pastures and the living waters, of which, if man drink, he should thirst no more for ever. He told them that while Swedenborg held converse with spirits, and spoke of men and women becoming angels in some far away future kingdom of Heaven, Ann Lee, baptised of Christ, testified that the kingdom of Heaven had come, and that men might and should become angels now, renouncing the world, the flesh, and the devil.

Spiritualism, by which I mean conscious intercourse under certain conditions between the visible and invisible worlds, is a demonstrated fact, a scientific fact, and a fact of vast importance so far as it helps to convince Atheists and Materialists of a future existence, but it is of no possible authority in the line of philosophy, morality, or religion ; and further, I say it in all deliberation, I have not a particle of sympathy with this modern, destructive, disorderly, disorganising, irreligious Spiritualism that denies the personality of God and the existence of Jesus Christ of the New Testament, that ridicules prayer, pronounces the Bible useless as an old almanac, and religion a silly superstition. Such Spiritualism is simply necromancy, black magic and demonism, and should be shunned as one would shun the dens and stings of slimy serpents. If Buddha was the light of Asia, Christ was the Light of the World.

During the private and public meetings that we held in Sunderland, Newcastle, London, Manchester, and elsewhere, the Elder's testimony as entertained by believers against war, intemperance, land monopoly, the unfruitful works of darkness, and sin of all kinds, was clear, scathing, and convicting. He was at times grandly inspired from the very Heavens, and his words seemed all alive with the power of love and truth. Returning as I before said by way of Manchester to Glasgow, we were met at the former place by sympathising friends, and, testing the public pulse, we were gratified at the great progress made since that darker historical period when the Manchester authorities imprisoned Ann Lee. Surely progress is a universal law. Reaching Glasgow on our way homeward bound, we again held public meetings, which were very pleasant and harmonious. Love and good will were the prevailing elements. These people gave us a most inviting soiree, and almost overwhelmed us with presents and kindnesses. Already the harvest was coming in. Some few resolved to come to Mount Lebanon, and more will follow. No note of music is lost, no spoken truth ever dies.

If it does not bear fruit to-day, it will to-morrow, and still more in the golden future.

The Elder has stood the voyage by sea, the travels by land, and the arduous lecture labours much better than I feared he would soon after our arrival. But owing to his methodical habits, and his careful vegetarian diet, he had a great storehouse of vitality to draw from. The fact of his physical health and keen mental powers at eighty is of itself a powerful testimony in favour of a celibate life and a rigid vegetarian diet, which he has strictly adhered to for the last fifty-five years.

Finally, considering the whole matter of this mission carefully, I feel that it has been a very successful one in many ways, and further, I feel that it is making practical the command of Jesus,—" Go ye into all the world and preach the gospel to every creature." A mission inaugurated and carried out in the near future with preaching, music, and worship, a mission made sufficiently practical to the eyes of England in her present condition of misery and unrest, would as far excel ours as the day excels the night. Personally, I only regret that I could not have done more for the Elder, more for the right and more for that truth which is the power of God unto salvation. It was hard to part with the good, kind-hearted friends in Glasgow. They spread before us their tables, they gave us gifts, and bade us good-bye with tears in their eyes. Gratefully recounting the past, we could only say "God bless you, God keep you, and God gather you into that Heavenly order of love, peace, and purity, an order that knows no night, but one eternal morning of youth, growth, and spiritual progress. Most sincerely yours,

J. M. PEEBLES.

THE OTHER SIDE.

" He that is first in his own cause seemeth right, but afterward his
neighbour cometh and searcheth him."

IN the foregoing letter the Doctor is first. He has
told the truth, but not the whole truth.

In most of the places we visited the Spiritualists
were the hosts, we the guests. Consequently Spiritualism was first and foremost. Shakerism they knew
little or nothing about, and what they did know was
to its disadvantage, being the product of ignorance
and prejudice. On the other hand, J. M. Peebles was
their hero and idol. His round the world travels, his
high literary reputation, the result of his many books
and publications treating of those travels and many
other topics, his well earned reputation as a popular
lecturer upon hygiene and physiology, and finally,
but not least, in the estimation of his personal friends,
his blameless life and high moral and religious character as a man, all combined to reflect credit and
honour upon Spiritualism and the Spiritualist. These
they stood in need of, while Shakerism they did not
need, there being no form or comeliness in it that
they should desire it. It was unpopular. In the
various meetings the Doctor delivered beautiful
addresses in an eloquent manner, proving that when
men and women die they are not dead, but still
living, sentient, intelligent, rational, social beings
— thus demonstrating the immortality of human
souls. Having thus excited their interests to the
highest degree, and carried them to the very gates of
Paradise, he would deftly spring upon them the question,—" What next?" What shall we do to make
that immortality a blessing and not a curse? In a
word, what shall we do to be saved? This question
he would leave the Shaker to answer as best he could.

True, as the Doctor has stated, in Manchester
vegetarianism took precedence of everything else.

My long life testimony as a practical vegetarian, extending over fifty-five years, was duly recognised and highly honoured. I was first on the list. All through the mission the Doctor was very helpful in opening the way and preparing the people to hear and receive the testimony of Christ's second appearing in the female order, as logically flowing from the revelation of the mother spirit in Deity.

J. M. Peebles bare repeatedly strong and feeling witness to what he had himself seen and experienced in his many visits to the various Shaker societies. And in his last and most Pentecostal meeting held in Glasgow, he boldly declared his faith in Shakerism, frankly stating that he belonged to the Order, and that nothing but the complicated condition of his family affairs prevented him from either founding or uniting with the Shaker family.

Truly, as J. M. Peebles has said, there has much seed been sown in England in the hearts of many seekers after righteousness. One sows and another reaps. God only can give the increase. For that increase, like the husbandman who ploughs and harrows, and casts his seed into the ground thus prepared, we must patiently wait. There cometh a time when the reaper will overtake the ploughman, and the sowers will have ceased their avocation, for on earth the Kingdom of Heaven will have come.

F. W. EVANS.

Mount Lebanon, Columbia County, N Y.

ELDER EVANS AMONG VEGETARIANS IN MANCHESTER.

MR. FREDERICK WILLIAM EVANS, an elder from the Shaker Settlement at Mount Lebanon, New York, was on Thursday entertained to dinner by the Manchester Vegetarian Society. The dinner took place in the Vegetarian Restaurant in Fountain Street, in this city, and was well attended. Mr. Evans, a man in his eightieth year, has for fifty-six years been a vegetarian and a teetotaller, and he is described as a temperance reformer, a prohibitionist, a land reformer, and a peace advocate. After the dinner a meeting was held. Mr. W. A. E. Axon presided, and was supported by the Rev. James Clark, Mr. C. Rowley, and others. The Chairman said that Manchester gave birth to the foundress of the Shaker sect, of which Mr. Evans was at present the leading expounder. Apart from the theological belief of the Shakers, they were an exceedingly interesting people, who had solved, apparently with success, some of the problems that were troubling the minds of the world to-day. In the Shaker community of America the problem of the application of co-operative labour had been solved. Whatever else might be said respecting the Shakers, it must be acknowledged that they paid great attention to hygiene. They were temperance people and peace folk, and they were engaged in a great many movements that were working for the regeneration of the world.

Mr. C. Rowley spoke of his recent visit to the Shaker Settlement at Mount Lebanon, and said that there it seemed that God's will on earth as it is in heaven had been accomplished. He never before saw so many happy people together.

Dr. Peebles, who has accompanied Mr. Evans from America, next addressed the meeting. He said the Shakers were ever struggling against the earthly and carnal, and trying to lead better lives. As a people they were healthy ; as individuals they had nothing, for they held all things in common. They were industrious, temperate, and well behaved.

Mr. Evans, in the course of his remarks, mentioned that he was brought up on an English farm. He did not claim that the views held by the Shakers were

new, but admitted that anything that was commend-
able in them was the result of the efforts of those who
had gone before. The Shakers were the outcome
of the progress of the whole human race. It was not
possible that every one should be a Shaker, because
all men were not fit for such a life, and in coming to
England he desired to gain the adherence only of
those whose hearts told them they were ripe for the
change. All the Shakers were not yet vegetarians,
but he believed that in course of time they would be.
They advocated the nationalisation of the land and
reform of civil government. The civil government of
the United States of America came nearest to their
ideal.

Mr. Evans went on to refer to the theological views
of the Shakers, and ridiculed some of the doctrines of
the " orthodox Christians," showing that he could not
understand how any one could swallow them. A
conversation followed, and afterwards a vote of thanks
was passed to Mr. Evans.

ELDER EVANS' FAREWELL MEETING
IN GLASGOW.*

WE have had quite a time of rejoicing in Glasgow,
having been privileged to see much of those estimable
men, Dr. Peebles and Elder Evans. It is not necessary that we agree intellectually on all points with
people to appreciate their moral and spiritual worth.
Had we as a body been at one with Shakerism, we
could not have loved the Elder more than we did.
More than one felt that here was not only a moral
force, but a man of ideas, and so we have all in a

* From Report by James Robertson, Glasgow, in *Medium* of 29th July,
1887.

measure been stirred by the sweet simplicity, the naturalness, and purity of the man. Altogether a striking figure is Elder Frederick, with his large fund of common sense, throwing light on ancient errors, thrashing the absurdities of the churches, and trying to work out the problem of a community in which righteousness and peace will reign. To get at the better way is the object and aim of all reformers, and the Shakers are surely entitled to the credit of doing something to help the world to get at a higher truth than has yet been reached. Hepworth Dixon, in his "New America," published over twenty years since, seemed to be much attracted to Elder Frederick and the people. "The people," he says, "are like their village: soft in speech, demure in bearing, gentle in face, a people seeming to be at peace not only with themselves but with nature and with heaven." And again, "After spending a few days among them, seeing them at their meals, and at their prayers, in their private amusements, and in their household work, I found myself thinking that if any chance were to throw me down, and I were sick in spirit, broken in health, there would be few female faces, next after my own wife and kin, that would be pleasanter to see about my bed. Life appears to move on Mount Lebanon in an easy kind of rhythm : order, temperance, frugality, worship, every one seems busy, every one tranquil." We may not comprehend Shaker theology, cannot make much out of the Second Advent, some of us may not be so certain of the first advent, but we can admit to the full that it is a sweet picture, which not only Hepworth Dixon, but so many other workers have drawn of their life, in marked contrast to what is got out of the gas-lighted and gas-inspired Christianity we are triumphant in. John Ruskin forcibly says,—"You might sooner get lightning out of incense smoke than true action or passion out of your modern English religion." The Shakers have, undoubtedly, made a road on which we can travel a long way ; they have given us many lessons as to life culture, given us many seeds of future life for our little garden. Men might go leagues to listen to such a man as Elder Evans, and come back well paid. One feels that the realisation of heaven on earth looks a bit nearer than ever it did before, and that it does not belong to dreamland, but is practical and present. " Measured against the millions of Christian people in the United States, six or seven thousand Shakers may appear of small account ; and this would be truth if the strength of spiritual and moral forces could be told in figures, but one man with ideas may be worth a parliament or army," says Dixon. The greatest work is one which the world does not talk about, does not even see. The Shakers soar above the level of all common vices and temptations, and from the height of their unselfish virtue offer to the worn and wearied spirit a gift of peace and a place of rest.

ELDER EVANS' WELCOME HOME AND REPLY.

ELDER FREDERICK,— Beloved Brother, your return from Great Britain is the accomplishment of a great and good work. For some years I have been impressed with the conditions of the people of that country, and felt that a field was open for us to work in.

Every movement among men that " makes for righteousness, its root, branch, and fruit, ought to be found in our novitiate orders. Should such not be the case, then that order is disqualified from being a minister of righteousness. Should there be a continuance in that state, any increase of testimony must come from without.

What is the meaning of an increase of testimony?
It is written,—"Of the increase of his kingdom to
order and establish it, there would be no end." Hence
it is desirable to know on what lines an increase of
Christ's kingdom operates. One of the lines marked
off by the prophet is,—" None shall say I am sick,"
and that a great age would be attained. This line
"*makes for righteousness*," — was clearly opened, de-
fined, and enforced by Moses; indorsed by Jesus
Christ and by the whole tenor of prophecy. On this
line there is at present great activity all through
modern civilisation. As a people what are we doing
on this line? Another movement that makes for
righteousness is Spiritualism. Modern thought has
been, and is being modified by its action to such
an extent, that materialism — *animalism*—is greatly
checked. This mighty movement went out from us.
Had it not, I am led to think we would have been
found shutting it off as the churches of the world have
done, on the ground that it is a disturbing element.
The Peace movement all are willing to accept as
making for righteousness. Lastly, we have the Land
movement—justice to every person.

All these movements are now in active operation.
Hence your visit abroad as a leading Novitiate Elder
was in season. With my whole heart I thank you.
You touched the current of human thought, and
turned it Godward! How does the Church respond
to these movements? On Peace, Spiritualism, and
the use of the land for ourselves, we stand somewhat
squarely. As regards hygienic law, the Church, east
and west, does not officially recognise it as one of the
foundations "of the city that lieth four square." Hence
she has no testimony against a destructive—an all-
pervading evil, attended by indescribable sufferings,
and the premature extinction of life of untold millions
of human beings! As regards that movement we are
as the heathen around us. It is the province of the

Church to live peace, and it is the province of the Novitiate Order to preach peace. It is the province of the Church to live a spiritual life, to the total exclusion of a materialistic—animal life. It is the province of said Order to preach that form of sound doctrine. The Church have lands in common. Hence it is the duty, and also *in the interest of the Church* that the Novitiate Orders should declare that all monopoly by corporations, or by individuals, of the elements of human subsistence, is contrary to God and godliness, and destructive of the means of right living and doing, and contrary to that "that makes for righteousness;"—not only retards the elevation of both rich and poor to the angelic order of Christ's kingdom, but also creates class distinctions among men, subversive of the fundamental principles of Christ's kingdom, and also of that of the United States.

If the Church stood in the testimony of right living —of hygienic law, as written by the finger of God on the nature of things, it would be the duty of the ministers of the Novitiate Order to preach a "full deliverance from all evil;" and that the testimony of the everlasting gospel is the testimony of a full salvation—a promise of the life that now is, and of that which is to come. But if the Church has no such testimony, then the testimony of a full salvation cannot be held forth.

Here is our friend the critic; he holds that our Church is lame — has not the power to insure its members of the fulfilment of "the promise of the life that now is." And being lame in one function, she is lame in all her functions. She having no such testimony, is a virtual declaration that she has no need of it. She sustains herself in that conclusion, say-ing,—"That the attempts to introduce that testimony had resulted in disturbance, and that her system of salvation is complete without it." Forthwith, she shuts up the heavens in the face of all the providential pointings at home and abroad.

This blindness of vision to the unfoldments of hygienic law, accounts for the indifference manifested by the Church east and west in the non-appreciating of the extraordinary activities "making for righteousness" in Great Britain, and, of course, of missionary labours there. Again our critic remarks,—" If the Church shuts up the heavens—declines to accept any influx in the matter of right living, which makes for righteousness, she will be under the necessity to shut the heavens against all revelation." Because, in the nature of things, all revelation, whether appertaining to the lower or the higher order of truths, is to disturb, to unsettle, to supplant, to overthrow. "*Behold, I create all things new,*" is a most revolutionary utterance. What could be more disturbing than,—" I will break in pieces man and woman, the young man and the maid, captains and rulers, nations and kingdoms." The ideas and thoughts of the Abolitionists disturbed more than one continent. The vast amount of property destroyed during the great rebellion was due to resisting the unfoldments of moral law. The awful destruction of human life was also due to that cause. On the afternoon of the last day of the battles of Gettysburg, within about forty minutes two thousand able-bodied men bit the dust. That settled the conflict ; the South, broken in pieces, turned their backs and fled.

These great calamities occurred because of resistance to the light which makes for righteousness. To the spiritually minded it is unnecessary to show that any neglect to incorporate the light of providential openings will be attended with serious difficulties: First, the inspired ones outside will get before us and be our ministers. When light is not improved within, there will be a conforming to the world, as is now the case to a small extent, in the form of singing-birds, personal adornments, etc., till we cannot tell some of our members from heathen gentlemen.

If there is no revelation to break the natural man into pieces, he will have revelations enough for us.

From a want of compliance with light "that makes for righteousness," I have been a sufferer for more than half a hundred years. In my old age, all I ask is, take away from before me the smell of dead fish and of land animals. The Holy Place was void of animal meats.

Again thanking you most cordially, I have the happiness to be, faithfully, your brother,

DANIEL FRASER.

NORTH FAMILY, August, 1887.

CRITICISM OF THE CRITIC.

DEAR BROTHER,—You are welcome to my effort to introduce the Gospel, in its second cycle, into the mother country—old England and Scotland. The first cycle in America was embraced by noble men and women, corresponding to the class who founded the American Government, which is not yet republican, only "in part."

Those first cycle believers have done a glorious work. They put the gospel axe to the root of the tree of human evil, and many thousands of souls have been saved "from the pollutions that are in the world through lust." These are now in spirit-life, and constitute a powerful battery of moral and spiritual forces which is acting upon the whole order of believers on earth. And through it, as a medium, they are shaking the old heavens and earth—church and state organisations—with the radical truths of Christianity and

18

the law of Moses, that have so long lain dormant. The "dark ages" are past. In them the sun of revelation was "darkened — black as sackcloth of hair," and the moon of church and state—civil governments—was "turned to blood"—war—as at this day. The scientific and mechanical power of the nations is pitted against each other ; and England manufactures the monitors and ammunition for the other nations to fight her with. Is not the boasted wisdom of this world foolishness? Jesus said,—"I am the way, the truth, and the life." He united in his character the substance of both the law and gospel. Who follows him? In the "kingdom" which has come, and for which saints have been instantly praying since his crucifixion, generative lust has no place ; war is not known. Private selfish property is prohibited — all things being in common ; each member is a labourer, and all enjoy the blessing of food, clothing, shelter, and the worship of God, as being in heaven.

Two Orders will be established, of which the Ann Republic and the United Society of Believers are the first Cycle of seven stages of progress through which they will both pass to a full millennial order. In it the earthly order of generation and the spiritual order of the resurrection, or regeneration, will have come to perfection—a perfect republic and a perfect kingdom of God on earth, the former being the seed bed of the latter. One will "sow the earth with the seed of man," the other harvest them from the lower to the higher order of human existence.

F. W. EVANS.

MOUNT LEBANON.

BY C. ROWLEY.

MANCHESTER has had a pre-eminence of which few of us were aware. In Todd Street, in the year 1736, was born Ann Lee, the foundress of the most successful body of religious communists which the world has ever seen. She had many revelations, and was often in an ecstatic condition. When she was twenty-three years old she joined a number of people who were members of the Society of Friends, and who were impressed mainly by the one idea that celibacy was an essential condition, if life was to be lived on the highest plane, if the mind was to be brought in contact with spiritual influences. She was imprisoned in Manchester because of her fervour and persistence in preaching this and other doctrine. According to her own account, she was wrought upon for nine years, and finally attained a state of perfect purity. She had only a few followers, and eight of them in all sailed for America in 1774. They founded a community, and there are now eighteen successful ones in the States. The foundress is, her followers claim, the type of Christianity in its second advent upon the earth. I have recently had the privilege of being a guest at their chief community at Mount Lebanon. They claim that the fundamental condition, celibacy, for all members was only possible in the last and final Church — the Millennial Church. They have no body of theology, being firmly impressed by the belief that it is theology that crushes out all vitality in religion ; but they have a few root principles, and these they hold in perfect freedom of thought and action. They are thoroughly wide awake to all that is going on in the world, and speak with remarkable intelligence about the questions which mankind keeps asking but cannot answer. They claim to have solved these burning and to us hitherto insoluble questions. They have no crime, no poverty, no idleness, no disease, no discontent, no filthy surroundings, no polluted air ; but the reverse of all this—pure and healthy bodies, abundance of good food, work for all, ample leisure, companionship, and an excellent home life, good health so as to need no doctors, no quarrels, and so they require no lawyers, and they have absolute cleanliness and comfort. Nothing can exceed the peaceful and happy expression on the faces of all the brothers and sisters— no sign of wear or worry, but constant cheerfulness in work. How different from the excited and disturbed expression of New York faces, for instance, or, indeed, of any that one sees in a great city, where the fight against each other and all others is keenest ! I said to the sister who attends to the guest-room,— "How happy everybody looks here." "Yes," she replied, "if we are not happy here, I don't know where we could be."

The community at Mount Lebanon, in New York county, consists of over 400 brothers and sisters. It has been founded about 100 years. The situation is most lovely ; it is 1000 feet above the sea, with high rolling land, and it is just on the borders of Massachusetts. There are six families or homes, each a distinct community, but each belonging to the whole, as do all the other seventeen settlements. Each home, however, takes a great pride in doing all it can to be up to the best style in all things, and this is encouraged by a series of visitations which the members make every year to each community and each home. There is no difficulty about the work, for nobody shirks it, and to be idle is to be miserable. They engage "world help" as occasion requires, and have outsiders almost continually on the farms and roads. They try, however, to do all their own labour. I asked the question which everybody puts when dis-

cussing this mode of life,—"What do you do with
your lazy or idle people?" They soon show you
that their communism has not "cut the nerve of industry." The incorrigible idler seldom inflicts himself
on them, and when by chance he does, it is he who
is the miserable person, for the whole tone is "work
and be happy," and so he finds no suitable environ-
ment, and soon departs. It is this gaiety of labour
which charms one most, I think, in this mountain
home. I visited the wash-house, where the sisters
were busy at work, and the dairy. It is just the same
here as at their meetings—a healthy cheerfulness and
constant activity. At Sunday's meeting the death of
a sister was spoken of, but there were no tears, no
regrets, but thankfulness that she had "passed the
river." In their laundry, dairy, and all their workshops, they have the best modern appliances, and an
abundant water power, which is admirably utilised
to save labour and to do most of the heavy work.
Their workshops are ample, and very clean and airy.
They have sawmills, planing machines, and, indeed, all
that a community requires to produce its necessities.
They have an abundance of timber on their extensive
lands, which extend over thousands of acres ; and
their fencing, their farming operations, and general
orderliness are the best and most complete that I
have seen in the States. In fact, as they produce
things for use and not for profit, they have enormous
advantages, and they are not stinted in the main
commodity, land. I need not say that they are all
ardent land reformers—passionately so, seeing clearly
that without this prime necessity men are more or less
the slaves of those who have secured it. They tell
me that their abundant crops are sometimes be-
wildering—so many apples, so many pears, so much
asparagus, and so forth. They send a good many
commodities to the world in exchange for their wants,
but they also sell large quantities of produce, such as

eggs, fruit, cattle, and they have a fame for seeds. Although they need, therefore, use no medicine themselves, they send great quantities of herbal preparations which outsiders sell and puff in a way very distasteful to their quiet and steady view of things. The preparations sold under the name of Mother Siegel, which are so well known in our own country, are produced here in bulk, but they are made up and puffed outside the community. They are nearly all Vegetarians, so their table is covered with a profusion of dishes which are very toothsome, though some of them are strange to a carnivorous feeder. I had the privilege of much companionship with Brother Daniel Fraser, a hale old man of eighty-three, and went over the proofs of a pamphlet he has just written in reply to some of Ingersoll's negations. Ingersoll has been asking in despair in one of his lectures how America is to face and solve her labour troubles, her cruel growing monopolies, her drift of poor and criminal into the great cities, her general low level of materialistic life. Daniel Fraser points in reply, to their settlements for a practical answer to the wail. Another brother is a young and handsome Russian of twenty-four. He was imbued with communistic ideas at eighteen, and felt his country to be unbearable ; so he left his university and family, and tried to get free. He was captured and sent back to his family. He escaped, however, and fled to America. He joined a Free Communistic Society in Oregon, but it did not hold together, having, he says, no religious bond. After this he joined a Positivist Communistic body out West, but hearing of the Christian Communists at Mount Lebanon, he came and has remained for two years, and feels that he is here for life. Another member, Daniel Offord, who has been here since a child, has developed a remarkable mechanical faculty, and most of the ingenious arrangements for utilising the water power are due to him. Music is much in use, and all the tunes are their own, as are the words. They call them both "inspirational." The music as I heard it rendered at their meetings is very sweet and simple, having its genesis, I imagine, in the good old hymnology of a hundred years ago—a music we are especially rich in, but which is much neglected for more fashionable but less worthy forms. A sister told me that they learn a new tune nearly every week.

These people, so bright, so busy, so rational in all their actions, do really seem to deserve the happiness they evidently possess. While here they have every comfort and every sane luxury ; they have no desire to have anything so long as obtaining it means in any way suffering to others. That one thought would vitiate their whole organism, and they would cease to exist. They believe that the world is troubled by problems which to them are easy of solution, and that they have patterns to show which should be convincing. With something like this in mind, Elder Frederick Evans and another brother are about to sail for England fully to explain their methods and their successes. Elder Frederick Evans, although close upon eighty, is ready to fight the battle of his faith. It is quite remarkable to hear him tell of the Shaker ideas which the world has adopted. This leads him to hope that we outsiders are ready for more, and that a considerable percentage may have the courage of their convictions. He made a suggestion which he requested me to pass on to our clergy of all denominations for the celebration of the Queen's Jubilee. This was to preach the Mosaic law of restitution of land to the people, which Moses commanded should take place at every jubilee year. He defends the adoption of their nickname, "The Shakers," as being, perhaps, the most expressive word in the language to explain their mission, which is to shake, to disturb all the evil and all evildoers, and compel the adoption of just, sound, and righteous laws, which shall result in the greatest good for the greatest number, and also the greatest good to the whole number.—(*Cutting from Manchester Guardian, 1887.*)

SHAKERS AND SHAKERISM.

BY HESTER M. POOLE.

A LATE visit to the Shakers at the instance of one of their elders, filled me with a desire to lay before your readers some account of these people so interesting to the thoughtful student of humanity, yet so little understood.

On the eastern boundary of the State of New York, twenty miles as the crow flies from the Hudson, and contiguous to the beautiful hills of Berkshire, in Massachusetts, lies about six thousand acres of land owned and tilled by the Shakers of Mount Lebanon.

A lonely and peaceful scene expands before the visitor who rides through these well-tilled farms and inspects workshops and dwellings. Along the street one group of buildings succeed another, five in all, containing three hundred or more of both sexes and all ages. Each group constitutes a family, presided over by two men and two women, whose wisdom, patience, and tenderness, are constantly challenged in administering more especially to the spiritual necessities of those under their charge. They are assisted in the temporal affairs by two deacons and two deaconesses, whose wisdom is available in all matters pertaining to the good of the society.

The family life is that of a religious communism, the intention being, as far as possible, to preserve and perpetuate primitive Christianity. Body and soul are consecrated to this purpose. It is a part of their un-

written creed to study the laws of hygiene and conform to them, to live in celibacy, and to exercise
justice in the earning, owning, and distribution of
property.

Among them are neither bond nor free, rich nor
poor. All are incited to industry, thrift, generosity,
and fraternity, and there is a strong psychologic power
in such sentiments, which, when exercised by masses
of people, produces an influence that not even the
stranger within the gate can quite escape. The
despot or the millionaire would feel out of place
among those "gentle ascetics," whose lives are a rebuke to that spirit of greed, selfishness, and love of
luxury, which is the curse of modern civilisation. We
find at Mount Lebanon several hundred people living
in a simple, pure, wholesome manner, without the
help of courthouse, jail, grog shops, or the three professions, so that even from an external point of view,
Shakerism is eminently successful.

All the buildings occupied by the respective families,
constructed of wood, brick, and stone, are commodious
and well ventilated. The arrangements for cooking
and eating are admirable ; in fact, in regard to appliances for comfort and sanitation they take the lead
among progressive peoples.

The table, almost entirely vegetarian, is perfect.
Food is fresh, abundant, exquisitely cooked and served
with care and intelligence. Cereals, with the excep-
tion of superfine flour, are cleansed and crushed in
their own mills and used in a variety of ways. There
is a large dairy and tons of fruit, deliciously prepared,
are ranged in storerooms for the winter's consumption.
Woman's work is simplified by curious machinery
invented and made by some of their leaders. All
work, but none overwork. Garments are homemade,
and until lately woollen clothing was homespun and
home-woven. An abundance of spring water is carried
into every building, ventilation and drainage are ex-

cellent, and sickness is almost a myth. Cleanliness of the person and of their dwellings is carried to its utmost extent. It follows that simplicity of furnishing is necessary, and that their apartments, in comparison with those of the world, look plain and bleak.

Yet recreation and rest, sunshine and cheerfulness, are terms having real meaning. "Age cannot stale nor custom wither " men and women who live so near to nature and in the exercise of such noble qualities. Accordingly, they very generally appear to be from ten to twenty years younger than they really are. Many reach extreme old age, and finally pass away from the natural decay of the body, with little sickness or pain. The expression of the face is mild, benignant, and serene, sometimes approaching high spiritual beauty.

So much for the religion of the body—the only basis of the scientific and enduring.

Before reviewing their religious tenets it may be well to state that their origin is found in the Revolutionists of Dauphiné and Nivarais, France, about the year 1689. Offshoots of the parent stock formed a society in England in 1747 ; and two years prior to the Declaration of Independence by the American colonies, Ann Lee, with seven of her followers, landed on these shores.

From the little spark brought over by them a fire was kindled which vivified many souls, and in New Lebanon over a century ago, these gathered together and built their first house for public worship. From that period they have acted as a leaven among the elements of progress.

Mother Ann, so called from that tender maternal love which would fain save a world from sin and suffering, was the first seer to enunciate the principle that the Great First Cause is dual—He and She— Father and Mother. It is certain that Theodore Parker obtained his conception of this deific attribute from the Shakers, as shown by his correspondence. This duality is now so generally accepted that church-men are apt to forget that the Jewish Jehovah and the Christian God was forceful, revengeful, and on occasion hateful. This one-sided Creator lacked all that sweet plenitude of womanly love, which united with a manhood of corresponding wisdom, would alone be worthy of reverence. And Christendom waited seventeen centuries for a woman to declare the duality of the Deific Essence.

This, then, is the central idea of Shakerism. Ranged about it are others, not the result of dry reasoning, but of experiences similar to those of Paul and the Pentecostal Church. Profoundly reverent by nature, they recognise a " divine afflatus," which is the inspiration of all real development. This divine ele-ment, they believe, has manifested itself whenever the condition of an individual or of society afforded occasion, from the beginning of history through Moses, Isaiah, Swedenborg, Whitfield, and others, down to the time of Mother Ann, and even since then. They declare that " the continuous revelations of truth will ever be the leading lines of human progress."

What is now known as Modern Spiritualism is ac-cepted by them as a fact. They assert that all phases of mediumship were common among them several years prior to the first rap heard at Hydeville, and that its advent to the general public was then foretold. In its higher phases, shorn of crudities and mon-strosities, it is still sometimes exhibited. Witness the sweet, pathetic, yet simple melodies which come, " the gift of the spirit," as they believe, to one or another, either in private or in public worship. A brother or a sister at such times is inspired to sing a new song to new music, which, when written down, becomes a permanent possession. A large book has been pub-lished consisting of these inspirational hymns, which is in constant use.

They do not generally believe in the miraculous birth or divinity of Jesus, but consider that he was divine in the sense of having power to rise above the lower propensities. His mission was "simply and fully to manifest the divine attributes to man more than any other one who has ever lived."

They also believe that the first wave of deific light sweeping over the earth after the Reformation began with the Quakers. Its mission was to "prepare the world for the divine form of human society," or the "kingdom of heaven on earth." The second appearance of this wave, or the "Christ-Spirit," was manifested in and through woman in the form of Ann Lee.

They accept the Christian Bible allegorically and literally, and include among Bibles the Koran, Talmud, Zendavesta, and other books sacred to various nations. They discountenance war, never go to law among themselves, and aim to act in a just, humane, and brotherly manner to all men.

In regard to women, "It is the only society in the world, so far as we know," said Eldress Anna, "where woman has absolutely the same freedom and power as man in every respect." And the world may well hail the advent of woman's era if it shall usher in such noble types of womanhood as we found at Mount Lebanon, hid under the quaint cap and staid dress of the gentle sisterhood.

In regard to the future, Elder Evans has declared their belief to be that "The old heavens and earth— united church and state—are fast passing away, dissolving with the fire of spiritual truth. Out of the material of the old, earthly, civil governments, a civil government will arise—is even now arising—in which right, not might, will predominate. It will be purely secular, a genuine republic. Men and women will be citizens. All citizens will be free-holders. They will inherit and possess the land by right of birth. War

will cease with the end of the old monarchical, theological earth. . . . In the new earth sexuality
will be used only for reproduction; eating for strength,
not gluttony; drinking for thirst, not drunkenness.
And property, being the product of honest toil—as
those who will not work will not be allowed to
eat — will be for the good of all, the young and
the old."

Purity of mind and body is necessary to Shakerism.
But virgin celibacy has in it nothing of moroseness or
asceticism. A pleasant relation is maintained between
the brethren and sisters, fostered by social meetings
in which reading, conversation and discussions upon
topics germane to the welfare of humanity take place.
In these, all who choose to do so, participate.

Believing that human theologies perish in the using,
while the revelations of truth are continuous and progressive, they earnestly watch and wait for every sign
of the domination of the spirit of truth and justice
over that of error and falsehood in the government
or in social life. As to them, the fall of man consists
in "disorderly relationships," and the serpent is the
sensuous nature. They are strenuous in the advocacy
of purity and temperance. And here it may be said
that the institution of marriage is not condemned by
the Shakers. All men, they consider, are bound to
make the animal propensities tributary to their higher
natures, while marriage is a purely worldly institution.
They are called to a higher order of life, to "come
out of the world and be separate."

The following description of this growth from a
lower to an upper plane, is from the pen of one of their
number who wears his eighty odd years as a crown of
wisdom and beauty.

"Allow me to assure you, scientific men, philosophers, doubters, and all interested, that whenever
human spirits are in the right condition and are about
to change from the animal emotional to the divine

emotional life, that there will be manifestations of intelligent spiritual affinities, forces, effusions of the Divine Spirit, producing extraordinary results as on the day of Pentecost. There will be deep conviction of sin, bodily agitations, gifts of tongues, curing diseases, discernment of spirits, and striking with fear the hardened sinner and unbelieving opposer."

Whatever may be thought of their beliefs, the catholicity of thought evinced by their leaders, the comprehensive grasp of affairs, the judgment of the trend and comparative value of social, political, and religious movements, the balancing of various reforms, the interest maintained in scientific discoveries and inventions, the depth and breadth of that love of humanity which dominates every motive, is something as surprising as it is delightful to the dispassionate visitor.

Professor Richard T. Ely, of Johns Hopkins University, who sojourned at Mount Lebanon for a few weeks, gives this testimony in regard to that visit,— "The feeling grew upon me that I was in a social observatory, viewing as from another planet the buying and selling, the hurrying to and fro, the marrying and giving in marriage, the toil, the pleasure, the vanity, the oppression, the good and the evil among men on earth."

There are seventeen communities of Shakers in this country, containing in all between four and five thousand individuals. These are situated in the States of New York, Massachusetts, Connecticut, New Hampshire, Maine, Ohio, and Kentucky. Elder F. W. Evans, the able and venerable senior elder at Mount Lebanon, has just returned from a visit to England, at the solicitation of sympathisers in Great Britain who desire to establish a community. Adherents are constantly joining them, though, in the nature of things, not in large numbers. Those who believe and work in unison with their aims, yet who remain without the fold, are more numerous. However this may be, these people who dispense with liquor and tobacco, who subsist on grains and fruits, and live near to the great heart of nature, practise as well as preach a temperance and a religion well worthy of respectful attention.—*From the Open Court, Chicago, 29th September, 1887.*

INFORMATION.

THE different United Societies of Believers in the Second Appearing of the Christ Spirit upon this earth are composed of three Orders; and these again are constituted of several families, each designed to be self-sustaining in temporal as well as Spiritual things—small communities.

The Novitiate Order receives and entertains strangers who are inquirers into the religious elements of the Shaker faith.

That the writer occupies the position of First Elder in the Novitiate Order of the Society at Mount Lebanon, is the reason so much prominence is given to his particular name and history in this publication; also, in order that seekers after spiritual truth may know to whom, in so large a Community, to apply personally, or address their letters.

The Society does not wish to receive children *under twelve years of age*, except when they come in with their parents. And children so taken are not expected to go out into the world visiting friends and relations. Nor are such relatives, when they come *merely* to visit such minors, or friends in general, expected to remain more than a very short time, as the Society keeps no female servants, and both the labour and expense are onerous to the Society members.

Strangers are not permitted to perambulate the premises of the Novitiate families, nor of the Office families of any of the Societies, without special permission from the proper authority of the family.

Wages are not paid to minors, nor to probationary members in the Novitiate Order (consisting of three families) any more than to Covenant members.

Inquirers and investigators may apply to

F. W. EVANS,

MOUNT LEBANON,

COLUMBIA CO., N.Y.

THE AMERICAN UTOPIAN ADVENTURE

sources for the study of communitarian socialism in the
United States 1680–1880

Series One

Edward D. Andrews THE COMMUNITY INDUSTRIES OF THE
SHAKERS (1932)

Adin Ballou HISTORY OF THE HOPEDALE COMMUNITY from its
inception to its virtual submergence in the Hopedale Parish. Edited
by W. S. Heywood (1897)

Paul Brown TWELVE MONTHS IN NEW HARMONY presenting a
faithful account of the principal occurrences that have taken place
there during that period; interspersed with remarks (1827)

John S. Duss THE HARMONISTS. A personal history (1943)

Frederick W. Evans AUTOBIOGRAPHY OF A SHAKER and revelation
of the Apocalypse. With an appendix. Enlarged edition (1888)

Parke Godwin A POPULAR VIEW OF THE DOCTRINES OF CHARLES
FOURIER (1844) DEMOCRACY, CONSTRUCTIVE AND PACIFIC
(1844)

Walter C. Klein JOHANN CONRAD BEISSEL, MYSTIC AND
MARTINET, 1690–1768 (1942)

William J. McNiff HEAVEN ON EARTH: A PLANNED MORMON
SOCIETY (1940) With "Communism among the Mormons," by Hamilton Gardner

Michael A. Mikkelsen THE BISHOP HILL COLONY. A religious,
communistic settlement in Henry County, Illinois (1892) With "Eric
Janson and the Bishop Hill Colony," by Silvert Erdahl

Oneida Community BIBLE COMMUNISM. A compilation from the annual
reports and other publications of the Oneida Association and its branches,
presenting, in connection with their history, a summary view of their
religious and social theories (1853)

Marianne (Dwight) Orvis LETTERS FROM BROOK FARM 1841–1847.
Edited by Amy L. Reed (1928)

Robert A. Parker A YANKEE SAINT. John Humphrey Noyes and the
Oneida Community (1935)

A. J. G. Perkins & Thersa Wolfson FRANCES WRIGHT: FREE
ENQUIRER. The study of a temperament (1939)

Jules Prudhommeaux ICARIE ET SON FONDATEUR, ÉTIENNE
CABET. Contribution à l'étude du socialisme expérimental (1907)

Albert Shaw ICARIA. A chapter in the history of communism (1884)